Process as Power

Process as Power

The Legitimacy of Indigenous Consultation in British Columbia Environmental Assessments

MINH THUY DO

UBCPress · Vancouver

Originally printed in Canada
Printed and bound by CPI Group (UK) Ltd, Croydon, CR0 4YY

UBC Press is a Benetech Global Certified Accessible™ publisher. The epub version of this book meets stringent accessibility standards, ensuring it is available to people with diverse needs.

Library and Archives Canada Cataloguing in Publication

Title: Process as power : the legitimacy of Indigenous consultation in British Columbia environmental assessments / Minh Thuy Do.
Names: Do, Minh Thuy, author.
Description: Includes bibliographical references and index.
Identifiers: Canadiana (print) 20250253062 | Canadiana (ebook) 20250258684 | ISBN 9780774872263 (hardcover) | ISBN 9780774872270 (softcover) | ISBN 9780774872287 (PDF) | ISBN 9780774872294 (EPUB)
Subjects: LCSH: Indigenous peoples—Civil rights—British Columbia. | LCSH: Indigenous peoples—Civil rights—Canada. | LCSH: Indigenous peoples—Legal status, laws, etc.—British Columbia. | LCSH: Indigenous peoples—Legal status, laws, etc.—Canada. | LCSH: Indigenous peoples—British Columbia—Government relations. | LCSH: Indigenous peoples—Canada—Government relations. | LCSH: Environmental impact analysis—British Columbia. | LCSH: Environmental protection—British Columbia.
Classification: LCC KEB529 .D6 2026 | LCC KF8210.C5 D6 2026 kfmod | DDC 342.71108/72—dc23

UBC Press gratefully acknowledges the financial support for our publishing program of the Government of Canada, the Canada Council for the Arts, and the British Columbia Arts Council.

This book has been published with the help of a grant from the Canadian Federation for the Humanities and Social Sciences, through the Scholarly Book Awards, using funds provided by the Social Sciences and Humanities Research Council of Canada.

UBC Press is situated on the traditional, ancestral, and unceded territory of the xʷməθkʷəy̓əm (Musqueam) people. This land has always been a place of learning for the xʷməθkʷəy̓əm, who have passed on their culture, history, and traditions for millennia, from one generation to the next.

UBC Press
The University of British Columbia
www.ubcpress.ca

To Mom, for your unwavering dedication and love
To Dad, for your courage to get on that boat

Contents

Acknowledgments

This book would not be possible without the sustained generosity and support of many mentors and friends. The intellectual foundation of this work is thanks to the careful guidance and encouragement of Andrea Olive and Robert Schertzer. Their insights at critical stages shaped my thinking in ways I could not have realized on my own. From our extensive chats and meetings, they have become cherished friends, and I will always appreciate their thoughtful investment in my growth as a scholar. I am also indebted to Sari Graben, Grace Skogstad, and Neil Craik, whose expertise helped refine my understanding of the relationship between law and policy-making.

Beyond academia, I had the privilege of learning from the lawyers, consultants, and policy officials who generously shared their knowledge with me. Their rich insights added an invaluable dimension to this work, and I remain inspired by their dedication to justice between Indigenous and non-Indigenous societies. I also acknowledge the Social Sciences and Humanities Research Council for its support through research funding.

This book would not have come to fruition without the guidance from Randy Schmidt, my editor at UBC Press. His patience and steadfast support made navigating the publishing process far less daunting, and I truly appreciated our coffee chats at conferences as well as our shared appreciation for Vietnamese cuisine. I am also immensely grateful to the two anonymous reviewers who generously took the time to thoroughly engage with my work and offered invaluable feedback to sharpen my theoretical arguments.

Throughout my academic journey, I have been fortunate to receive the wisdom and mentorship of many scholars. At the University of Toronto, I am grateful for the intellectual support of Ran Hirschl, Linda White, Andrew McDougall, and Kate Neville. The Courts and Politics Research Group, led by Emmett Macfarlane and Kate Puddister, provided me with a vibrant scholarly community in which to share ideas and grow. Emmett and Kate are my greatest champions, and their mentorship deeply inspires me. At the University of Guelph, I am equally thankful for the support and collegiality of Leah Levac, Jordi Díez, Tamara Small, Nanita Mohan, Carmen Ho, Dennis Baker, and Troy Riddell, who did not hesitate to welcome me and offer guidance on navigating academia.

I also had the joy of learning from and alongside brilliant colleagues. Eve Bourgeois, Sophie Borwein, Elena Goracinova, Meghan Snider, Jason VandenBeukel, Heather Millar, and Amy Janzwood – thank you for answering my endless questions, reading early drafts, and keeping me motivated. I will always remember working and talking together in the dark computer lab on the third floor of Sidney Smith.

This book has been shaped by many remarkable thinkers, but I would not have completed it without my family and friends. Mom, Dad, Quyen, and Nhi – thank you for believing in me, even if it was not always clear exactly what I have been doing all these years. I am grateful for the care and support of my extended family – Kim Ha, Thong Do, Kim Dang, Kim Phuong, and Dung Dang – as well as my cousins Annie, Henry, and Lily for motivating me with joy and laughter. My in-laws, including Terry, Alicia, and Pechill, thank you for unreservedly welcoming me into your family and encouraging my pursuits. Thank you to Madeliene Merrick and Inas Ettayebi for your wise counsel that kept me focused and grounded. Michael Ng's steadfast support and confidence in me through all the highs and lows of research and writing made all the difference. Mike endured my endless whining and protestations with good-natured jokes and an unhealthy supply of bubble tea. And a heartfelt thank you to Michelle Fung, my most trusted confidante, whose good judgment, unwavering integrity, and sharp wit continually inspire me to pursue my passion.

Process as Power

Introduction

The potential of the law to radically transform the state's governance over policy areas has been thoroughly debated – most notably, with the advent of bills of rights and the judiciary's role in interpreting those rights.[1] In Canada, the *Canadian Charter of Rights and Freedoms,* passed in 1982, outlines individual fundamental freedoms and allows citizens to use the Charter to challenge government actions that violate their rights.[2] Both optimism and anxiety surrounded the inclusion of a new bill of rights and the court's ability to strike down government legislation that is found to be inconsistent with the Canadian Constitution. Although this power of judicial review existed long before 1982, the addition of a bill of rights was thought to introduce political, policy, and moral issues before the courts, thus potentially bypassing democratic decision-making processes. The courts could serve as a powerful corrective to unjust government legislation or undemocratically thrust their own political agenda through the guise of rights interpretations. Despite the judiciary's heightened political importance, studies suggest that governments are successful at managing the threat posed by increased litigation and judicial oversight. Canadian governments have the resources to engage in long-term legal battles and are reinforced by an executive-driven parliamentary system to protect their legislative agenda.[3] The Charter revolution altered state governance, but state power was not rendered impotent.

Much of the scholarship that evaluated judicial power after 1982 focused on how the judiciary shaped policy-making through their interpretation of Charter rights. But, in addition to a bill of rights, Canada's constitutional order after 1982 also included an explicit recognition of Aboriginal[4] rights under section 35 of the *Constitution Act, 1982.* This section recognizes that Aboriginal rights, as exercised by First Nations, Métis, and Inuit, are "recognized and affirmed." These rights flow from Indigenous peoples' prior occupancy of the land before the assertion of the Crown's sovereignty. Through consistent litigation, section 35's scope and content have developed over time. Many of these cases dealt with interpreting treaty rights or how Indigenous peoples can claim recognition for rights that have not been extinguished by the Crown. As Indigenous peoples asserted more rights to activities over contested land and water, state governance has shifted in response, although in a piecemeal manner. One response includes Indigenous and state governments negotiating comprehensive agreements and modern treaties to realize Indigenous self-government. Studies have shown that section 35 and judicial decisions have prompted settler governments to consider entering negotiations with Indigenous groups to settle land claims, but, although legal victories may explain how negotiations are brought about, the outcomes of comprehensive agreements are better explained by political factors like the role of Indigenous political leadership.[5]

In addition to using section 35 to clarify the scope and content of Aboriginal and treaty rights, Indigenous peoples have also sought to change government decision-making. The Haida Nation brought a novel legal claim before the judiciary by asserting that the Crown's action to authorize the continuation of a logging license that affected claimed Haida territory violated section 35. The Supreme Court of Canada (SCC) agreed with the Haida Nation and asserted that the Haida were entitled to consultation.[6] The duty to consult is a unique constitutional obligation that compels the Crown to consult, and, if necessary, accommodate, relevant Indigenous groups when the Crown's[7] conduct may negatively affect an Indigenous group's Aboriginal rights. Although the duty emerges from section 35, it is not a typical right that curtails the exercise of the Crown's power. Instead, the SCC conceptualized the duty as a key mechanism of advancing reconciliation. By incorporating Indigenous parties into the Crown's decision-making when those decisions could have an impact on Aboriginal rights, both the Crown's and Indigenous participants' authority is legitimated: the Crown's actions are legitimated when the exercise of power is consistent with respecting and upholding Aboriginal rights and title that flow from Indigenous peoples' prior occupancy on the land; through the duty, Indigenous peoples' distinct role in executive decision-making is also legitimated as a constitutional imperative.

The duty to consult is conceived by the SCC to change the Crown's decision-making processes; by encouraging honourable negotiations, questions about how Aboriginal rights and the Crown's governance can best interface, particularly before formal agreements are finalized, can be resolved without the use of adversarial litigation.[8] This approach appears consistent with some Indigenous scholars' assertions that negotiations, rather than litigation through Canadian courts, can open jurisdictional space for Indigenous peoples to exercise governing powers.[9] Analyzing the legal scope of the duty to consult and its implementation by policy actors is a clear place to understand the degree to which the courts can shape the policy process and the intersection of law and politics more generally.

Despite this promise of managing conflict through political negotiations, the Crown's decisions over major projects that could affect the exercise of Aboriginal rights have not been met consistently with Indigenous support after consultations have taken place. Sometimes, consultative measures have resulted in substantial efforts by all the parties to balance competing interests, but, at other times, they have resulted in distrustful interactions. For instance, the Galore Creek mining project in 2007 in northwestern British Columbia is considered a positive example of meaningful consultation, whereby the Tahltan Nation had their concerns and interests accommodated through private agreements and through the provincial environmental assessment process.[10] In contrast, the Trans Mountain Pipeline expansion project, which was finalized in 2017, provoked an intense backlash from Indigenous nations in British Columbia, even though the project had also undergone a similar regulatory review process. These different outcomes indicate that the way in which the duty to consult is implemented by governments matters in explaining the right's effectiveness to improve Indigenous-state relations.

These cases involved similar policy actors – most notably, the Crown, the industry actors, and the affected Indigenous peoples. These projects also underwent similar institutional processes and constraints, such as regulatory review taking place before the Crown's decision-making and the threat of litigation should the duty remain unfulfilled by the Crown. And, yet, the variation in consultation successes is surprising given the high stakes for governments; governments have much to lose when major projects are stalled and mired in legal challenges. A perceived failure of the Crown to uphold honourable conduct, as required by the duty to consult, can lead to contentious politics and time-consuming and expensive litigation. Such a contentious and litigious policy environment may threaten the country's resource extractive industries since companies may decide to withdraw major projects or rethink Canada as an attractive place for their ventures. It is in the interests of the Crown to ensure Indigenous consultation garners legitimacy for its decisions, but this does not consistently occur. This variation in Indigenous acceptance of the Crown's decisions after consultation suggests that the implementation of the duty to consult is shaped by additional forces other than the legal rules conveyed by the judiciary.

This book answers the following questions about the duty to consult's implementation in the Crown's decision-making processes: Does the implementation of the legal duty to consult transform state governance over major projects that may affect the exercise of Aboriginal rights? What do these effects reveal about the ability of constitutional law to produce political change? What are the effects of these changes on Indigenous-state relations? Although the 2004 case of *Haida Nation v British Columbia (Minister of Forests)* held great promise to change the Crown's decision-making, the duty has now been largely dismissed by Indigenous groups as simply window dressing before the Crown pursues its preferred course of action, regardless of the substantive concerns raised by Indigenous participants in consultation.[11] More recently, the governments of British Columbia and Canada have passed legislation that commits to aligning existing and future laws with the *United Nations Declaration on the Rights of Indigenous Peoples* (*UNDRIP*) in 2019 and 2021 respectively.[12] *UNDRIP* appears more robust than the section 35 duty to consult because it requires governments to "consult and cooperate in good faith with the indigenous peoples concerned through their own representative institutions in order to obtain their free, prior, and informed consent."[13] Nevertheless, the Canadian government has also stated that the implementation of *UNDRIP* will maintain the framework already set out in section 35,[14] which may signal an intention to limit the transformative potential of *UNDRIP* in favour of prioritizing existing approaches to consultation. Therefore, even though many Indigenous groups may be ready to abandon the duty to consult in favour of *UNDRIP*, understanding the way in which the government manages their legal obligations, such as the duty to consult, may reveal how the state will continue to practise and guard its decision-making powers in response to the changing legal obligations towards Indigenous peoples, including *UNDRIP*. Indeed, the federal government committed $11.4 million over three years to Crown-Indigenous Relations Northern Affairs Canada in its 2023 budget to create new duty-to-consult guidelines.[15] These changes aim to support the implementation of *UNDRIP* and will be created with Indigenous engagement.[16] The findings from this book will reveal some of the factors that explain whether changing the legal obligations will produce changes in the Crown's decision-making processes and in Indigenous-state relations more broadly.

The Approach

This book explores the relationship between judicial decisions and policy-making by employing an explicit policy lens,[17] treating courts as one potentially significant factor in the broader array of political, legal, social, and economic forces that shape policy-makers and their decisions. By interpreting the Canadian Constitution, courts present ideas about both the normative goals of the duty to consult and rules over how the duty must be practised. These legal rules limit policy alternatives for policy-makers over how to structure decision-making to meet the duty to consult. Although the law, as interpreted by the judiciary, is a powerful constraint on the Crown's decision-makers, the Crown still exercises agency to structure consultation processes, particularly how consultation is integrated in decision-making processes. For instance, policy actors resisting radical institutional change to existing norms or practices may only minimally adopt or layer consultative obligations to seek the least disruptive forms of change. Alternatively, policy actors could be willing to embrace significant institutional change in light of new objectives as signalled by the judiciary, such as calls for a renewed relationship and reconciliation between the state and Indigenous peoples.

Because of the judiciary's role in providing the legal framework for the duty to consult, this book first analyzes the duty's jurisprudence. The judiciary – specifically, the SCC – explained in *Haida Nation* that the duty to consult is a procedural right intended to ensure that the process of the Crown's decision-making meaningfully considers Aboriginal rights, but the court further elaborated that the right does not entail a duty on the part of the Crown to reach an agreement between the participating policy actors. The scope of consultation can vary depending on the strength of the Aboriginal rights at stake and the potential negative impacts on those rights: the high likelihood of a negative impact on established or strong rights claims would entail a more expansive consultative measure than a lower risk to weaker Aboriginal rights claims. How the court has developed the legal rules of the duty to consult over time undoubtedly shapes the policy tools that are available for governments to meet their constitutional obligations. To this end, this book analyzes the duty-to-consult case law from 2004 to 2018 to show how the SCC has defined and prescribed the Crown's appropriate behaviour and actions to advance the duty to consult and the broader political goal of reconciliation.

The analysis of the case law on the duty to consult only partially explains the duty's effects on the Crown's decision-making. In this book, I also evaluate the Crown's decision-making process during the approval of major projects to uncover how the duty is practised and implemented. Within this process, there are various stages leading up to when the Crown makes the final decision to approve or decline projects. Consultation with the relevant Indigenous peoples can take place throughout these stages. The primary goal of the duty to consult is to use negotiations to ensure that the exercise of Aboriginal rights informs the Crown's decision-making; when these interactions are underpinned by honourable dealings, the Crown's actions are considered legitimate since Aboriginal rights are protected. In other words, practising the duty to consult compels governments to explicitly demonstrate their legitimacy to the affected Indigenous groups by including them in the decision-making and ensuring that their section 35 rights are considered.

This demonstration of legitimacy can be evaluated by the courts as they created the legal parameters of the duty that the Crown must meet. But legitimacy is ultimately a subjective concept, and the views of the governed are crucial to evaluating whether governments are acting legitimately, independently of whether the judiciary views state actions as consistent with the duty-to-consult case law. This point is especially pertinent in the context of Indigenous-state relations in Canada, where Indigenous peoples contest the legitimacy of the state to govern any matter in the territory now called Canada due to the state's colonial and unlawful acquisition of territory. The court's interpretation of the Crown's conduct in consultation evaluates whether governments meet the standards of Canadian law, but this does not necessarily mean that those actions are legitimate from the perspective of Indigenous groups. Since reconciliation purports to bring about a nation-to-nation relationship, any evaluation of the duty's implementation and its ability to produce legitimate decision-making must include the perspective of Indigenous nations throughout consultation.

Given the goal of the duty, which is to compel governments to demonstrate their legitimacy to Indigenous peoples, each stage of the Crown's decision-making is evaluated using a public policy framework that helps identify the acquisition of legitimacy throughout these phases. Public policy scholars Fritz Scharpf and Vivien Schmidt differentiate between input, throughput, and output legitimacy as representing the different ways in which the state can attain legitimacy depending on the stage of the decision-making process.[18] This framework's focus on distinguishing these various decision-making phases can be applied to how the duty to consult must be upheld as the Crown engages in decision-making. Input legitimacy is concerned with the inputs of decision-making, mainly ensuring that the relevant actors are included in the decision-making process at the outset and have the requisite resources to participate. Obtaining throughput legitimacy requires meaningful interactions between the actors in the decision-making process, such that the inputs from the policy actors are shaping the form and content of the final decision. Then, output legitimacy addresses whether the outputs of decisions are responsive to the demands of the participants, which in this case includes Indigenous groups. Identifying the barriers or issues that prevent the Crown from attaining legitimacy can explain why Indigenous groups sometimes reject the Crown's decision-making despite their participation in the consultation activities. Based on the scope of duty to consult, success and failure of the duty cannot only be measured by assessing the attainment of various policy preferences. Rather, it must be evaluated based on the goals of the duty: the attainment of the Crown's legitimacy for decisions that may impact Aboriginal rights *throughout* the decision-making phases.

This study focuses on analyzing the Crown's consultation when major projects are proposed in British Columbia. British Columbia is a jurisdiction where many Indigenous nations have not yet resolved rights and title claims with the Crown because few treaties were signed in the province. The duty to consult first emerged to address the possibility that rights claims may be unduly disturbed by the Crown's action before formal recognition of those rights are attained. As such, British Columbia is an important jurisdiction to analyze the implementation of the duty to consult as the duty arose to address the very circumstances faced by many First Nations in that province. Although smaller in number, there are also Indigenous groups who have treaty relationships with the Crown, both historical and modern. Treaty 8 is a historical treaty that covers parts of the northeast region in the province and includes eight First Nations within British Columbia. Modern treaties like those signed with the Nisga'a Nation and Tsawwassen Nation are also present in this jurisdiction. Thus, British Columbia is home to many First Nations with different legal relationships with the Crown, providing a suitable setting to test if these relations affect the Crown's practice of the duty.

Nevertheless, the findings from this study may not perfectly mirror the experience of other Indigenous groups: some nations may generally have more difficulty proving the existence of their rights, as experienced by Métis groups across the country.[19] That being said, interactions between the Crown and First Nations in British Columbia are worth investigating because this jurisdiction is understood by practitioners as a leader in implementing duty-to-consult processes in existing regulatory reviews such as the environmental assessment (EA) process.[20] As such, any issues with the Crown's consultation in this context will likely be apparent in other jurisdictions. Moreover, British Columbia has also approved more salient major projects that have produced high levels of Indigenous resistance in comparison to other regions,[21] revealing the high political stakes when consultation fails. Consultation in British Columbia represents a wide range of cases where the government is arguably well placed to learn best practices for implementing the duty, especially considering that the majority of duty-to-consult cases at the SCC level began in this province. Thus, the lessons learned in British Columbia regarding how the duty is implemented in EA processes remain valuable in other jurisdictions, despite different Indigenous-Crown relationships. Because this analysis of the duty to consult's implementation is focused within British Columbia, the study also includes judicial rulings on the duty from the BC Court of Appeal (BCCA) from 2004 to 2020. This provincial court may produce more specific rulings relevant for the implementation of the duty within this province's EA process.

I evaluate the Crown's performance in consultation within the context of the BC EA process. In addition to analyzing the duty-to-consult case law from the SCC and the BCCA from 2004 to 2020, this study presents a content analysis of 126 EA reports from 2004 when the duty to consult was first established to 2019 when the EA process underwent significant reforms. These reports reveal how the duty to consult was practised by policy actors within the EA process. The EA process is a valuable institutional venue to analyze the implementation of the duty because major projects, which are more likely to trigger the duty, must undergo an EA review. This analysis of the EA reports goes beyond an examination of the duty-to-consult case law to understand how consultation is practised. These archives were supplemented with interview data from twenty-eight key policy actors who have experience working with Indigenous parties and the Crown in consultation.

The Argument

The argument of this book is that the Crown is failing to live up to its duty to consult in British Columbia, largely because the process is not legitimate from the perspective of its key partner, Indigenous peoples. I make this case by exploring both the judiciary's legal framework for the duty to consult and how the Crown has sought to uphold this legal obligation through the EA process in British Columbia, as analyzed through the lens of input, throughput, and output legitimacy. Input legitimacy is compromised because Indigenous parties have not been given the supports to effectively participate in consultation activities; the Crown does not consistently incorporate and address Indigenous parties' feedback throughout the entire assessment, which is a core tenet of throughput legitimacy;

and the Crown's rationales underpinning decisions made by the BC Environmental Assessment Office (EAO) are not communicated transparently, including explaining why one outcome is chosen over the alternatives. This issue undermines output legitimacy as the Crown does not explain how its decisions are responsive to the interests of the governed.

Investigating why these legitimacy deficits appear consistently across various environmental assessments reveals that the duty changes some aspects of state governance but in ways that do not consistently include Indigenous forms or ideas about governance. This is consistent with the critical settler-colonial literature, which posits that the state's main objectives to dispossess and eliminate Indigenous peoples are not radically disturbed through state-based instruments such as legal rights.[22] This book reveals how challenges against settler-colonial legitimacy and authority are managed, with the result that state decision-making power is largely intact and that standards of what constitutes legitimate conduct remain under the control of the state itself. Given the state's focus on mainly pursuing the court's standards of legitimate conduct, it is not surprising that Indigenous participants remain open to challenging the state's actions through litigation if they have a record that shows bad faith negotiations. Overall, I have found that governments can resist challenges against their authority brought upon by the duty to consult by (1) institutional layering driven by key judicial rulings, whereby consultation duties are added onto existing state decision-making processes without the engagement of Indigenous perspectives, and by (2) focusing on managing potential litigation risk to meet the court's arguably deferential standards of adequate consultation. As a result, state legitimacy is reproduced according to the state's own metrics.

Although the creation of the duty to consult has induced changes in governance, the state can resist more transformative changes because the SCC has layered the obligation of the duty onto existing state-based decision-making processes. This institutional layering dampens the transformative potential of the duty because the state and Indigenous parties are not co-creating new processes or standards of legitimate conduct and policy outputs. Instead, additional actors and instruments are simply layered onto processes like the existing regulatory review to produce incremental change that protects the core state institutions.[23] In British

Columbia's EA context, there is an absence of clear legislative frameworks that provide guidance and empower the province's EA actors to comprehensively engage with Indigenous perspectives and world views throughout the assessment. As a result, British Columbia's EA actors avoid overstepping their roles and potentially threatening the policy and negotiating positions of other government actors in future interactions with Indigenous groups. Without a clear change in their mandates, these actors do not exercise the discretionary power to adapt the duty to consult beyond the formal legal requirements as outlined by the courts. This low level of discretionary power among policy actors is a typical condition for institutional layering.[24]

Instead, British Columbia's EA actors closely follow the court's standards of consultation to ensure that litigation risk is managed. For example, the general guidelines on the duty to consult at the provincial and federal levels simply mirror the legal principles outlined by the courts in duty-to-consult jurisprudence and are not targeted towards directing specific agencies like the EAO. Furthermore, without clear statutory or political direction, EA actors do not depart from the status quo EA processes that they have been conducting before the consultative duties were layered since many of those practices are deemed adequate in meeting the Crown's legal obligations under the duty.

EA officials thus meet the judiciary's standards of adequate consultation but do not actively open space for conversations about how to respect Indigenous governance. By largely excluding Indigenous perspectives on governance, consultation and accommodation negotiations resemble a series of performative actions where the actors use the process to best position themselves for the possibility of a legal battle, while the substantive issues of concern are not adequately addressed.[25] Legal victories may compel the opposing party to perform more steps in the consultation performance, but this often does not lead to the integration of Indigenous practices of governance within the Crown's decision-making process. These dynamics strongly suggest that the Crown's policy actors do not practise the duty to attain legitimacy from the perspective of Indigenous peoples but are mainly motivated to meet their own standards of legitimate conduct. This result is paradoxical and politically suspect since the state is identified by the court as suffering from legitimacy deficits, and yet the state institutions unilaterally decide the standard of legitimate behaviour.

These troubling effects are facilitated by the judiciary's conceptualization of the duty to consult, which presents an inadequate and inconsistent baseline to uphold legitimacy from the perspective of Indigenous peoples. The case law does not disturb the Crown's substantial degree of discretion to structure consultative processes and balance competing societal interests. The court's interpretation of the duty incrementally layers some additional rules for the state to follow throughout the consultations, but these rules permit the state to maintain its decision-making processes without Indigenous involvement. Legal scholars have identified how, within the duty-to-consult case law, the SCC has maintained the primacy of the Crown's sovereignty in decision-making, turning the duty to consult as a way for the Crown to consider Aboriginal rights but ultimately maintaining powers to unjustifiably infringe those rights.[26] The SCC's protection of the Crown's sovereignty is evident in its section 35 jurisprudence more generally,[27] suggesting that the duty to consult, like so many early section 35 cases, holds some promise to enforce political change but has been curtailed by the court itself over time. Contrary to public policy studies that show layering as being driven by policy actors, the practice of the duty to consult shows how court rulings can incrementally change certain aspects of the decision-making process while foreclosing opportunities for transformative change. This study's investigation of the duty's implementation in British Columbia's EA process shows that this process has been adjusted to consider Aboriginal rights but not always in ways that align with the perspective of Indigenous rights holders.

This finding is supported by the fact that no major project that has undergone British Columbia's EA process has been rejected principally on the grounds that the exercise of Aboriginal rights was compromised. The two projects that have been rejected had other issues in addition to having a negative impact on Aboriginal rights – largely meaning that the projects were assessed as producing marginal economic benefits[28] or that other non-Indigenous communities would also be adversely affected.[29] This finding is troubling considering that a majority of Indigenous peoples have explicitly opposed forty-one projects out of the 126 assessments (33 percent) conducted by British Columbia's EA process from 2004 to 2019.[30]

These key findings show that the duty to consult alters state governance to focus on the management of legal risks and thus allows the state to resist transformative changes to their governing authority. Despite its promise, the duty does not compel the state to structure consultative mechanisms to address the settler state's legitimacy deficits. The Crown must now show that consultation has taken place with relevant Indigenous groups before decisions are made that affect claimed and proven Aboriginal rights, but these standards to show that adequate consultation has taken place are deferential to the Crown's decision-makers and are interpreted by a state institution. Moreover, this constitutional legal obligation is not paired with legislative reforms to further shape the behaviours of British Columbia's EA officials. Although British Columbia's EA officials are motivated to ensure that the duty to consult has been met, they typically do not exercise their powers to engage with Indigenous perspectives beyond the confines of existing EA statutory mandates.

It is not surprising that Indigenous nations will continue to use even the highly imperfect tools and processes available to them to live and act according to their legal and political obligations. But this resolve does not mean that Indigenous groups are satisfied with the duty-to-consult framework, as evidenced by the most recent efforts to enforce changes to British Columbia's EA process to align with *UNDRIP*. The BC and federal governments' commitments to align laws with *UNDRIP* are more promising precisely because legislative action may realize *UNDRIP*'s legal principles. The new statutory changes to British Columbia's EA process appear to give the EAO more direction regarding how to engage with Indigenous groups, including beginning negotiations with the assumption that they hold Aboriginal rights. Nevertheless, as this study shows, the Crown can use institutional layering to limit transformative disruptions and protect its governing powers. The state's current institutional processes will maintain the Crown's authority at the cost of enduring legitimacy deficits that could erupt in future legal and political conflict, particularly if *UNDRIP* is simply layered onto the framework of section 35's duty to consult.

Chapter Breakdown

This book will substantiate its argument in the following chapters. Chapter 1 explains how consultation is typically used in the policy process to gain legitimacy for policy decisions and that this objective takes on a distinct importance in settler-colonial contexts like Canada. This chapter shows how the colonial relationship between the Crown and Indigenous peoples has de-legitimated the Crown's decision-making authority. As a result, the judiciary has created the duty to consult as a necessary corrective to foster reconciliation or improved relations between Indigenous peoples and the state. The duty is an instrument that could cultivate the Crown's legitimacy and, in turn, legitimate Indigenous peoples' role in executive decision-making. The chapter concludes by presenting the input, throughput, and output legitimacy framework as a useful analytical tool to assess the Crown's performance during consultations with Indigenous participants. Attaining legitimacy throughout the various stages of the decision-making process requires different actions; the Crown's actions towards Indigenous participants in consultation can be examined to determine whether the Crown attains these different, but equally integral, aspects of legitimacy.

Chapters 2 and 3 detail the legal parameters of the duty to consult and explain the findings from the case law analysis. Chapter 2 presents the analysis of eleven duty-to-consult cases rendered by the SCC from 2004 to 2018, and Chapter 3 illustrates the key findings from the sixteen duty-to-consult decisions that were brought before the BCCA between 2004 and 2020. When the duty to consult was established in 2004, the SCC's vision of the goals of reconciliation was a balance between Indigenous and non-Indigenous interests. This vision has remained consistent throughout the duty-to-consult case law. The practices prescribed by the SCC, however, have the potential to undermine the very goals set out by the court to advance reconciliation. In particular, reconciliation is threatened by the inconsistent guidelines that steer how the Crown can implement a fair process for consultation. The BCCA, being a lower court, has not departed from the SCC's articulation of the duty as a tool of reconciliation by balancing Indigenous and non-Indigenous interests. Instead, this court has offered additional specifications around how the Crown can fulfill the duty, particularly within regulatory review processes. The BCCA has also shown deference to the Crown's decision-making, particularly when the Crown must negotiate accommodation measures. This deference may give additional latitude for the Crown to approve major projects without adequate safeguards and accountability measures to ensure that impacts to section 35 rights are avoided or mitigated. The recent decision in *Yahey v British Columbia* by the BC Supreme Court in 2021 is also examined in Chapter

2, as this ruling, which has not been appealed, could have profound effects on how higher courts treat cumulative impacts in future consultation processes. Additionally, the federal court's 2025 decision in *Kebaowek First Nation v Canadian Nuclear Laboratories* explains how *UNDRIP* is to be incorporated in the duty-to-consult framework. The reasoning presented in this decision demonstrates a similar pattern of institutional layering identified in this book, mainly that *UNDRIP* is changing state decision-making in ways that build on the existing duty-to-consult framework rather than replacing the duty altogether.

Chapters 4, 5, and 6 outline the analysis and findings from the 126 EA reports. These reports illustrate in detail how the duty-to-consult process is implemented within the EA process from 2004 to 2019. Moreover, these chapters show how different types of legitimacy – specifically, input, throughput, and output legitimacy – can evaluate the Crown's performance in fulfilling the duty. These chapters assess the Crown's performance according to this framework. The three main stages of the EA process – the application information requirements phase, the application review stage, and the decision stage – mark various decision points where the Crown can attain legitimacy. Specifically, the application information requirements phase is analyzed to consider the Crown's performance in attaining input legitimacy; the application review phase illustrates whether the Crown upholds throughput legitimacy; and the decision phase helps identify any issues with output legitimacy. The study reveals that the Crown in the EA process does not attain key aspects of input, throughput, and output legitimacy. The deferential provisions outlined in the duty-to-consult case law and the absence of additional legislative guidance for British Columbia's EA actors can explain the Crown's inconsistent performance in consultation from the perspective of Indigenous participants.

Chapter 7 examines how Canada's adoption of *UNDRIP* might change current consultation practices. At the end of 2019, the BC government introduced significant reforms to its EA process to align regulatory review with the principles found in *UNDRIP*. This chapter details and analyzes these reforms and their potential to garner more input, throughput, and output legitimacy in the practice of Indigenous consultation. The commitment to provide consistent funding for Indigenous participants, options for Indigenous-led assessments, explicit agreements on the methodology underpinning studies to assess a project's impacts, and consensus-seeking practices appear to be promising measures to attain key aspects of input and throughput legitimacy that have been missing in previous EA processes. Nevertheless, it remains troubling that the decision-making minister's power is still undisturbed, despite *UNDRIP*'s insistence that Indigenous consent is required for project approval on traditional territory. The very layering that diminished the duty to consult's potential to radically change government decision-making may be present in the ways *UNDRIP* appears to be integrated in the new EA process.

The book concludes with some final observations and reflections on the relationship between the judiciary, constitutional law, and policy-making. The judiciary may be an important driver to help ensure Aboriginal rights are not disregarded by the state, but favourable judicial rulings alone are unlikely to compel respect for Indigenous governance alongside the Crown's processes of decision-making.

1

Legitimacy Deficits in Settler-Colonial Canada

Can state-based processes of decision-making ever be perceived as legitimate by Indigenous peoples? Legitimacy is evaluated based on normative standards and moral values underlying the political decisions being taken.[1] Political decisions are generally perceived as legitimate if the process and outcome of decisions solve policy problems. In modern democratic systems, legitimacy is attained through democratic processes, such as having decisions taken by a representative and accountable government. The legitimacy of such a "social contract"–based state system is undermined by the actions and goals of settler colonialism. Settler-colonial states seek to supplant and eliminate Indigenous societies and replace them with a settler population and governance system. From the perspective of Indigenous peoples who resist these colonial forces, the imposition of the state is an illegitimate act of force that has no foundation of consent, implicit or explicit. The settler-colonial state's political claims to sovereignty do not necessarily align with the cultivation of legitimacy from those who would be governed; settler-colonial states attained external acceptance of their claims to control territory from other colonizing states despite the internal rejection and claims of illegitimacy from Indigenous peoples.[2] Colonizing powers created legal rules that suited their interests and facilitated their acquisition and control over territory, even though they did not meet the legal standards of attaining territory through conquest, cessation, or settlement.[3] Concepts like *terra nullius* and the doctrine of discovery were conjured to legally justify settler-state domination by treating lands occupied by Indigenous peoples as constituting "empty lands" that could be discovered and settled by colonizing powers.

It is largely accepted that Canada is an example of a settler state that used force and fraud to impose Crown sovereignty onto pre-existing Indigenous societies and nations. The settler myth is that British and subsequent Canadian officials signed treaties with various Indigenous nations, whereby the Indigenous signatories agreed to surrender their political authority over their lands and people to the Crown in exchange for small reserve lands and became absorbed into the settler body politic. According to this myth, Indigenous peoples exercised sovereign authority insofar as that authority was used to extinguish their political status as self-determining peoples.[4] Contrary to the interests of the settler-colonial state, Indigenous sovereignty has never been eliminated. Instead, it is nested within and alongside the settler state as both Indigenous and non-Indigenous sources of authority have developed overtime.[5] Interactions between sovereign authorities is inevitable and likely to be characterized by conflict if the dominant settler society continues to constrain the exercise of Indigenous self-determination. Indeed, the ongoing resistance of Indigenous peoples has challenged explicit colonial modes of governance and rejected the authority and legitimacy of the settler state. For example, the Red Power movement in the 1970s ensured that Indigenous rights, nationhood, and self-government were never going to be ignored by the state in future interactions and policy-making.

Due to the resistance and mobilization of Indigenous communities and nations, settler-state political institutions and actors are shifting away from overt colonial policies. Since the Indian Residential School Settlement was completed in 2007, Canadian governments have embraced the politics of reconciliation, which seeks to establish a new relationship between Indigenous and non-Indigenous peoples. Although many scholars remain sceptical about the state's intentions to radically change its mode of coexistence with Indigenous peoples,[6] the politics of reconciliation may open opportunities for Indigenous peoples to strategically use state-based interactions like negotiations to secure powers to actualize self-determination.[7] As the state is pivoting to pursue a politics of reconciliation, Indigenous nations are adopting a spirit of resurgence, whereby Indigenous ways of being such as the pursual of their legal and political traditions animate continuing strategic interactions with the state.[8] It is virtually impossible for Indigenous nations to extricate themselves from all interactions with the state, but the resurgence movement posits that Indigenous world views should ground those interactions to prevent cooptation by settler-colonial forces and interests.

From the settler side of the relationship, reconciliation is an opportunity for the state to attain internal legitimacy for future decisions and policy-making. State actors can decide that treaties and agreements have value beyond a means to commit fraud to maintain unilateral control over all territory.[9] The conundrum is whether a settler-colonial state can change its modus operandi to become a more just expression of a political community that shares sovereign authority with the multiple nations in the territory. This means radically transforming Canadian state institutions and processes such that Indigenous nations can exercise decision-making authority over matters that are most pressing to those communities. In other contexts, the state has reorganized to include private and civil society actors in policy-making circles because the state's decision-making authority overall has diffused over time. Given the pressures of the market economy, globalization, and localization, the state has reoriented itself to steer and coordinate new governing arrangements that include actors that exercise and represent various types of authority,[10] such as expert, market, and popular sources of authority.[11]

Public policy and public administration literature have been attuned to these disruptions to state authority, but they have often neglected to evaluate Indigenous challenges to settler states' hierarchical decision-making when assessing the transformation of state power. For example, the literature suggests that pressure to improve the processes of decision-making increase when the state experiences a serious loss of legitimacy,[12] but few have directed attention to Indigenous-led challenges against state-imposed legitimacy. Indigenous peoples' right to govern over matters that are most significant to their communities directly challenges the Canadian state's legitimacy to govern Indigenous nations and lands unilaterally and hierarchically.

Evolving Indigenous-State Governing Arrangements

In the Canadian context, some scholars have employed public policy concepts to understand the changing patterns of governance between Indigenous groups and settler governments, such as how the loci of authority can shift away from the state to Indigenous nations. For example, some have applied the multilevel governance (MLG) framework to describe Indigenous peoples' changing relationship with the Canadian state and other policy actors.[13] Alongside the pursuit of inducing the state to honour treaties and Indigenous peoples' inherent right to self-government, Indigenous nations are also asserting a more dominant role in the design, decision-making, and implementation of policy that affects their interests and communities.[14] This scholarship identifies how these changes in patterns of governance affect existing institutions, like Canadian federalism and intergovernmental relations, and the delivery or management of specific policies and programs. MLG is also evaluated based on whether it can incrementally increase Indigenous participation and autonomy in various policy areas. However, it is important to remember that these patterns of collaborative policy-making occur "in the shadow of hierarchy," whereby the state can leverage its significant resources and power to act unilaterally when collaborative solutions are elusive.[15] Moreover, these arrangements rarely disturb the legitimacy of the Canadian state in making policies concerning Indigenous peoples and lands overall.[16]

The same critique that collaboration with the state rarely disrupts Crown sovereignty over Indigenous peoples and lands can also be applied to the processes in place to settle land claims and new comprehensive governing agreements. It is well known how state-based negotiations like those governing the modern treaty process are fraught with issues relating to uneven bargaining power, such as how, for many years, First Nations were forced to take on loans to participate in negotiations. Only in 2021 did the Trudeau government end this practice and open a process to reimburse those nations who had taken out loans. When outlining the terms of a modern agreement, Indigenous nations are still expected to extinguish claims to title in exchange for clearly defined rights within treaty settlement lands.[17] Due to the devasting effects of colonial policies, many Indigenous governments and communities lack the capacity to negotiate with governments over long periods of time to settle outstanding questions relating to jurisdictional control and authority over land and other key policy areas of interest. Those nations that secure a modern treaty can exercise jurisdictional control over various policy areas, albeit within the broader framework of Canadian federalism.

Beyond political negotiations over managing territory and policy, the judiciary is also used strategically by Indigenous actors as a key venue to help advance Indigenous nations' ability to assert governing authority. The Supreme Court of Canada (SCC) acknowledged in its decision in *Calder et al v British Columbia (Attorney General)* that Indigenous peoples' legal rights are not derived from the *Royal Proclamation* and common law.[18] As such, reconciliation entails a legal component, including ensuring that the common law respects Indigenous rights that flow from Indigenous peoples' prior occupancy before the assertion of Crown sovereignty. Reconciliation can be defined as both "a juridical concept developed by the judiciary to ascribe meaning and purpose to [the] recognition [of Aboriginal rights]" as well as "acts and processes that seek to bring justice to Indigenous-settler relations."[19] From the judicial side, reconciliation must start with acknowledging "the historically-based rights of the Aboriginal group concerned," but then enduring action to bring justice to Indigenous-settler relations entails that the interpretation of those rights "must strike a balance between the need to remedy past injustices and the need to accommodate the full range of contemporary interests."[20] Such legal rights grounded by reconciliation can help shield Indigenous peoples and interests from being neglected and overrun by the state's interests. This idea was the court's initial understanding of section 35 of the *Consitution Act, 1982,* such that the constitutional status of Aboriginal rights can constrain Crown legislative power.[21]

The judiciary's primary function to resolve conflict as an independent institution makes it an optimal body to ensure that governments do not violate rights protected by the Canadian Constitution. However, the judiciary itself does not escape the conundrum of settler colonialism, as courts are a settler-state institution that arguably has a highly limited capacity to challenge the Crown's sovereignty in order to give space to Indigenous legal orders or political authority. This has not stopped the judiciary from pronouncing on the scope and limits of section 35 rights; courts have interpreted section 35 rights like Charter rights that can be justifiably infringed by governments rather than jurisdictional rights exercised by governments that must be negotiated between sovereign authorities.[22] As a result, some Indigenous groups can attain victories before the courts but are ultimately hindered by colonial assumptions around the legitimacy of the Crown's sovereignty as derived from *terra nullius* and the doctrine of discovery.[23]

Although the SCC's decisions construe Aboriginal rights as the rights to engage in cultural practices rather than as expressions of Indigenous legal authority,[24] the SCC has more recently asserted that the Crown's sovereignty must be reconciled with section 35 rights; only when the Crown's exercise of sovereignty respects and upholds section 35 rights is the Crown acting honourably and legitimately.[25] Indeed, the duty to consult arguably emerged as a tool to ensure that the Crown's legitimacy is attained internally across participating policy actors throughout decision-making contexts. The duty emerges in recognition of the fact that Indigenous nations may hold historic rights that have not yet been recognized and that the Crown must seek to find compromises when pending rights may be negatively impacted by contemporary decisions by the Crown. Since the introduction of the duty as a right under section 35, reconciliation "is now something that structures the processes of current interaction between the Crown and Aboriginal peoples."[26] The recognition of Aboriginal rights under section 35 and the duty to consult have resulted in questions about the state's legitimacy in decision-making when Indigenous peoples' rights are at stake. The court's assertion that the Crown must act honourably and with good faith towards Indigenous peoples[27] means that legitimacy must be explicitly demonstrated throughout the decision-making process to show that the state is protecting and honouring Aboriginal rights. When the state upholds Aboriginal rights, then the state can be perceived by internal policy actors as acting legitimately and consistently with the Canadian Constitution. This approach to legitimacy cultivation through piecemeal government decision-making has the potential to transform relationships between Indigenous nations and the state over time, even as the primary conflict between competing conceptions of sovereignty and authority remain.[28] Indeed, the court's promotion of the duty to facilitate reconciliation within the Crown's decision-making suggests that the court itself prefers political actors to negotiate how the Crown's policy-making and Indigenous rights interface, thus requiring the actors to reaffirm the terms of coexistence[29] rather than relying on the zero-sum nature of litigation.[30]

The duty to consult is a constitutionally mandated requirement, meaning that governments uphold the duty when their actions are consistent with broad constitutional principles like those that animate the purpose of section 35, including the objectives of reconciliation. The judiciary has imposed this legal obligation onto governments, but assessing whether policy-making has changed requires analyzing how other policy actors react to these judicial pronouncements.[31] Governments can alter how they govern in areas that affect Indigenous peoples by changing not only the variety of actors, such that Indigenous peoples are now more formally included in decision-making but also the very process by which decisions are made. Decision-making is critical because "it is about making final priorities and allocating public resources to various programs and purposes, [and] it is also about settling disputes, enforcing rules, and bringing closure to issues."[32] Decolonizing the site of state decision-making can radically alter governance over key policy areas that affect or implicate Aboriginal rights. If the judicial evaluation of specific Aboriginal rights cannot produce a comprehensive acceptance of Indigenous legal and political authority, focusing on opening the decision-making process to Indigenous leadership who can assert their rights and interests may be a more effective measure to produce nation-to-nation negotiations across a variety of policy areas.

Scholarship in Canada, focused on understanding the evolving power and role of the judiciary, has evaluated the courts' influence over policy-making, which is considered a highly political domain of activity.[33] This literature has found that additional judicial oversight has led to executive-driven policy-making,[34] whereby the Department of Justice plays a crucial role in ensuring that policies are in compliance with the Canadian Constitution.[35] And yet, even with judicial oversight, Canadian governments continue to pass constitutionally vulnerable legislation because the government's primary objective to pass its preferred legislation is often not outweighed by the risk that the courts will strike it down. Due to its expense, litigation may not be pursued against legislation at all; the process of litigation is lengthy, which gives governments time to entrench support for their legislation or avoid blame altogether if a new government takes over; and, in the context of legislation that violates individual Charter rights, courts employ a proportionality assessment that could ultimately protect the government's primary legislative objective.[36] Although this literature does not employ policy theories or theories of institutional change, it highlights how judicial powers, and the availability of rights protections, change state governance but do not necessarily ensure stronger compliance with the Canadian Constitution. These lessons concerning the extent to which litigation risk induces changes in governance have yet to be tested in the specific context of Aboriginal rights or linked with policy theories that identify changes in state governance.

This book aims to answer the question whether the duty to consult produces sufficient institutional change to legitimate the Crown's decision-making from the perspective of the participating Indigenous policy actors. The duty's main objective is to foster internal legitimacy for the state and its decisions affecting Aboriginal rights, but it must be evaluated whether this legitimacy is attained or whether the state continues to use such legal rules, like the duty to consult, to simply justify continued state control over decision-making while managing litigation risk. Consequently, the judiciary's rulings on duty-to-consult cases over time are also scrutinized in this study. Although the judiciary intends the duty to produce fruitful negotiations between the Crown and Indigenous parties, the reluctance of the courts to directly challenge the Crown's decision-making authority may give the state grounds to cultivate its own legitimacy rather than use the duty to attain legitimacy from Indigenous leaders and groups. In this way, the legal parameters of the duty to consult, as they are articulated by the judiciary, can influence how the Crown implements consultation to either introduce significant change in governance or manage challenges to state legitimacy by minimizing the duty's transformative potential.

Public Policy Approaches to Assessing Legitimacy

Assessing how decision-making processes and actors may have shifted as a result of the duty to consult is the first step to assessing whether and how the Crown's consultation cultivates internal legitimacy for its decisions. A focus on the decision-making process reveals "what must be done to govern" in a particular policy area,[37] which can then reveal the type of actors involved and their respective roles.[38] Crucially, analyzing the policy process can reveal whether certain actors or groups are excluded, repressed, or treated unequally compared to others.[39] Scrutinizing the potential for exclusion may be especially pertinent in the context of Indigenous-Crown relations as there are significant power imbalances between the state and Indigenous actors. Despite the ideals of the duty to consult, the Crown may continue to maintain unilateral control over key policy decisions.

Importantly, the various phases that comprise the decision-making process can produce different sets of processes and actors. The extant literature on Canadian and European network governance have closely analyzed how policy actors can attain legitimacy across these different phases of decision-making. Fritz Scharpf distinguishes two types of legitimacy that is produced throughout the decision-making process, specifically input and output legitimacy.[40] Input legitimacy is gained "when individuals believe that those who make legally enforceable decisions have a right to do so."[41] In contrast, output legitimacy refers to "the outputs of governing – public policies and other decisions – meet[ing] social standards of acceptability and appropriateness."[42] Following Scharpf's elaboration of these concepts, many scholars have evaluated whether various governance networks have upheld input and output legitimacy and tested whether there are trade-offs or interaction effects between the two types in Canadian[43] and European contexts.[44] In addition to input and output legitimacy, Vivien Schmidt introduces an additional type of legitimacy, called throughput legitimacy. According to Schmidt, this type of legitimacy directs attention to the quality of interactions between actors throughout the policy process, requiring scholars to open and investigate this "black box" of governance.[45] Evaluating throughput legitimacy entails examining the administration of complex decision-making processes and the behaviours of these actors throughout.[46] Specific criteria to evaluate the quality of throughput legitimacy include: inclusiveness, transparency, accountability, and effectiveness.[47] Other scholars have similarly analyzed the processes of decision-making beyond their participatory quality and output.[48] Figure 1 provides a summary of the relationship between input, throughput, and output legitimacy according to the literature on comparative network governance.

Within decision-making processes, policy actors can use various tools and instruments to promote or discourage interactions between actors. The choice of what instruments are employed to facilitate actors' interactions can provide insight into how the state may use its coordinative

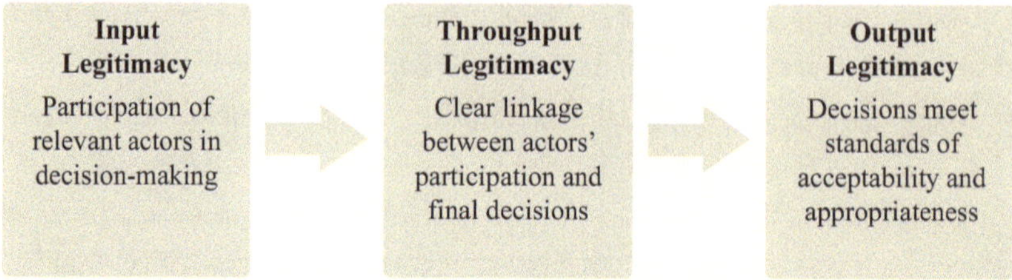

Figure 1 Summary of relationship between input, throughput, and output legitimacy

powers to attain different types of legitimacy across decision-making phases.[49] For example, state decision-makers can use instruments to manipulate the type and number of policy actors involved in decision-making or the structure or sequence in which actors participate.[50] These types of instruments that alter the process of decision-making are conceptualized by Michael Howlett as procedural instruments.[51] According to Howlett, procedural instrument choices are made "in order to retain the political trust or legitimacy required for governments to govern."[52] Procedural instruments may include tools that enhance or repress participation and policy-relevant knowledge.[53]

Interestingly, the network governance literature does not often examine the effectiveness of participatory instruments to increase state legitimacy.[54] This oversight is surprising given that participatory instruments like consultation are intended to obtain legitimacy for the state in the decision-making process. The first objective of consultations is functional, which is to provide information to decision-makers.[55] Providing relevant information to decision-makers may produce more responsive policies as policy-making venues are opened to consider additional perspectives.[56] But, importantly, the second objective of consultation is to add legitimacy to policy outcomes.[57] The scholarship suggests that consultative processes can best attain legitimacy and improve policy outputs when consultees are representative of their group,[58] there are equal participation opportunities, including the provision of adequate resources,[59] and transparent rules and expectations are established at the outset.[60] If the state effectively designs participatory consultative practices, the state is arguably well positioned to attain input and throughput legitimacy.

The potential for consultative measures to produce legitimacy and responsive policies also depends on the interaction dynamics between participants. For instance, principles of deliberation, such as communicative rationality, are seen as ideally situated to increase the likelihood of consultation facilitating both legitimacy and policy responsiveness.[61] Under a deliberative system, actors enter institutional decision-making processes and then actively deliberate with one another by using reasoning to work through opposing or varied positions.[62] Through reason giving, various parties can reach compromises by learning and adjusting their positions throughout interactions with one another. Due to this emphasis on productive interactions between the participants, settings that facilitate deliberative dynamics are also seen as conducive to producing throughput legitimacy.[63] Deliberation between participants is considered ideal, but consultation may also resemble utility-maximizing negotiations or be guided by established rules and organizational templates that are not amenable to learning or change.[64]

Participatory instruments like consultation can open state decision-making processes to include various actors with their own sources of authority and therefore increase both policy responsiveness and legitimacy. But the potential of these types of participatory instruments to garner meaningful engagement from varied actors – most notably, among groups that experience marginalization – is highly contested. Even tools that aim to facilitate deliberation have been critiqued as simply perpetuating exclusion, particularly if the goals of engagement are not directed at anti-oppression and social justice.[65] There is a risk that participatory tools may proceduralize engagement to seek "box ticking" rather than meaningfully include the various perspectives being sought. Without carefully structuring consultation processes, its goals, and how it is implemented within the broader state decision-making process to address power disparities, even deliberative forms of participation will simply "fold people and ideas into a flawed system."[66] These important critiques demonstrate the need to critically examine how participatory tools are implemented and their effects to ensure that participants are meaningfully included in the state's decision-making. A pathway to design decision-making processes that reflect meaningful exchanges between policy actors could involve including the various participants' standards of what is deemed to be legitimate practices of decision-making.[67] In the case of Indigenous participants in settler-state decision-making contexts, the importance of respecting

Indigenous perspectives, including those perspectives that challenge the state's authority itself, is crucial to developing legitimacy.

The inclusion of Indigenous peoples into existing state processes raises questions about whether it is possible to significantly transform state-based decision-making as directed by the duty to consult.[68] It is the objective of this project to empirically assess whether the duty to consult as a legal obligation produces change in the Crown's decision-making. Answering this question reveals the extent to which the judiciary, and its articulation of legal obligations, can compel changes to the state's policy process. For example, the effects of the duty to consult on the Crown's decision-making can present strategic opportunities for Indigenous policy actors to assert their authority and interests. Through political negotiations that are structured by honourable consultations, it is possible that Indigenous nations' governance over people and territories is asserted to constrain the Crown's power. Procedural tools by themselves may not resolve deep political conflicts, such as conflicts over authority,[69] but implementing the duty can be an important step in opening the process itself to scrutiny from Indigenous participants to reject and contest unilateral Canadian governance.

On the other hand, the settler state can strategically produce legitimacy to support the continued dispossession of Indigenous nations under a framework of "recognition."[70] The Crown's policy actors may take measures to protect their policy-making authority and colonial interests over land. It is debated in the public policy literature whether new sources of authority limit the state's power[71] or whether the state has simply been directed to achieve different aims with its power.[72] This debate is particularly pertinent in the context of settler-colonial states, as the duty may not effectively constrain state power to give space for the exercise of Indigenous authority but, rather, redirect state power to manage Indigenous involvement in policy decisions while ensuring colonial interests are served.

The policy literature concerned with legitimacy and the participatory tools to attain legitimacy can be applied beyond the context of policy networks to assess the implementation of court-mandated changes to decision-making, like the duty to consult. This approach to evaluating the implementation of the duty is novel but promising as the concern for input, throughput, and output legitimacy aligns with the procedural and substantive objectives of the duty. One objective of the duty to consult is a fact-finding purpose, which is to identify the relevant Aboriginal rights that may be negatively affected by the Crown's action.[73] This goal is achieved by structuring a fair process for relevant Indigenous actors to participate in decision-making so that they can express their rights claims to the Crown's actors. The characteristics of input legitimacy lend guidance concerning what a fair process can look like for participants: inviting and communicating with the relevant and representative Indigenous leadership when consultative activities are happening; providing the adequate resources for groups to participate; and ensuring that the rules and processes that structure the consultations are clear and agreed upon by the participants.

Another key characteristic of the procedural aims of the duty is to facilitate meaningful and informed interactions between the Crown's representatives and Indigenous parties as they dialogue with one another with the aim to address Aboriginal rights.[74] As such, the primary focus of throughput legitimacy, with its emphasis on the quality of interactions between actors, may be an essential element to ensure that the inputs of decision-making are meaningfully considered to produce responsive policy outputs. It has been suggested that the quality of interactions in fulfilling the duty to consult should reflect "deliberative characteristics of participatory decision-making."[75] Although dialogue sometimes is used synonymously with negotiations in the context of the duty to consult,[76] how policy actors interpret the goal of dialogue may influence the quality of the interactions between the Crown and the Indigenous actors in consultation. Instrumental understandings of dialogue may simply require the actors to understand the position of others, while deliberative understandings of dialogue include the possibility that preferences and ideas can change through introspection and persuasion.[77] The court has only stated that consultation must entail the possibility that final decisions may be altered,[78] but policy actors must interpret the court's rules when practising the duty, including the prescription for dialogue to take place. How the Crown's policy actors choose to engage with Indigenous perspectives will likely have an impact on the extent to which Indigenous participation is linked to the final decision, thus influencing the attainment of throughput legitimacy.

Finally, the duty to consult also has a substantive dimension, whereby consultation efforts may lead to the creation of accommodation measures that mitigate or compensate for the potential negative impacts to the exercise of Aboriginal rights. Under the duty, the Crown retains its decision-making authority if it acts honourably by making appropriate accommodation measures given the identification of the Aboriginal rights at stake. Only honourable actions from the Crown, such as meaningfully trying to incorporate Indigenous peoples' concerns through the fulfilment of the duty, are viewed by the SCC as legitimate.[79] There are no legal expectations around the kinds of accommodation measures that would best meet Indigenous parties' concerns and protect the exercise of their rights. It may be the case that more long-term agreements around pursuing joint decision-making between the state and Indigenous peoples over a geographic area or over the management of a specific resource may be put forward. In this way, the duty could help facilitate piecemeal arrangements that shift authority towards Indigenous communities as a means of mitigating negative effects on the exercise of Aboriginal rights.

Unlike consultations between decision-makers and citizens or stakeholders, the duty to consult engages input, throughput, and output legitimacy in unique ways due to the constitutional status of Indigenous consultation and its purpose of protecting Aboriginal rights. For instance, Indigenous peoples' expectations about how institutions and decision-making processes attain input, throughput, and output legitimacy is crucial since the objective of the duty is to attain internal legitimacy for state action by protecting Aboriginal rights. Legitimacy must be acknowledged by the participating Indigenous policy actors in order to advance reconciliation;[80] the state's authority is not legitimate unless it is recognized as such by the Indigenous parties. Otherwise, the cultivation of unilateral legitimacy that follows the court's interpretation of legitimate conduct will continue the colonial trajectory of the state guarding authority over decisions affecting Indigenous peoples. Moreover, the scope and nature of Aboriginal rights are determined by both Indigenous perspectives and the common law.[81] Without the effective inclusion of Indigenous perspectives, the Crown may not grasp the full scope of the Aboriginal rights that are at stake across various major projects. Finally, since reconciliation entails relationship building between the Crown and Indigenous peoples, the perspective of

Indigenous parties in their interactions with the Crown is significant to evaluate whether reconciliatory actions animate the practice of Indigenous consultation. Figure 2 summarizes how input, throughput, and output legitimacy can be attained in the context of the duty to consult.

The framework of input, throughput, and output legitimacy is a set of normative criteria that evaluates whether the Crown's decision-making can be considered honourable towards Indigenous peoples. It is a useful framework to adopt in the settler-colonial context because it does not presuppose hierarchical patterns of decision-making. Instead, the framework captures that the onus is on the state to include and interact with additional policy actors because the state suffers from legitimacy deficits. Moreover, this framework can be applied to emphasize the Indigenous participants' perceptions in measuring the various aspects of legitimacy. Legitimacy is a constructed and contested concept; including Indigenous participants' perceptions of legitimacy may reveal crucial differences between their understanding of honourable dealings and the Crown's position. Indeed, even the concept of what constitutes legitimate actions may need to be decolonized to account for Indigenous perspectives of good governance.

Analyzing both the legal structure of the duty-to-consult case law and how it has been implemented within state-based policy processes can reveal the extent to which settler institutions, both legal and policy oriented, can produce opportunities for Indigenous policy actors to assert their rights and governing authority. Indigenous peoples will continue to contest colonial acts, but changing state decision-making to explicitly address

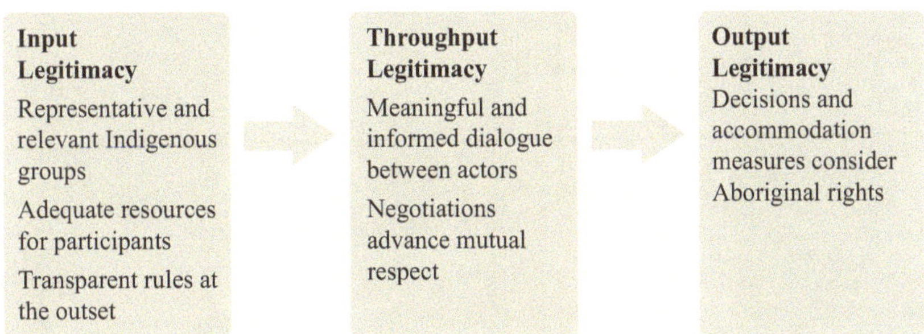

Figure 2 Input, throughput, and output legitimacy in the context of the duty to consult

Aboriginal rights and include Indigenous leadership can open the possibility of transforming colonial processes in a piecemeal fashion. If the duty to consult does not present these opportunities for Indigenous groups to strategically engage with the state in protecting their rights and promoting shared governance structures, then it is pertinent to understand how the state uses and construes the legal rules and policy instruments to maintain control over decision-making.

2

The Supreme Court of Canada and the Duty to Consult

The duty to consult is a legal mechanism introduced by the judiciary to facilitate political negotiations between Indigenous and non-Indigenous societies. The duty emerges in recognition of the fact that Indigenous nations hold historic rights; it seeks to find compromises when rights that are not yet recognized by the state may be negatively impacted by the Crown's contemporary decisions. The Crown experiences legitimacy deficits if it does not seek to recognize and respect Aboriginal rights, making reconciliation through political negotiations crucial. Arguably, since the introduction of the duty under section 35 of the *Constitution Act, 1982,* reconciliation "is now something that structures the processes of current interaction between the Crown and Aboriginal peoples,"[1] with the aim of promoting reconciliation "through negotiated settlement[s] of outstanding claims."[2]

The Supreme Court of Canada (SCC) has elaborated how the duty fits within Canadian constitutionalism by linking the duty to the honour of the Crown and the goal of reconciliation. This overarching goal of reconciliation helps contextualize the judiciary's evaluation of how the Crown should implement and practise the duty and the standards by which to evaluate the Crown's performance in consultation. Decisions at the SCC level must be closely examined because its decisions are binding on all other courts, the SCC rules on issues of public importance, and this court's rulings contribute to the development of all areas of law in Canada. Since the aim of this book is to identify the legal parameters within which policy actors can fulfill the duty to consult, identifying the rules outlined by the SCC are most relevant because they cannot be further appealed and contested. Moreover, the BC government's guiding documents that discuss how government bodies can implement the duty to consult also focus on the case law at the SCC's level, further demonstrating its relevancy in this jurisdiction.

The duty to consult is understood by the SCC to advance reconciliation by balancing the interests of both Indigenous and non-Indigenous societies and to reconcile the Crown's asserted sovereignty and Indigenous peoples' prior occupancy. The court understands this balancing to take place within the existing decision-making processes, with the obligation of the duty layered on top of those existing processes. The SCC has thus incrementally driven the duty's layered implementation in Crown decision-making by articulating the main goal of the duty, which is to advance reconciliation through honourable decision-making processes, and the rules and procedures to meet this goal.

With regard to articulating the rules of honourable consultation, the SCC presents a vague standard for the Crown to meet the procedural and substantive dimensions of the duty to consult. For instance, the Crown can exercise discretion over how transparently it communicates its decision-making to Indigenous parties, thereby diminishing the goal of upholding procedural fairness. Indigenous parties cannot claim a particular outcome from consultation, and the judiciary itself faces institutional limitations in reviewing the Crown's various activities. These factors lead to the Crown facing fewer constraints to approve major projects since the Crown's decision-makers can claim to balance Aboriginal rights without clearly incorporating the perspectives of Indigenous peoples about the exercise of those Aboriginal rights. As a result, the implementation of the duty can lead to an asymmetrical version of reconciliation whereby Indigenous peoples must reconcile themselves to the Crown's power. Under such a view of the duty, consultation could become an ineffective check to ensure that the Crown produces legitimate decision-making. A failure to produce legitimate decision-making may cause Indigenous parties to reject consultation altogether as it appears to simply make post-hoc justifications for the Crown's decisions. This result would delegitimize Canadian constitutional law to adequately protect Indigenous peoples' rights, delegitimize the decision-making actions of the Crown, and delegitimatize the judiciary itself as a key interpreter of Canadian law and Aboriginal rights.

To show how the judiciary produces this problematic foundation for the duty to consult's implementation, this chapter investigates all eleven SCC decisions about the duty to consult. The duty became a definable stream of Aboriginal law in the *Haida Nation* trilogy, which includes *Haida Nation v British Columbia (Ministry of Forests)* in 2004, *Taku River Tlingit First Nation v British Columbia (Project Assessment Director)* in 2004, and *Mikisew Cree First Nation v Canada (Minister of Canadian Heritage)* in 2005.[3] Following this trilogy, the SCC has clarified in what contexts the duty is triggered and has elaborated on key parts of its nature, thus refining the rules surrounding its implementation incrementally over time. The role of regulatory bodies was addressed in *Rio Tinto Alcan v Carrier Sekani* in 2010, and the duty in the context of a modern treaty was covered in *Beckman v Little Salmon/Carmacks First Nation* in 2010.[4] In *Behn v Moulton Contracting* in 2013, the SCC stressed that all parties have an obligation to uphold the principles of due process to maintain good faith but left open the question of whether a smaller group within a larger Aboriginal group could trigger the duty.[5] *Tsilhqot'in Nation v British Columbia* in 2014 referenced the duty in the context of justifying infringements to Aboriginal title.[6] The SCC assessed the adequacy of the Crown's consultation efforts in *Chippewas of the Thames First Nation v Enbridge Pipelines*, *Clyde River (Hamlet) v Petroleum Geo-Services*, and *Ktunaxa Nation v British Columbia (Forests, Lands and Natural Resource Operations)* all in 2017.[7] Finally, *Mikisew Cree First Nation v Canada (Governor General in Council)* in 2018 presented questions about whether the duty or other obligations grounded in the honour of the Crown is triggered in legislative contexts.[8]

The introduction of the duty to consult is an important turning point in reconciliation and section 35 rights. Literature that examines the development of the duty to consult as its own area of Aboriginal law considers the duty's role in advancing reconciliation either directly or indirectly. This scholarship analyzes the duty in various contexts such as its scope and level[9] and its relationship with administrative law[10] as well as questions surrounding the role of industry actors.[11] Although this scholarship is insightful and important, this chapter will analyze the duty-to-consult case law by considering the consequences of the law's development on political actors' choices to implement the duty.[12]

Scholars have considered many different consequences that emerge from the duty-to-consult case law, such as the Crown's power in negotiations;[13] the Crown's balancing of Indigenous and non-Indigenous interests;[14] the capacity of Indigenous peoples to participate in consultation, particularly over time and across different projects;[15] and whether the duty can promote "economic reconciliation."[16] This literature depicts the various challenges that might arise when the duty to consult is practised. A potentially more systematic way to analyze these various consequences of the case law is to distinguish between procedural and substantive concerns that may arise from the duty.[17] Thus, an additional aim of this chapter is to differentiate between the procedural and substantive consequences of the duty-to-consult case law over time. This distinction will help identify how to evaluate the Crown's performance in meeting its procedural and substantive obligations towards Indigenous peoples in the environmental assessment (EA) process.

The Duty to Consult as an Aboriginal Right: *Haida Nation, Taku River,* and *Mikisew Cree*

In the *Haida Nation* trilogy, which includes the cases of *Haida Nation, Taku River,* and *Mikisew Cree,* the duty to consult formally articulates the right of Indigenous nations to be consulted in situations other than when the Crown justifies infringements to Aboriginal title. In *Haida Nation* and *Taku River,* the SCC stated that the duty is triggered when the Crown's action may adversely impact unproven Aboriginal rights.[18] In *Mikisew Cree* 2005, the SCC deemed that the duty to consult is also triggered when the Crown's action could impact existing treaty rights, even if the Crown's interference is outlined in the treaty itself.[19]

The SCC reiterated in all three cases that reconciliation is required between the Crown's *de facto* sovereignty and Indigenous peoples' prior occupancy and that the duty can facilitate this goal of reconciliation.[20] Reconciliation is necessary since "Canada's Aboriginal peoples were here when Europeans came, and were never conquered."[21] The duty to consult can facilitate reconciliation because it incentivizes governments to negotiate unsettled claims over territory and governance; since the SCC found that the Crown cannot unilaterally pursue actions that may adversely impact unclaimed Aboriginal rights,[22] negotiations are required before claims are settled and long after settlements are formalized. In this way, the duty prevents reconciliation from being treated as a "distant legalistic goal."[23] This understanding of reconciliation also reflects the idea that the Crown and Indigenous parties must enter political negotiations to redefine, or to find, new terms of coexistence with one another. Indeed, the SCC explained that the Crown is required to participate in these negotiations.[24] The duty to consult is one legal mechanism to ensure that these political interactions occur to sort out how the protection of Aboriginal rights interfaces with the Crown's decision-making.

Since the duty to consult is meant to manage Indigenous-Crown interactions within political decision-making processes, the SCC explained how Crown and Indigenous parties are required to behave towards one another in this process. The Crown is expected to uphold the honour of the Crown, which is at stake in all dealings with Indigenous peoples.[25] The court clarified that upholding the honour of the Crown means that the Crown must intend to fulfill its promise to recognize Aboriginal rights through negotiations.[26] The SCC also stated that both Crown and Indigenous parties are expected to act in good faith to resolve conflicts throughout any negotiations.[27] On the part of the Crown, acting in good faith means taking Aboriginal rights claims seriously and meaningfully attempting to address the concerns that arise. The Crown's sovereignty remains unchallenged in the *Haida Nation* trilogy, but the court acknowledged that the Crown's sovereignty is simply "asserted"; in order to remain legitimate, the Crown's sovereignty must be exercised honourably. The Crown meets the standard of an honourable sovereign authority when the Crown "determine[s], recognize[s] and respect[s]" Aboriginal rights, and the duty to consult and accommodate can facilitate these ongoing political negotiations aimed at respecting Aboriginal rights.[28] Thus, the Crown can demonstrate its *political* legitimacy to govern by maintaining honourable conduct towards Indigenous peoples and upholding their rights in decision-making contexts; this imperative to explicitly demonstrate honourable conduct is *legally* required due to the asserted nature of the Crown's sovereignty. Moreover, this honour requires the Crown to "balance societal and Aboriginal interests in making decisions that may affect Aboriginal claims."[29] This call to balance Indigenous and non-Indigenous interests shows that the court understands that Indigenous rights and societies are a part of a broader Canadian society that needs reconciling.

On the part of Indigenous peoples, they are expected to "not frustrate the Crown's reasonable good faith attempts, nor should they take unreasonable positions to thwart government from making decisions."[30] The SCC also clarified that Indigenous peoples do not have a veto power over decisions about land and resources.[31] It is the court's belief that, if both parties are motivated by good faith, then it is possible for them to "understand each other's concerns and move to address them."[32] Therefore, the practice of the duty to consult is guided by the honour of the Crown and good faith dealings. It is also crucial to note that "mov[ing] to address" the concerns of Indigenous parties means that the duty has a substantive component to negotiate accommodation measures if potential impacts to Aboriginal rights have been identified.[33] The Crown cannot simply identify impacts without considering measures to address those impacts. Nevertheless, the court is clear that the duty to consult does not entitle any party to a particular outcome or a "duty to agree" but, instead, ensures a "meaningful consultative process."[34]

Additional practices required to fulfill the duty to consult relate to identifying the appropriate scope and content of consultation. The duty is triggered when the Crown has knowledge of an Aboriginal rights claim and when the Crown's conduct may adversely impact an Aboriginal rights claim.[35] The scope of the duty depends on both the severity of the Crown's potential adverse impact and the strength of the Aboriginal rights claim. A dubious claim with minimal risk of infringement may only involve a duty to give notice of a proposed action,[36] while a strong rights claim and serious infringements to the rights claim may require more substantive forms of consultation, including accommodation.[37] When the Crown has identified the proper scope of consultation, the adequacy of this consultation is adjudicated based on the broad goals of balancing and finding a compromise between the competing interests.[38] Although the purpose of the duty laid out in *Haida Nation* was clear, the court maintained that the scope and practice of adequate consultation should be evaluated on a case-by-case basis.[39]

The SCC further asserted that the Crown "is not rendered impotent" and "may continue to manage the resource in question pending claims resolution."[40] At the same time, the court stated that Indigenous peoples can still engage in "hard bargaining" in the consultative process.[41] The SCC's lack of specificity over how compromises are reached enables the parties to exercise flexibility in negotiations guided by honourable, good faith efforts. The focus of negotiation within the duty to consult can open the possibility of a "generative dialogue," which has the potential to creatively weave together Indigenous and non-Indigenous forms of governance. Although not mandated by the SCC, the Crown may find that respecting Indigenous-led processes of decision-making can effectively meet the requirements of honourable dealing and advance a vision of reconciliation where Indigenous and Crown authority are considered equal. Such an approach may also be more likely to find acceptance among Indigenous nations, as their approaches to governance would be respected. James (Sa'ke'j) Youngblood Henderson defines generative dialogue in the following terms:

> Generative dialogue is a conversation in which people think together in a constitutional relationship. Thinking together implies that you no longer take your own legal tradition or parallel position as final. You relax your grip on certainty and interests and listen to the genuine legal possibilities that result simply from being in a relationship with others, possibilities that might not otherwise have occurred. These processes will generate a demand for learning new skills and methods that are different from existing legal and political knowledge.[42]

Balancing Indigenous and non-Indigenous interests, as advocated by the SCC to maintain the honour of the Crown, can be informed by engaging with Indigenous decision-making and legal traditions. Although the court did not adopt the language of a nation-to-nation relationship when describing the process of Indigenous consultation, the duty to consult does not preclude the possibility of equal collaboration from Indigenous parties to meet the duty's aims to reconcile varying rights and interests.

Despite the promise that a renewed decision-making process can recognize Aboriginal rights and uphold the Crown's honour, the duty to consult may still not dramatically alter decision-making outcomes following consultation. The Crown remains the final decision-maker, and the Crown itself has interests in pursuing its own proposed conduct. Moreover, the court placed the onus on creating consultative processes with the Crown alone,[43] which may mean that the Crown will not incorporate Indigenous views of legitimate conduct or honourable dealing in consultative schemes. The duty may facilitate fruitful negotiations between the Crown and Indigenous peoples, or it may only change how the Crown's decisions are put into operation.[44] Although the honour of the Crown requires the balancing of interests to account for Indigenous perspectives, there is no guarantee a change in the process will amount to adequate changes in the outcome. Table 1 summarizes the key findings from this trilogy of cases.

Table 1: Summary of *Haida Nation, Taku River,* and *Mikisew Cree* 2005 cases

Case name	*Year*	*Legal issue(s)*	*Key duty-to-consult principles*
Haida Nation v British Columbia (Ministry of Forests)	2004	Whether the government has a legal duty to consult and accommodate the Haida Nation with respect to harvesting timber on lands claimed by the Haida Nation	• The duty to consult is grounded in the honour of the Crown and facilitates reconciliation between the Crown's asserted sovereignty and Aboriginal rights. • The duty to consult is triggered when the Crown has knowledge that their proposed action could affect Aboriginal rights or title that are claimed or recognized. • The scope of the duty is based on an assessment of the seriousness of the potential impact and the strength of the Aboriginal rights or title claim. • It is the Crown's responsibility to create regulatory schemes to fulfill the duty. • There is no duty for all parties to reach an agreement.
Taku River First Nation v British Columbia (Project Assessment Director)	2004	Whether the government's consultation efforts in the EA process adequately meet the duty to consult	• The case reaffirmed principles from the *Haida Nation* case.
Mikisew Cree First Nation v Canada (Minister of Canadian Heritage)	2005	Whether the duty to consult applies to treaties that stipulate the terms of the Crown "taking up" lands	• The duty is triggered in treaty contexts even where "taking-up" clauses are outlined.

The Duty to Consult in Administrative Law and Title Contexts: *Rio Tinto, Beckman, Behn,* and *Tsilhqot'in*

After the *Haida Nation* trilogy entrenched the duty to consult as its own area of Aboriginal law, the subsequent duty-to-consult cases further shaped the rules of how the duty is practised. In particular, the SCC turned to other areas of common law, such as administrative law, to help inform how the Crown can implement the duty and evaluate its adequacy. The *Rio Tinto* case was the next SCC decision relating to the duty to consult. In this decision, the SCC clarified "what triggers a duty to consult, and the place of government tribunals in consultation and the review of consultation."[45] In terms of what triggers the duty, the SCC created a three-step procedure that builds on the framework outlined in *Haida Nation*. The Crown must have knowledge of an Aboriginal right or rights claim, the Crown must have demonstrated a proposed conduct, and this proposed conduct must adversely impact the Aboriginal right or rights claim.[46] These steps ensure that there is "a causal connection between the proposed Crown conduct and a potential adverse impact on an Aboriginal claim or right."[47] The court also clarified that the duty cannot be used to address underlying infringements, historical grievances, or the "larger adverse impacts of the project of which [the Crown's specific action] is a part."[48]

Crucially, this decision addressed the role of tribunals. Up to this point in the SCC's duty-to-consult decisions, the cases involved disputes between one of the Crown's decision-makers and an Indigenous party. In *Rio Tinto*, the decision-maker was a tribunal, which is not a representative of the Crown because of its quasi-judicial status to consider questions of law. The SCC explained that tribunals' powers depend on the mandates conferred to them by statute; if a tribunal is expected to evaluate the adequacy of consultation, or engage in consultation itself, then the legislatures must give them the jurisdiction to perform these tasks.[49] This decision reveals a crucial development concerning the duty's implementation because the court acknowledged that Indigenous consultation can be fulfilled by existing Crown institutions and decision-making processes. Rather than encourage a generative decision-making process that reflects patterns of governance by Indigenous groups and the Crown, the court affirmed that the duty can be layered onto state-based processes even if they have not been initially designed to evaluate or address concerns related to Aboriginal rights.

In contrast, the *Beckman* decision explained how the duty applies in the context of modern treaties and is compatible with administrative law.[50] Specifically, administrative law principles were drawn on to evaluate the adequacy of consultation. In the *Haida Nation* decision, the SCC explained that because "the government is required to make reasonable efforts to inform and consult," it makes more sense to use a standard of reasonableness rather than a standard of correctness.[51] In contrast, when determining whether the duty is triggered and how the Crown determines the scope of consultation, the standard of correctness applies.[52]

The adoption of a standard of reasonableness may give rise to the concern that the court will be more deferential to the Crown's judgment in judicial review.[53] These concerns could be assuaged by the Crown's requirement to act honourably towards Indigenous peoples. This unique relationship that is underpinned by honourable conduct may entail further obligations on the part of the Crown to consider the contextual factors of a decision's impacts, including "the vulnerability of the affected parties."[54] Although such an interpretation of a standard of reasonableness in the context of the honour of the Crown may be more robust than mere deference,[55] the SCC avoided devising a framework to evaluate the outcomes of consultation. Consultation must be meaningful, but the court did not suggest that it would closely assess the Crown's efforts to balance the competing interests, apart from determining its reasonableness. This aversion may reflect the highly contextual nature of adjudicating reasonableness as well as the court's hesitancy to mandate policy outcomes.

In *Beckman*, the SCC also explicitly stated that the duty to consult could be informed by administrative law principles such as procedural fairness. The court referenced *R. v Van der Peet* from 1996, which states that "Aboriginal rights exist within the general legal system of Canada,"[56] meaning that both the common law and Indigenous perspectives should inform Aboriginal rights. The SCC rejected the Little Salmon/Carmacks First Nation's assertion that there should be distinct constitutional remedies, and it remained convinced that "administrative law is flexible enough to give full weight to the constitutional interests of the First Nation" and so "there is no need to invent a new 'constitutional remedy.'"[57] This idea that common law concepts can adequately capture Aboriginal rights claims continued from the *Van der Peet* decision, which arguably diminished the importance of uncovering the Indigenous perspective of their rights, including those perspectives grounded in Indigenous legal traditions. The court continued that, under the principles of procedural fairness, the impact of an administrative decision is of interest to all the parties involved, Indigenous and non-Indigenous.[58]

Another way in which the SCC has shown the intersection between the duty to consult and administrative law principles is in the importance placed on procedural justice when reviewing duty-to-consult cases. The *Behn* case involved members of the Fort Nelson First Nation, who were blocking access to a logging site, claiming that the duty to consult was not met before the logging licenses were issued.[59] The court found that the Behn family's actions constituted an abuse of process because they did not raise their concerns with the logging licenses at the appropriate time, such as when the BC government granted them to the proponent.[60] Due to the Behn family's lack of intervention when the authorizations were issued, the court claimed that the Behn family's actions "amount[ed] to an abuse of process" and that "allow[ing] the Behns to raise their defence ... at this point would be tantamount to condoning self-help remedies and would bring the administration of justice into disrepute."[61] Moreover, the court also explained that the Behn family did not act in good faith, which animates the duty to consult.[62] Acting in good faith involves observing deadlines and opportunities to put forward concerns. This decision demonstrates that the court strictly upholds procedural fairness and does not tolerate any party appearing to circumvent the established consultation process.

The use of administrative law principles like procedural fairness and the aversion of the SCC to evaluate the outcome of consultation could be a way for the court to account for the highly contextual nature of the Crown's decision-making. The SCC appears to understand reasonableness as ensuring that the Crown equally accounts for the interests of all relevant groups that may be impacted by a proposed project. Equally considering impacts to various groups may entail differential calculations when balancing interests. For instance, upholding reasonableness in the context of the Crown's honourable relationship with Indigenous peoples may require the Crown to consider the different levels of vulnerability that groups experience and how that vulnerability may be exacerbated by the Crown's decision.[63] This more "purposive approach" to consultation would focus reconciliatory efforts on the outcomes of consultation, such as the accommodations made to address Aboriginal rights, in addition to securing opportunities for Indigenous parties to express their interests throughout the decision-making.[64] Accommodation should "incorporate the concerns" of Indigenous peoples rather than simply allowing the Crown to "unilaterally determin[e] the value of the Aboriginal interests at stake" when the Crown balances competing societal interests.[65] By treating Aboriginal rights as equal to other stakeholder interests, there is a risk that consultation will inadequately protect rights that hold constitutional status.[66] Practising procedural justice without seriously considering the obligations owed specifically towards Indigenous peoples that are required to maintain the honour of the Crown could allow the Crown to ignore or misunderstand the unique claims of Indigenous parties. This neglect would not only undermine the pursuit of reconciliation but also fail to correct the Crown's unique legitimacy deficits vis-à-vis Indigenous peoples.

The *Tsilhqot'in* case is the first decision to grant an Indigenous nation title through judicial review and was considered a highly positive development in Aboriginal case law for Indigenous peoples.[67] The Tsilhqot'in Nation, a semi-nomadic First Nation, disputed the issuing of logging licenses on lands claimed to be its traditional territory.[68] Although this case is an Aboriginal title case, the SCC also addressed the issue of consultation. Affirming *Delgamuukw v British Columbia* from 1997, the court affirmed that consultation in the context of claimed Aboriginal title could be used as part of the justification process to infringe title.[69] The SCC further explained that "after Aboriginal title to land has been established by court declaration or agreement, the Crown must seek the consent of the title-holding Aboriginal group to developments on the land."[70] If consent is not acquired, then the Crown must discharge the duty and justify its infringements in order to pursue its conduct.[71] Moreover, the court added that "governments and individuals proposing to use or exploit land, whether before or after a declaration of Aboriginal title, can avoid a charge of infringement or failure to adequately consult by obtaining the consent of the interested Aboriginal group."[72]

The SCC strongly signalled to the Crown that seeking consent is the best practice to ensure that litigation is avoided, the duty is discharged, and reconciliation is advanced. Nevertheless, these statements are merely prescriptions, and the court does not enforce any standards to suggest that consent is required to fulfill the duty in the context of Aboriginal title. It may be unlikely, then, that the suggestion for consent will be pursued by the Crown when measures apart from obtaining consent can still justify infringements to title. Nevertheless, since the judiciary is now an avenue for Indigenous groups to claim title, it may be possible that title claims from Indigenous parties may induce the Crown to seek consent as a prudent measure to avoid litigation.[73] Table 2 summarizes the main ideas from these four cases.

Table 2: Summary of *Rio Tinto Alcan*, *Beckman*, *Behn*, and *Tsilhqot'in Nation* cases

Case name	*Year*	*Legal issue(s)*	*Key duty-to-consult principles*
Rio Tinto Alcan v Carrier Sekani Tribal Council	2010	Whether the change in the energy purchase agreement between BC Hydro and Rio Tinto Alcan required consultation with the Carrier Sekani Tribal Council	• The duty to consult is not used to address underlying infringements, historical grievances, or the broader adverse impacts of a project in which the Crown's specific action is a part. • Tribunals can evaluate the adequacy of the Crown's consultation or engage in consultative activities, but it requires a statutory mandate to do so.
Beckman v Little Salmon Carmacks	2010	Whether the duty to consult is triggered in modern treaty contexts that stipulate a "taking-up" clause	• The duty to consult applies in modern treaty contexts, even where "taking-up" clauses are outlined. • The case confirmed that a standard of reasonableness applies to evaluating the adequacy of the Crown's consultation, while a standard of correctness applies to evaluating the scope of consultation. • The duty to consult can be informed by administrative law principles like procedural fairness.

(*Continued*)

Table 2: (Continued)

Case name	*Year*	*Legal issue(s)*	*Key duty-to-consult principles*
Behn v Moulton Contracting	2013	Whether individuals from the Fort Nelson First Nation can raise a breach of Aboriginal rights, such as the duty to consult, and whether the Behn family's actions constitute an abuse of process	• An abuse of process occurs when a party does not observe official processes when raising concerns about the Crown's action. • The question about whether members of a larger Aboriginal community can claim Aboriginal rights is not directly answered.
Tsilhqot'in Nation v British Columbia	2014	Whether the Crown breached the duty to consult by issuing logging licenses on lands claimed by the Tsilhqot'in Nation to be their traditional territory	• If the Crown seeks to infringe Aboriginal title, the Crown must seek the consent of the title-holding Aboriginal group. • Without consent, the Crown must discharge consultation and justify its infringements.

Adjudication of Crown Conduct: *Clyde Rider, Chippewas,* and *Ktunaxa*

The more recent cases in duty-to-consult law reveal how the SCC adjudicates whether the Crown's decision-makers have met the appropriate scope of the duty and reasonably addressed the affected Indigenous parties' interests. These cases emerged in 2017 after Canada officially endorsed the *United Nations Declaration on the Rights of Indigenous Peoples* (*UNDRIP*) in 2016.[74] Although the federal government pledged to adopt *UNDRIP* in a manner that was consistent with the Canadian Constitution and the Truth and Reconciliation Commission of Canada called upon all orders of government to implement *UNDRIP*,[75] the court did not reference these legal developments in these duty-to-consult cases. Instead, the court continued to evaluate the quality of Indigenous consultation through the existing duty-to-consult framework. The *Clyde River* and *Chippewas* cases show that the court has presented inconsistent criteria to uphold procedural fairness throughout consultation, particularly when expressing how the Crown should maintain transparency in decision-making. *Ktunaxa* is an additional case that evaluates the adequacy of the Crown's consultation. This case shows how the court's assessment of reasonable accommodation may not adequately consider the contextual nature of the Aboriginal rights claim, thus potentially diminishing the standard for honourable dealing.

In the *Clyde River* case, the SCC further clarified the role of tribunals in the Crown's fulfilment of the duty, mainly that they can be relied upon to fulfill the duty in whole or in part.[76] The court stated that the National Energy Board's (NEB) approval process triggered the duty even though tribunals are not agents of the Crown.[77] The court stated "that a regulatory agency that exists to exercise executive power as authorized by legislatures" is "the vehicle through which the Crown acts" and that it must fulfill the duty before the final decision is made.[78] The concern that the NEB cannot effectively assess the adequacy of the duty to consult and Aboriginal rights was also disregarded by the court. The SCC reiterated that the public interest and the duty do not operate in conflict with one another, making the NEB capable of making a recommendation while accounting for a variety of societal interests.[79] Nevertheless, the degree to which the NEB considers Indigenous interests depends on the scope of consultation. The court claimed that "deep consultation" will "usually oblige the NEB, where its approval process triggers the duty to consult, to explain how it considered and addressed those concerns."[80] Here, the court confirms in stronger terms what was expressed in the 2010 *Rio Tinto* case, which is that existing institutions, like administrative tribunals, can partake in the duty to consult and that no new institution or co-created process with Indigenous parties is needed. Thus, the court fully accepted that the obligation of the duty can be layered onto the Crown's existing decision-making processes.

The SCC found that the Crown had failed to meet the procedural obligations of consultation. For instance, the NEB authorized seismic testing regardless of the fact that the proponents could not answer basic questions about how their activities would have an impact on the surrounding environment.[81] When the proponent attempted to address the Inuit's concerns, its responses were communicated in an inaccessible document that could not be downloaded by the Inuit leaders and was not translated into Inuktitut.[82] There is little possibility that a mutual understanding of the issues between the parties occurred under these circumstances. The court also took issue with the direction of the NEB's inquiry because it did not directly assess the impact of the seismic testing on the Inuit's rights.[83] Moreover, the SCC found that the Inuit were not told that the Crown would rely on the NEB to discharge the duty and that the Inuit did not receive adequate funding or opportunities to meaningfully participate in the consultation.[84] The Crown could not have addressed the Inuit's interests because the consultative process did not allow the Inuit to adequately present their concerns.

The SCC employed the same reasoning in *Chippewas,* the companion case, but, in this decision, the court found that the participation of the Chippewas was substantial and adequate because they were afforded opportunities to communicate their concerns to the Crown's decision-makers. Significantly, the Court stressed the importance of written reasons for facilitating reconciliation because written reasons reveal whether Aboriginal rights and interests are addressed.[85] However, the SCC also stated that the NEB did not have to present a full *Haida Nation* analysis,[86] which would entail making explicit the strength of claim of the Aboriginal right that informed the final decision.[87] This part of the decision may have serious implications because it appears to diminish the Crown's obligations to transparently explain how it will structure consultative activities with the participating Indigenous nations.

Indigenous parties cannot properly determine whether their participation was meaningful without knowing how their rights claims were assessed and treated by the Crown. The lack of a *Haida Nation* analysis removes an important mechanism that Indigenous parties can use to hold the Crown accountable. Obliging the Crown to perform a *Haida Nation* analysis would help ensure that the Crown transparently assesses the strength of the Aboriginal rights claims during consultation. This analysis is significant since assessing the strength of an Aboriginal rights claim is crucial to appropriately determining the scope of the consultative measures. Indeed, because the scope of consultation is assessed based on standards of correctness, it should be required for the Crown to show that its strength of claim assessment is appropriate. Without a requirement for a *Haida Nation* analysis, the Crown can limit the scope of the Indigenous parties' participation in the consultative process and then assert in writing that Aboriginal rights have been addressed at the decision-making phase. The main objective of the duty to consult is to ensure an honourable process to guide Indigenous-Crown interactions, but the inconsistent obligations on the part of the Crown to be transparent in various decision-making points undermine this purpose.

The SCC's emphasis on upholding transparent decision-making and its statement that a tribunal does not always have to disclose how it evaluated the validity of the Aboriginal rights claim appear to be at cross purposes with one another. Given this lack of information,

Indigenous parties may be even more likely to litigate if they disagree with how the Crown has addressed Aboriginal rights. The court recognized that "adequate Crown consultation *before* project approval is always preferable to after-the-fact judicial remonstration following an adversarial process."[88] Although it is known that litigation is not preferable for any party, it appears to be the only alternative for Indigenous parties if they perceive their rights claims are not taken seriously or misunderstood by the Crown. The court's interpretation on how to fulfill the duty to consult and practise reconciliation has cast doubt on whether the Crown's decision-making will be perceived as legitimate by Indigenous participants.

In *Ktunaxa*, the SCC agreed with the Crown's decision and its balancing of competing interests.[89] The *Ktunaxa* decision concerned both the duty to consult and a *Canadian Charter of Rights and Freedoms* claim under section 2(a), which upholds the right to freedom of religion and conscience.[90] The Ktunaxa Nation disputed the approval of a ski resort development on their traditional territory. The Ktunaxa Nation argued that a ski resort would drive away the Grizzly Bear Spirit, which is "a principal spirit within Ktunaxa religious beliefs and cosmology."[91] The majority of the SCC stated that the Ktunaxa's religious claims fall outside the scope of protection within section 2(a) and that the decision of the minister of forests, lands, and natural resource operations to approve the project, given the attempts to accommodate the Ktunaxa, was within reason, thereby discharging the duty.[92] Central to the SCC's decision was the characterization of the Ktunaxa's position as a claim for a specific accommodation, which is not the aim of the duty to consult.[93] For this reason, the SCC sided with the minister, who characterized the Ktunaxa's changed position as a "weak claim" because the Ktunaxa did not provide evidence that this claim about the Grizzly Bear Spirit was based on a pre-contact practice that was integral to the Ktunaxa's culture.[94] The court believed that the Ktunaxa's broader spiritual concerns were adequately addressed and accommodated because "specific changes to protect the grizzly bear population ... as well as extensive environmental reserves and monitoring" was made.[95] Although the court was aware that these measures were inadequate from the perspective of the Ktunaxa, the SCC restated that the duty can be discharged even if the parties cannot reach an agreement.[96]

The SCC's decision in *Ktunaxa* reveals serious problems with the judiciary's reticence to evaluate whether the Crown's accommodation measures adequately address the Aboriginal rights at stake. Allowing Indigenous parties to assert a preferred type of accommodation alongside their rights claims could be perceived as giving Indigenous parties a veto over decision-making, which was rejected by the court. Nevertheless, some rights may entail certain forms of protection for those rights to be meaningfully exercised. In this case, if the ski resort development drives out the Grizzly Bear Spirit, the Ktunaxa's "prayers, ceremonies, and rituals in recognition of Grizzly Bear Spirit would become nothing more than empty words and hollow gestures."[97] Even if other accommodation measures are implemented, they may fail to mitigate the main adverse impact, leading to disastrous outcomes for the Indigenous party.[98] Inadequate accommodation to protect the meaningfulness of a right leads to the same outcome as the Crown "run[ning] roughshod over Aboriginal interests" before formal settlements are pursued.[99] This outcome could be avoided if the court more explicitly considered evaluating the substance of the Crown's accommodation measures to protect Aboriginal rights and not just whether it balanced the minister's own objectives to "encourag[e] outdoor recreation."[100] The SCC appears to be actively eschewing a role for the judiciary to evaluate the Crown's accommodation measures.

This case exposes another potentially problematic development with regard to the quality of the Crown's accommodation measures. In this case, the minister characterized the Ktunaxa's new position as a "weak" claim because it was not accompanied by evidence to demonstrate that it was a pre-contact practice integral to the Ktunaxa's distinct culture. This categorization then influenced the minister's final decision that the accommodation measures were adequate, even though, from the Ktunaxa's perspective, the accommodation measures were wholly insufficient. Although the duty was created to ensure that the Crown's decision-makers do not run roughshod over "unproven" Aboriginal rights, tests to validate Aboriginal rights, such as *Van der Peet*'s distinctive culture test, are relied upon to also determine the strength of an Aboriginal rights claim. This determination then influences the scope of the accommodation measures that will be pursued by the Crown. Relying on the strict standards of the *Van der Peet* test to judge the strength of claim is inappropriate because the test is used to determine the scope and content of an Aboriginal right. This objective is unrelated to the aims of the duty to consult, which is to protect not yet recognized Aboriginal rights. The use of the *Van der Peet* test in contexts of Indigenous consultation may further limit the duty's effectiveness to secure substantive protections for claimed Aboriginal rights.

In the *Clyde River* and *Chippewas* decisions, the SCC showed some inconsistency with regard to the procedural obligations of the Crown, such as performing transparent decision-making. In contrast, the *Ktunaxa* case demonstrates the shortcomings of the court's reluctance to evaluate accommodation measures using the perspective of Indigenous rights claimants. In cases where adequate accommodation measures are not reached, the consequences for the affected Indigenous party may be "unsatisfactory, indeed tragic."[101] If decision-making outcomes are the site where reconciliation is ultimately judged and advanced, then the point of the duty to consult and its focus on ensuring an honourable decision-making process without equal attention to accommodation measures is called into question. These layered rules may guide the Crown further away from the goal of reconciliation. Table 3 outlines the main points addressed in the three 2017 cases.

Table 3: Summary of *Chippewas, Clyde River,* and *Ktunaxa* cases

Case name	*Year*	*Legal issue(s)*	*Key duty-to-consult principles*
Chippewas of the Thames First Nation v Enbridge Pipelines	2017	Whether the Crown's consultation can be conducted through the regulatory process – in this case, the NEB's approval to modify a pipeline – and whether the Crown's consultation efforts adequately discharged the duty to consult	• A full *Haida Nation* analysis, which includes an explicit strength of claim assessment, is not required to fulfill the duty.
Clyde River (Hamlet) v Petroleum Geo-Services	2017	Whether the Crown's consultation can be conducted through the regulatory process – in this case, the NEB's authorization of seismic testing for oil and gas reserves; and whether the Crown's consultation efforts adequately discharged the duty to consult	• A regulatory agency can be the vehicle for the Crown's conduct, enabling it to fulfill the duty to consult.

(*Continued*)

Table 3: (Continued)

Case name	*Year*	*Legal issue(s)*	*Key duty-to-consult principles*
Ktunaxa Nation v British Columbia (Forests, Lands, and Natural Resource Operations)	2017	Whether the minister's decision that the Crown fulfilled the duty to consult is reasonable and whether the minister's decision violates section 2(a) of the *Canadian Charter of Rights and Freedoms*	• It is reiterated that the duty to consult does not entail a duty to reach an agreement. • The final decision is deemed reasonable because of the balance between Aboriginal rights and the minister's statutory objectives.

Questions About the Scope of Crown Conduct: *Mikisew Cree* 2018

The *Mikisew Cree* 2018 case revisits a question left unanswered from previous decisions about whether legislative action constitutes conduct by the Crown that is subject to the duty to consult. This case illustrates a potential new line of inquiry: whether the honour of the Crown produces different obligations beyond the duty to consult, and how the duty is balanced alongside other constitutional principles, such as the separation of powers and parliamentary privilege in constitutional law. The main question in the case was whether legislative action, such as the drafting and introduction of bills, constitutes conduct by the Crown that is subject to the duty. The majority of the SCC asserted that the duty only applies to the Crown's executive conduct and that ministers drafting bills are acting in their legislative capacity rather than as the executive.[102] The majority of the court agreed that the law-making process is distinct from the implementation of bills and policies.[103]

By distinguishing between legislative and executive functions, the principles of the separation of powers and parliamentary sovereignty were found to protect Parliament from judicial oversight of the law-making process.[104] The majority were especially concerned with maintaining institutional boundaries and referred to the judiciary's long tradition of refraining from interfering with legislative processes.[105] In contrast to the majority, Justice Rosalie Abella and Justice Sheilah Martin were not convinced that insulating Parliament from judicial oversight balances the Crown's honourable obligation owed to Indigenous peoples. They found it "quite ironic that parliamentary sovereignty would now be used as a shield to *prevent* the Mikisew's claim for consultation," when, "in *Sparrow*, the Court found it impossible to conceive of s. 35 as anything *other than* a constitutional limit on the exercise of parliamentary sovereignty."[106] Abella and Martin JJ recognized the need to "reconcile, not choose between, protecting the legislative process from judicial interference and protecting Aboriginal rights from the legislative process" but in a manner that also upholds the honour of the Crown.[107] Therefore, they interpreted the honour of the Crown as encompassing parliamentary sovereignty to ensure Parliament also acts honourably towards Indigenous peoples.

The decisions of Justices Andromache Karakatsanis, Richard Wagner, and Clément Gascon also reveal an expansive interpretation of the honour of the Crown. Although they found that the duty to consult does not apply to the law-making process, they stated that the honour of the Crown and section 35 rights are not limited by the separation of powers or parliamentary sovereignty.[108] Indeed, Karakatsanis J stated that other remedies or processes besides the duty to consult, which are grounded in the honour of the Crown, may be available to Aboriginal peoples in the context of legislative processes.[109] Justices Russell Brown, Malcolm Rowe, Michael Moldaver, and Suzanne Côté disagreed with this position, with Brown J writing that allowing judicial oversight in any form into parliamentary law-making processes amounts to a "potential engorgement of judicial power."[110] Instead, these judges stated that consultation during the legislative process, although not mandated by the duty, should still be pursued as a matter of good practice and is an important consideration in justifying infringements to Aboriginal rights.[111] Finally, uncertainty in the law would only consume Indigenous peoples' time and resources to litigate the possibility that judicial recourse in legislative contexts could be provided.[112]

This decision demonstrates that the justices are divided over how to strike the appropriate balance between various constitutional principles like the honour of the Crown, the separation of legislative and executive powers, and parliamentary sovereignty. The division also reveals the disadvantages with relying on the judiciary as the primary body designated to hold the Crown accountable to Indigenous peoples and their rights. On the one hand, for one set of judges, pursuing more litigation for the possibility of outlining additional legal rights or protections is antithetical to the purpose of reconciliation as a process of Indigenous-Crown interactions and negotiations.

On the other hand, for other judges, unduly restricting legal mechanisms available to Indigenous peoples to protect their rights also undermines the goal of reconciliation to recognize Aboriginal rights within the Canadian Constitution. The SCC is simultaneously aiming to create a constitutional framework to promote reconciliation between the Crown and Indigenous groups while also trying to minimize judicially mandated outcomes and their overall involvement. Minimizing the burdens of Indigenous peoples as they interact with the Crown will undoubtedly be difficult given that the judiciary itself must contend with its institutional limits and capacity to oversee the actions of the Crown. These conflicting goals within the judiciary may also be a factor in the court's aversion to evaluate the Crown's accommodation measures, as the judiciary may want to avoid the perception that the court is willing to advance or promote specific policy preferences. Table 4 details these key ideas in the 2018 *Mikisew Cree* case.

The Canadian Judiciary and *UNDRIP*

To date, the SCC has yet to explicitly rule on the implementation of *UNDRIP*. The federal court is the first court to have engaged with *UNDRIP*'s implementation in the context of the duty to consult in its 2025 decision *Kebaowek First Nation v Canadian Nuclear Laboratories*. In this case, the Canadian Nuclear Laboratories sought to develop a Near Surface Disposal Facility to dispose nuclear waste.[113] The Canadian Nuclear Safety Commission approved the project, but the Kebaowek First Nation contested this decision, arguing that the commission did not consider *UNDRIP* when assessing the Crown's duty to consult.[114]

Table 4: Summary of the *Mikisew Cree* case

Case name	*Year*	*Legal issue(s)*	*Key duty-to-consult principles*
Mikisew Cree First Nation v Canada (Governor General in Council)	2018	Whether the duty to consult applies to the law-making process	• The duty is triggered during executive conduct, not legislative contexts such as the law-making process. • There may be other duties that flow from the honour of the Crown that are available to Aboriginal peoples seeking to influence the legislative process.

The court argued that *UNDRIP* became a part of Canadian law when federal legislation to implement *UNDRIP* passed on June 21, 2021.[115] Consequently, the court reasoned that *UNDRIP* "is an interpretive lens to be applied to determine if the Crown has fulfilled its obligations" but "does not create new law or statutory obligations."[116] This means that section 35 of the *Constitution Act, 1982,* should be interpreted in a manner that conforms with *UNDRIP* principles.[117] Although the federal court fully acknowledged that *UNDRIP* is a part of Canadian law, the court asserted that "the international understanding of FPIC [free, prior, and informed consent] seems to align more with the justified infringement framework" because the principle of free, prior, and informed consent is "not intended to be a general 'veto power.'"[118] Although *UNDRIP* requires a shift from the status quo of a section 35 framework, it entails "a right to a robust process ... not a veto or a right to a particular outcome."[119] In this case, the court found that the Canadian Nuclear Safety Commission could have adopted procedural practices to enhance the Kebaowek First Nation's participation, like organizing some hearings in Kebaowek communities, extending the time for oral submissions, and incorporating traditional knowledge-sharing practices.[120] The federal court emphasized that "process rights must be considered from the perspective of the rights holding collective and must consider the customs, traditions, and laws of the Indigenous rights holders."[121]

As such, the court ordered the commission to use *UNDRIP* as an interpretative framework and reassess whether the Crown fulfilled its duty to consult, but it did find the commission's assessment of the proposed impacts on Kebaowek's section 35 rights to be reasonable.[122] This decision suggests that *UNDRIP* provides Indigenous peoples robust procedural rights to engage in Crown decision-making, but it does not appear to change who makes the final decision and the standard to evaluate the final decision's reasonableness. Future decisions that specify the degree to which Indigenous perspectives on participation can change the design of decision-making processes themselves may lead to more transformative changes to the duty-to-consult framework.

Apart from this decision, some other legal developments are occurring that may significantly shape the Crown's approach to Indigenous consultation. Of particular importance in British Columbia is the *Yahey v British Columbia* decision by the BC Supreme Court (BCSC) in June 2021.[123] This decision will likely fundamentally alter the approval process for extractive resource projects. The *Yahey* case concerns whether the Crown infringed on treaty rights due to the cumulative effects from ongoing industrial development. The argument that cumulative effects from major projects constitute infringements to Aboriginal rights is novel. The Blueberry River First Nations (BRFN) is a party to Treaty 8. The BRFN claim that the cumulative impacts of industrial development create "significant adverse impacts on the meaningful exercise of their treaty rights," which culminate in a breach of Treaty 8 and an infringement of the BRFN's rights.[124]

The BCSC agreed with the BRFN's argument, asserting that "the Province puts forward an approach to infringement that essentially relies on an unfettered taking up clause and disregards the essential element of Treaty 8."[125] The essential element of Treaty 8 is the Crown's promise to the First Nations signatories and adherents "that their way of life based on hunting, fishing and trapping would not be interfered with."[126] Given this interpretation of Treaty 8, the province's argument that there were no treaty infringements was rejected.[127] A key point made by the BCSC was that infringements to treaty rights require a balance between the Crown's power to take up lands and the right of the BRFN to meaningfully exercise their rights.[128] When making this balance, the BCSC asserted that greater emphasis should be placed on the Indigenous perspective, "especially as it relates to understanding what it means to still have a 'meaningful' right."[129] This judicial ruling may significantly alter how actors within regulatory review must evaluate impacts to Aboriginal rights. This ruling arguably changes the threshold for considering whether Indigenous nations can continue to meaningfully exercise their rights. Evidence that Indigenous nations continue to exercise certain rights in some fashion may not be sufficient to justify a project, particularly if Indigenous parties' understandings of what a meaningful exercise of their rights entails must be given more weight in the decision-making process.

In addition to clarifying the threshold for treaty infringements, the BCSC also critiqued the province of British Columbia's heavy reliance on the duty to consult to address potential treaty infringements, as this court asserted that the duty is ill-suited to address cumulative impacts. For instance, the BCSC stated that "consultation is often marred by both procedural and substantive defects."[130] A major defect is that consultation is structured to consider specific projects in isolation from the overall pattern of development in a region. As a result, consultation "has not served as an appropriate way of addressing Blueberry's [the BRFN's] concerns about the cumulative impacts to the Blueberry Claim Area, and on the exercise of its treaty rights."[131] Therefore, "acting with good faith and ordinary prudence in relation to Blueberry's treaty rights required the Province to use more than just the usual process."[132] In this case, the province did not create another process or additional measures to adequately protect treaty rights from the cumulative effects of industrial development.[133] Indeed, the decision-makers admitted that they did not have the required tools to address or evaluate the cumulative impacts on rights; they instead opted to find ways to mitigate the adverse effects from specific projects through accommodation measures.[134] Even though the province could point to numerous decision-making bodies tasked with reviewing major projects, it could not show how these various bodies prevented the BRFN's concerns from falling through the cracks.[135] As a result, the BCSC agreed with the BRFN that the cumulation of adverse negative effects over time constituted "death by a thousand cuts."[136]

This part of the ruling is especially significant and has the potential to alter the province of British Columbia's current course with Indigenous consultation in regard to assessing cumulative effects. A new process may be established within the province's regulatory review to specifically account for cumulative effects. It is worth noting that the *Yahey* decision is a treaty rights case. It remains to be seen whether the province will treat groups with asserted Aboriginal rights with the same rigour as situations involving Aboriginal treaty rights.

Apart from influencing the process of consultation, the ruling could also provide leverage for Indigenous nations to change the structure of land planning in certain regions before specific projects are proposed. Indeed, after the BCSC's ruling, the province of British Columbia finalized a new agreement with the BRFN in January 2023 that commits both parties to change wildlife management practices, land use plans, and the planning of future projects in petroleum, natural gas, and forestry.[137] The BRFN now plays a key role in future land use planning using approaches that are consistent with the BRFN's stewardship practices. In order to address negative impacts that impair the exercise of Treaty 8 rights, the province has committed to a two hundred million dollar restoration fund by June 2025 that aims to repair damage from previous industrial activity.[138] Additionally, the BRFN and the province have signed an initial agreement that funds the BRFN with sixty-five million dollars to help with land restoration efforts, wildlife stewardship, and investments in general capacity building.[139]

The *Yahey* decision may also be used as a precedent to overturn more recently approved projects in other contexts. The West Moberly First Nations (WMFN) launched a lawsuit in January 2018 to challenge several projects including the Site C Dam, the W.A.C. Bennett Dam, and the Peace Canyon Dam. In the lawsuit, the WMFN planned to argue that the impacts from the three projects constitute an unjustified infringement on their Treaty 8 rights.[140] The *Yahey* decision would undoubtedly lend credence to the argument that part of those unjustified infringements is the result of cumulative effects that render the WMFN's treaty rights meaningless. However, the legal challenge against the Site C Dam was withdrawn, and the matter was settled out of court. The proponent, BC Hydro, and the province of British Columbia negotiated several agreements, including an impact benefit agreement with the WMFN, contracting opportunities, and a tripartite land agreement.[141] In turn, the WMFN released their claims against the Site C Dam, the province, and the federal government.[142] The remainder of the civil claim has been put in abeyance, with the province and the WMFN entering confidential government-to-government negotiations to resolve the remaining matters.[143] In this case, the province was able to avoid litigation to protect the project, but the changing legal landscape may generate future legal challenges against both existing and proposed major projects.

British Columbia and the federal government have committed to aligning their laws with *UNDRIP*. British Columbia's new *Environmental Assessment Act* is meant to reflect this commitment as the process is aimed at providing an opportunity for Indigenous participants to give or withhold their free, prior, and informed consent.[144] Although these commitments to *UNDRIP* will remain, the way in which these changes are implemented will determine whether Canadian governments are willing to radically adjust status quo decision-making processes to reflect evolving legal obligations to Indigenous peoples. Since there are no internationally recognized tools to measure states' compliance with *UNDRIP*,[145] Canada's adoption will likely be based on piecemeal negotiations between Indigenous and Canadian leadership. For instance, the agreement between British Columbia and the BRFN after the

Yahey decision includes new approaches to land use planning that reflect a respect for the BRFN's rights that are indicative of the *UNDRIP* principles. However, the reliance on political processes to implement *UNDRIP* rather than the judiciary may also seem alarming since political actors can more easily avoid having *UNDRIP* enforce upon them new legal standards, arguments, and remedies.[146] The recent *Yahey* case in the BCSC shows that Indigenous nations are challenging major projects without making arguments about Canada's adoption of *UNDRIP*, possibly because it is not certain how the Canadian judiciary will interpret *UNDRIP* given the existing section 35 case law. Table 5 summarizes the key ideas outlined in the *Yahey* and *Kebaowek First Nation* decisions that could further alter British Columbia's EA process.

Table 5: Summary of *Yahey* and *Kebaowek First Nation* cases

Case name	*Year*	*Legal issue(s)*	*Key duty-to-consult principles*
Yahey v British Columbia	2021	Whether the cumulative effects of industrial development breached the BRFN's treaty and Aboriginal rights	• When contemplating infringements to treaty rights, a balance must be struck between the Crown's power to take up lands and the right of the Aboriginal nation to meaningfully exercise their rights; greater emphasis should be placed on the Indigenous perspective. • It is the Crown's responsibility to devise processes to review cumulative impacts on Aboriginal and treaty rights
Kebaowek First Nation v Canadian Nuclear Laboratories	2025	Whether the Canadian Nuclear Safety Commission has the jurisdiction to determine if *UNDRIP* applies to the duty to consult	• The commission has the jurisdiction to apply *UNDRIP* as an interpretative lens to determine if the Crown met its duty to consult. • The standard of free, prior, and informed consent in *UNDRIP* entitles Indigenous peoples to a robust process but not to a particular outcome. • *UNDRIP* requires process rights within the duty to consult to be considered from the perspective of section 35 rights holders.

Conclusion

Reconciliation was adopted by the judiciary to explain the relationship between Aboriginal rights and the Crown's asserted sovereignty. The duty to consult is meant to facilitate reconciliation by requiring the Crown to consult with Indigenous parties when Aboriginal rights or rights claims may be adversely affected by the Crown's proposed conduct. By incorporating Aboriginal rights in policy decisions, the Crown's decision-making is legitimate. This chapter has included an analysis of eleven SCC cases to identify how the court has incrementally shaped the goals and rules of the duty to consult. The court has consistently expressed that the purpose of the duty is to reconcile Indigenous peoples' prior occupancy with the Crown's sovereignty and to balance Indigenous and non-Indigenous societal interests.

The SCC's assertions about how the Crown can fulfill the duty, and, by extension, advance reconciliation, may not achieve a symmetrical balance between Indigenous and non-Indigenous societal interests. As a result, the Crown can follow the court's standards of what constitutes legitimate behaviour, but it is not sufficiently compelled to engage with Indigenous perspectives of legitimate conduct. The content of the SCC's decisions limits the possibility of legitimating the Crown's decisions and Indigenous peoples' unique role in executive decisions in some key ways. To start, the court has permitted the Crown to create consultative processes without Indigenous involvement. This onus on governments to devise regulatory schemes to fulfill consultation reflects the fact that the duty is the Crown's obligation, but it consequently allows the Crown to layer the duty onto existing state decision-making processes that remain largely intact. These processes do not reflect Indigenous values or perspectives, and the procedural and substantive obligations of the duty may not compel decision-making actors to thoroughly engage with Indigenous perspectives either. Procedurally, the Crown, in certain decision-making contexts, is not required to employ a *Haida Nation* analysis to demonstrate the rationale for the appropriate scope of consultation or its decision. Despite the focus of the duty to create a procedurally fair process to identify Aboriginal rights, the Crown does not have to consistently act with the utmost transparency to explain how those Aboriginal rights claims are evaluated.

This procedural shortcoming is compounded by the substantive limitations of the duty. The SCC has consistently rejected the idea that Indigenous parties can claim a particular outcome after consultation. And yet, the Crown can exercise its discretion to reach its own determination of the balance between Indigenous and non-Indigenous interests at stake. The judiciary's own aversion to evaluate Crown decision-making means that the Crown is not required to clearly show that Indigenous perspectives on their rights have been taken into consideration during the decision-making. This practice seems to be an extension of problematic practices outlined in cases such as *Van der Peet,* whereby the perspective of Indigenous peoples regarding their rights is moderated in favour of considering common law concepts and approaches. Due to these shortcomings in the case law, Aboriginal rights may be unjustly eroded over time before they are formally recognized, which is contrary to the purpose of the duty to initiate interactions and negotiations before and after the formal claims process.

The SCC's duty to consult decisions must be analyzed because, as an apex court, it establishes the main rules about how the Crown can fulfill the duty and the responsibilities between the Crown and Indigenous parties in consultation. However, it may be useful to also analyze the rulings produced by a provincial appeal court to identify whether lower courts have added supplementary guidance over how the Crown can fulfill the duty to consult. Since this book assesses the implementation of the duty to consult in British Columbia's EA process, the appeal court in this province may have produced rulings that specifically target how the EA process has integrated this duty.

3

The BC Court of Appeal and the Duty to Consult

In addition to the Supreme Court of Canada (SCC), the BC Court of Appeal (BCCA) also renders decisions that inform provincial policy-makers in British Columbia on how to fulfill the Crown's duty to consult. The provincial and federal guidelines on consultation are drawn from the SCC's decisions, but court decisions at this level can further clarify the goals and rules of Indigenous consultation and accommodation. To this end, this chapter examines all sixteen cases at the BCCA level from 2004 to 2020 that are directly related to the Crown's duty to consult. The aim is to identify if this court provides additional guidance about how provincial actors like the BC Environmental Assessment Office (EAO) can discharge the duty. Duty-to-consult cases that were appealed to the SCC have not been included as decisions of the SCC supersede the decisions of the BCCA. Apart from these sixteen decisions, twenty-seven additional BCCA cases in the same period were analyzed where the duty to consult was referenced in different contexts, such as cases related to the granting of interlocutory injunctions or the interpretation of Aboriginal rights and title. Although these twenty-seven cases do not involve the judiciary assessing the Crown's adequacy of consultation, they were analyzed since the BCCA may still have discussed and commented upon the scope and nature of the Crown's duty to consult Indigenous parties within these different contexts. In this chapter, one of those twenty-seven cases is referenced to provide additional analysis of the BCCA's position on matters related to the duty to consult. One case before the 2004 period is also analyzed to provide some contextual information about the BCCA's stance on the role of tribunals in Aboriginal rights and title cases. Of the sixteen duty-to-consult cases, eight are explicitly referenced in this chapter as they reveal significant insights into the development of key duty-to-consult practices.

The BCCA has not provided a different interpretation of the goals of the duty to consult established by the SCC. Since the *Haida Nation* case was decided by the SCC, the BCCA accepts that the duty is necessary to uphold the Crown's honour as the Crown negotiates with Indigenous groups to reconcile Aboriginal rights claims with asserted Crown sovereignty.[1] Moreover, the BCCA acknowledges that another goal of the duty is to balance or find a compromise between competing interests.[2] Throughout the cases in the 2000–20 period, the BCCA has not disturbed these interpretations of the duty's main goals. Instead, the BCCA has ruled extensively on how actors should practise the duty to consult and elaborated on additional rules regarding how the duty can be discharged in more specific contexts. The BCCA's rulings on the duty to consult can be distinguished from the SCC's decisions about the procedural requirements of the duty and the substantive dimension of the duty – mainly, with respect to accommodation measures.

However, despite providing additional clarity about how the Crown can discharge the duty to consult, the decisions reveal that the BCCA does not create rules that ensure that the Crown consistently acts in good faith during both the procedural and substantive phases of consultation. With regard to the process of consultation, the BCCA also does not fully obligate the Crown to ensure that principles of procedural fairness are upheld to a high standard, such as transparency and facilitating the participation of Indigenous parties. Within the substantive phases of consultation, the BCCA has deemed any role for itself, and the judiciary in general, inappropriate, making it easier for the Crown to justify its decisions. These shortcomings can lead to Indigenous participants perceiving the process to be illegitimate from the start as the legal framework to guide good faith interactions with the Crown does not appear to compel the government to consistently engage with Indigenous perspectives. Similar to the potential issues with the SCC's decisions, the BCCA has also incrementally layered on some additional rules surrounding consultation without obliging the state to transform its decision-making processes to encompass Indigenous expectations of good governance.

Role of Tribunals

Tribunals play an increasingly significant role in assessing the adequacy of the Crown's consultation as these bodies regularly make decisions that can affect Aboriginal rights and title claims. The SCC's decision in *Rio Tinto Alcan v Carrier Sekani* states that the regulatory review process is adequately flexible to incorporate the Crown's duty to consult and that it is open to governments to establish regulatory schemes to fulfill the requirements of consultation.[3] The BCCA further affirmed the suitability of regulatory review in its 2011 decision in *Nlaka'pamux Nation Tribal Council v British Columbia (Environmental Assessment Office)*.[4] In this decision, the BCCA stated that a new, complex regulatory process is not necessary to uphold the honour of the Crown and avoid the exercise of unstructured discretion.[5] The BCCA added that the decision-maker in a tribunal can structure the terms of how to include and consult with Indigenous participants.[6] Interestingly, the BCCA did not always view tribunals as a suitable venue to make decisions relating to Aboriginal rights and title. Before the SCC confirmed the establishment of the duty to consult in *Haida Nation*, the BCCA's 2001 decision in *Paul v British Columbia (Forest Appeals Commission)* shows some concerns surrounding the appropriate role of tribunals to determine questions about Aboriginal rights and title.[7]

In the *Paul* case, the BCCA discussed whether the province of British Columbia had the constitutional capacity to confer jurisdictional authority to the Forest Appeals Commission to decide questions relating to Aboriginal rights and title, such as extinguishment, infringement, and justification.[8] This question is distinct from whether tribunals should evaluate the Crown's consultation efforts with Indigenous parties, as a tribunal in consultation contexts would not determine the scope or nature of Aboriginal rights and title. Yet the substance of the BCCA's reservations about tribunals is significant and could be applied to tribunals assessing the duty to consult. Writing a concurring decision, Justice Ian Donald expressed his concern with the fact that members of administrative tribunals are appointed through an order in council and that tribunals carry out government policy as outlined in legislation.[9] Since tribunals appear to be closely connected to the government, the perception of impartiality may be compromised when tribunals "decid[e] cases of Aboriginal rights when that same government may be an adversary in the dispute."[10]

In contrast, the SCC in *Rio Tinto* explained that tribunals are suitable to evaluate the Crown's duty to consult and balance competing interests because they have a mandate to uphold the public interest, which includes upholding constitutional duties and responsibilities towards Indigenous peoples.[11] Therefore, the government and Indigenous parties are not understood as adversaries when consultation is underway as it is the Crown's duty to adequately consider various societal interests. Nevertheless, the concerns of the BCCA in the *Paul* decision about tribunals' close association with the government may still be valid in the duty-to-consult context. Legislatures may confer authority to tribunals to uphold constitutional obligations towards Indigenous groups, but these decision-makers are appointed solely by the government without Indigenous input. The specific backgrounds and experience of the individuals that comprise the tribunal may lead to a perception that these decision-makers are seeking to advance a particular agenda or favour certain interests over others, thus contributing to a lack of legitimacy for the final decision that they produce.

Strength of Claim

Within the *Rio Tinto* case, the SCC firmly established the three-step process to determine when the duty to consult is triggered and how the Crown can determine the scope of appropriate consultation. A key part of this test is the assessment of the strength of claim, which is an initial determination of the strength of an Aboriginal rights claim. If the claim is deemed strong, then the scope of consultation will entail more opportunities for Indigenous peoples to participate in decision-making. A weak rights claim may only include a duty on the part of the Crown to give notice and share information about a proposed action.

The BCCA initially placed substantial weight on the importance of the strength-of-claim assessment in duty-to-consult contexts. According to the BCCA, without a strength-of-claim assessment, "there can be no precise determination of the extent of the Minister's obligations to consult and to seek accommodations."[12] If the scope of consultation is not sufficiently determined, the Crown is likely to inadequately discharge the duty. However, after the SCC released its 2010 decision in *Beckman v Little Salmon/Carmacks First Nation,* the BCCA adjusted its stance on the primacy of the strength-of-claim assessment.[13] In *Beckman,* the SCC asserted that, although the decision-making actor – in that case the director of the Agricultural Branch of the territorial Department of Energy, Mines and Resources – failed to understand that the province must carry out consultations to fulfill a legal obligation, the resulting process of consultation did adequately address the concerns of the Little Salmon/Carmacks First Nation. After this decision, the BCCA aligned itself in *Halalt First Nation v British Columbia* with the view that the strength-of-claim assessment is less important than the quality of the subsequent consultation efforts.[14]

After 2010, both the SCC and BCCA contended that the Crown could adequately consult Indigenous parties throughout the consultation process with a mischaracterization of the strength of claim. Yet it is difficult to see how this mischaracterization would not then affect the process by which decision-makers balance competing interests before rendering a final decision. It is reasonable to assume that the strength of the Aboriginal rights claims is a key factor in determining the rights at stake and the effects of the Crown's proposed action on those rights. For instance, an Indigenous group's strong rights claim to hunt in traditional territory may be more significant to uphold than enhancing local tourism in a region. In this scenario, the Indigenous group should be afforded many opportunities to directly participate in decision-making processes. This extensive participation is then matched by an expectation that such strong rights claims will be protected in the final decision. However, the participation of the Indigenous group may be adjusted if that group's rights claims were weak; then, the group's tenuous claim to a practice may be outweighed by considerations to develop local tourism, thus affecting their overall role in decision-making and how they are likely to shape the final outcome. The procedural requirements to determine the scope of consultation directly influence the substantive outcomes that arise from consultation processes.

Apart from asserting that the quality of consultation is more important than a correct strength-of-claim assessment, the BCCA also stated in *Halalt First Nation* that Indigenous parties are "not entitled as a matter of law to an assessment of the strength of claim."[15] This point would also be affirmed in the SCC's 2017 decision in *Clyde River v Petroleum Geo-Services* as the SCC states that tribunals are not always required to produce a "*Haida* analysis" in all circumstances.[16] The BCCA arrived at this conclusion because divulging the reasoning behind a strength of claim assessment may violate solicitor-client privilege.[17] Such a violation could hurt both the Crown and Indigenous parties; as rights and title negotiations are ongoing, neither party has an interest in disclosing sensitive information that could change their negotiating positions. For this reason, the BCCA also cautioned that courts should not engage in thorough strength-of-claims assessments during judicial review.[18] Although maintaining solicitor-client privilege is a justifiable concern, the strength-of-claim assessment has been emptied of its potential to hold the Crown accountable to correctly identify the scope of consultation. It is possible that the Crown could give due consideration to Indigenous concerns regardless of how the scope of consultation is initially determined. But if the process begins with the parties fundamentally disagreeing on the scope of consultation because the Crown is not required to disclose the strength-of-claim assessment, then the process could become delegitimized from the perspective of the Indigenous participants regardless of their subsequent participation.

Assessing Potential Impacts on Aboriginal Rights and Title

The *Rio Tinto* case was also significant because it confirmed that past grievances do not trigger the duty to consult. The SCC's blanket statement is concerning because determining the nature of the potential negative impacts from a proposed Crown action on Aboriginal rights may entail considering past and future development. Previous development on claimed traditional territories may have already produced negative effects that impact Aboriginal rights and title. And, thus, the negative impacts that may arise from new projects may compound with previous projects due the cumulative effects of development over time. The BCCA first considered the importance of cumulative effects in *West Moberly First Nations v British Columbia (Chief Inspector of Mines)*.[19] This 2011 case involved a proponent engaging in exploratory mining operations that could negatively impact the exercise of Treaty 8 rights. The majority's decision asserted that, because the current project under consideration by the Crown may have an adverse impact on Aboriginal rights, "the historical context is essential to a proper understanding of the seriousness of the potential impacts on the [Aboriginal rights]."[20]

Although it was accepted that establishing the historical context is important, the decision revealed divisions over how past impacts should be treated in the consultation process. The concurrent decision presented an alternative perspective about how to consider past impacts, stating that this historical context should inform the scope of consultation, but it does not create any obligations on the Crown to redress past losses.[21] The SCC later affirmed the perspective of this concurrent decision in *Chippewas of the Thames First Nation v Enbridge Pipelines* in 2017.[22] The SCC confirmed that cumulative effects must be considered to "recognize an existing state of affairs," which then "inform[s] the scope of the duty to consult."[23] There remains little guidance from the appellate courts over how this historical context then informs the determination of the severity of potential impacts on Aboriginal rights, if at all. In contrast, the 2021 decision by the BCSC in *Yahey v British Columbia* presents a much more robust treatment of how cumulative effects should shape determinations of negative impacts on Aboriginal rights.[24] Since this case was not appealed, it remains to be seen whether an appellate court confirms, adjusts, or rejects this stance.

Apart from past actions, future potential impacts may also be relevant in the duty to consult. Also in *West Moberly First Nations,* the judges disagreed on how potential future impacts should be incorporated in the consultation process.[25] The majority's decision stated that meaningful consultation in this context requires considering "the possibility of a full mining operation" as a full-scale mine is "the whole object of the Bulk Sampling and Advanced Exploration Programs."[26] The dissenting opinion took a different view, stating that "it was not wrong for the decision makers to limit their inquiry to the adverse effects of the permits under review, and decline to consider possible future scenarios on a hypothetical basis."[27] The SCC has not yet addressed the issue of future impacts on Aboriginal rights in the duty to consult. The divisions in the BCCA over the decision in *West Moberly First Nations* demonstrates that this issue may be contested in the future.

Funding

The BCCA has addressed certain procedural issues within the duty to consult that have not yet been answered by the SCC. One of these issues is the Crown's obligation to fund Indigenous participation in consultation.

The BCCA mentioned that upholding meaningful consultation entails providing Indigenous participants with "the necessary information and technical assistance" and "resources to facilitate [consultation] meetings."[28] This statement suggests that the BCCA acknowledges that adequate resources to participate in consultation are a factor in ensuring a meaningful process. Yet the BCCA has not ruled whether the Crown failed to discharge the duty on the grounds of insufficient resources. In the 2015 case of *Chartrand v British Columbia (Forests, Lands and Natural Resources Operations),* the BCCA found that the Kwakiutl First Nation requested "staff to assist them in understanding the information because it was not prepared to rely on [the proponent] or Provincial Crown staff to advise it ... and required independent and impartial assistance."[29] The BCCA did not engage with this issue and instead ruled that the Crown did not adequately consult the Kwakiutl First Nation because the province misunderstood the scope of the Kwakiutl First Nation's rights. The question of whether an Indigenous party is entitled to third-party personnel to interpret information remains unanswered, but Indigenous parties certainly perceive independent expertise as crucial to a meaningful consultation process.

The issue of who provides funding for Indigenous participants has also been discussed before the BCCA, but the court has not ruled on this issue either. In the 2013 case of *Louis v British Columbia (Minister of Energy, Mines, and Petroleum Resources),* the BCCA noted that the province of British Columbia did not provide funding; instead, the proponent granted some modest funds to facilitate Indigenous participation.[30] From the perspective of the court, the lack of financial support from the province to the Stellat'en First Nation in this case did not affect the Stellat'en First Nation's capacity to participate because the proponent supplied funds. The question of whether funding is part of the Crown's legal obligation remains unresolved. And yet these cases show that the BCCA acknowledges the importance of resources for Indigenous groups to effectively participate in information sharing and gathering, which is an integral initial step in consultation. Without adequate resources, Indigenous peoples cannot meaningfully express their concerns to the Crown. The judiciary's lack of guidance on the question of funding may leave Indigenous parties in a vulnerable position to accept resources that are not perceived to be independent, or be susceptible to insufficient or inconsistent funds, in order to participate in consultations.

Internal Divisions within Indigenous Groups

The final procedural issue within duty-to-consult processes that the BCCA reflected upon is the problem of internal divisions within Indigenous groups participating in consultations with the Crown. The BCCA noted in two different cases how upholding the honour of the Crown and respecting Indigenous self-government may be difficult when there is no clear Indigenous representative body that speaks for an Indigenous group. This issue arose in the 2011 case of *Nlaka'pamux Nation Tribal Council*.[31] In this case, the proposed project affected territory claimed by two First Nations: the Nlaka'pamux Nation and the Secwepemc First Nation. The BCCA noted that neither First Nations "have any governing body that unequivocally speaks for the nation."[32] Moreover, the situation was further complicated because there were "different entities that arguably speak for portions of the nations [that] do not take compatible positions."[33] For instance, the Ashcroft Band, which is a Nlaka'pamux group that may have been directly affected by the proposed project, objected to the participation of the Nlaka'pamux Nation Tribal Council (NNTC), an organization created to protect the Nlaka'pamux Nation's rights and title.

Although not a case relating to the duty to consult, similar issues of internal divisions also arose in *Spookw v Gitxsan Treaty Society* in 2017.[34] This case involved certain Gitxsan Chiefs, First Nations Chiefs, and Gitskan local services petitioning the judiciary to dissolve the Gitxsan Treaty Society because they claimed the organization did not have a proper mandate and that it did not represent them.[35] The BCCA ruled that neither the judiciary nor governments should interfere in the internal affairs of Indigenous groups as such an intervention would violate the principles of Indigenous self-government.[36] Based on this ruling, which emphasizes non-interference, the Crown should likely not pick and choose of its own accord which Indigenous groups and organizations to include in consultation if there are internal divisions. Indeed, in the 2011 case of *Nlaka'pamux Nation Tribal Council*, the BCCA sympathized with the difficult position of the EAO's project assessment director but stated that the consultation process cannot be compromised to prioritize efficiency.[37] Therefore, the failure of the project assessment director to reform the scope of consultation to include the NNTC once it had stated that it wanted to be a part of the assessment process led the BCCA to rule that the Crown did not honourably discharge the duty.[38] The BCCA did not address the situation of Indigenous groups contesting the participation of other Indigenous organizations. Since the duty is an obligation placed on the Crown, it would be prudent on the part of the Crown to include all Indigenous groups that seek to be involved in consultations.

Assessing the Adequacy of Consultation and Accommodation Measures

The duty to consult entails substantive requirements in the form of accommodation measures if the adverse impacts from the Crown's proposed action negatively affects the exercise of Aboriginal rights or title. One of the primary consequences of meaningful consultation is to identify accommodation measures that find a compromise between upholding Aboriginal rights and title and balancing other societal interests. The SCC actively eschewed the creation of a framework or test to determine the adequacy of the Crown's accommodation measures. The highly contextual nature of decisions that affect Aboriginal rights and title may make a common framework untenable. Unsurprisingly for a lower court, the BCCA has followed this aversion to create a standard framework that evaluates accommodation and has reiterated that the process of identifying appropriate accommodations is best decided through political negotiations. This position is reflected within the ways in which the BCCA has explained the appropriate standard of review to assess the adequacy of consultation; has reiterated the importance of preventing judicial intervention in the accommodation phase; and has shown reticence over creating guidelines about what the Crown's decision-maker should include in their final decision.

The SCC explained in its decision in *Haida Nation* that the process of consultation should be examined on a standard of reasonableness.[39] The BCCA has since articulated additional rules regarding how to apply a standard of reasonableness in the context of evaluating the duty to consult. First, a dissenting opinion in the 2001 *Paul* decision noted that employing a standard of reasonableness gives some deference to statutory decision-makers as "courts should give considerable respect to the decision maker when reviewing the manner in which discretion was exercised."[40] However, the exercise of this discretion must be consistent with section

35 of the *Constitution Act, 1982*, including its aim to reconcile Crown sovereignty and Aboriginal peoples' rights that flow from their prior occupancy.[41] Second, employing a standard of reasonableness entails recognizing that "there may be more than one reasonable outcome" and that a decision-making process is deemed reasonable if it is consistent with "the principles of justification, transparency, and intelligibility."[42] Third, consistent with the idea of giving statutory decision-makers deference, the reviewing court should not substitute its own evaluation "to re-weigh relevant considerations to arrive at a different result."[43]

Given that the standard of reasonableness provides a high degree of deference to statutory decision-makers, a reviewing court will most likely not re-weigh the balancing between competing social interests conducted by a decision-maker. If the final decision is transparent, is intelligible, and is accompanied by some form of justification, a reviewing court will most likely accept the decision as reasonable. For example, final decisions must include clear reasons to show how Indigenous concerns were incorporated. These reasons should persuasively explain why the Indigenous actors' course of action is deemed "either not necessary, ... impractical, or ... otherwise unreasonable."[44] The stipulation that the exercise of statutory discretion must be consistent with section 35 appears to be one of the few ways in which a reviewing court can deem a decision as being unreasonable. Therefore, the statutory decision-maker would have to make no attempt to reconcile Aboriginal rights claims with other social interests to be found unreasonable. However, if the decision-makers concede to some level of compromise in the form of accommodation measures, even if those measures are deemed inadequate from the perspective of the affected Indigenous participants, it is likely that the reviewing court will accept the decision as being within a range of reasonable outcomes.[45] The very standard of review that the courts have decided to employ to evaluate the adequacy of consultation prevents the courts from actively shaping the content of accommodation measures. It is also a highly flexible standard of review that permits a wide range of justifications from state decision-makers without necessarily engaging with the core substantive concerns of Indigenous participants.

Interestingly, the BCCA has also expressed the idea that the judiciary itself has limitations and should not interfere in the process of negotiating accommodation measures. In *Musqueam Indian Band v British Columbia (Minister of Sustainable Resource Management)*, the concurrent opinion stated that the BCCA should not be involved in deciding what accommodation measures are most appropriate.[46] Such an intervention would be inappropriate because "the courts, required ... to attempt to enunciate principles and pass judgment on disputes concerning aboriginal rights and title have sufficient to do without injecting themselves into treaty processes and negotiations."[47] A dissenting opinion in *West Moberly First Nations* affirmed this stance again by stating that "it is not for a court on judicial review to mandate specific accommodation measures."[48] The BCCA has expressed that the negotiations for accommodations is primarily a political exercise.

In more recent decisions, the BCCA explained some additional principles surrounding how final decisions can be considered reasonable. For instance, when a treaty right may be infringed by the Crown, the BCCA stated that a decision-maker is not required to engage in a *Sparrow*-level justification test[49] because a statutory decision-maker's mandate may not include the constitutional powers to determine whether a project constitutes an unjustifiable treaty infringement.[50] Instead, the concern for a potential unjustifiable infringement of treaty rights is considered throughout the consultation process, such as through deep engagement with the affected Indigenous party. The BCCA explained this reasoning in its 2017 decision in *Prophet River First Nation v British Columbia (Environment)*.[51] It ruled that the Environment Assessment Office was far from indifferent as the Prophet River First Nation's concerns about a potential unjustifiable treaty infringement "informed the recognition of the need for consultation [which then] drove the extent to which it was undertaken in discharging the duty owed by the Crown."[52] Based on this decision, it appears that Indigenous groups with treaty rights are not treated with much distinction within the consultation process if it involves a statutory decision-maker. These Indigenous groups may be entitled to more extensive consultation opportunities, but the threshold to meet a justifiable infringement is not significantly raised.

The BCCA also explained in *Prophet River First Nation* that it remains an open question whether the duty "requires the consideration of alternatives to any given project."[53] The court only cautioned that the duty to consult must be connected to the scope of the project under consideration so that alternatives to the project must also be considered in this context.[54] The court emphasized the causal connection between the scope of the duty and the proposed action to avoid forcing the Crown to exhaustively consult and address issues that fall far beyond the proposed action. However, in

Prophet River First Nation, the BCCA's rules surrounding how project alternatives are considered may have been too restrictive. Essentially, the court asserted that the Prophet River First Nation needed to present another viable project that met the Crown's agenda.[55] The burden of the Crown to produce a persuasive rationale explaining its rejection of the Indigenous party's position becomes significantly less burdensome if the Crown is not required to explain why its agenda is important enough to potentially produce negative impacts on constitutionally protected Aboriginal and treaty rights. In other words, because the Crown's objectives are not contested in duty-to-consult processes, the Crown can simply explain why the Indigenous position is unreasonable given the stated objectives of the Crown. This interpretation of how to evaluate the Crown's accommodation measures especially maintains the Crown's decision-making authority and limits how Indigenous participation can alter the Crown's proposed action. Table 6 summarizes the most relevant duty-to-consult decisions, the BCCA's corresponding interpretations of the case law, and how these interpretations affect an element of the Crown's consultation.

Table 6: Summary of the BCCA's decisions that affect the implementation of the duty to consult

Characteristics of the duty to consult	*Key ideas from the BCCA*	*Case name*
Role of tribunals	• Initially presented reservations about the impartiality of tribunals to decide Aboriginal rights cases (2001) • Accepted tribunals' role in evaluating and conducting the duty to consult (2011)	• *Paul v British Columbia (Forest Appeals Commission)* (2001) • *Nlaka'pamux Nation Tribal Council v British Columbia (Environmental Assessment Office)* (2011)
Strength of claim assessment	• Initially asserted the importance of the Crown correctly determining the strength of claim (2002) • Adopted the stance that Indigenous parties are not entitled to a strength of claim assessment (2012)	• *Lax Kw'Alaams Indian Band v British Columbia (Minister of Forests)* (2002) • *Halalt First Nation v British Columbia* (2012)

(*Continued*)

TABLE 6: (Continued)

Characteristics of the duty to consult	*Key ideas from the BCCA*	*Case name*
Assessing potential impacts on Aboriginal rights and title	• Past, cumulative impacts should shape the scope of present consultative processes but do not create obligations to redress past losses (2011) • Division over how potential future impacts should shape consultation processes (2011)	• *West Moberly First Nations v British Columbia (Chief Inspector of Mines)* (2011)
Funding Indigenous participants	• Acknowledge the importance of resources to facilitate effective consultation (2011) • No answer to the question of whether the Crown can fail to discharge the duty on an account of insufficient funding (2013, 2015)	• *West Moberly First Nations v British Columbia (Chief Inspector of Mines)* (2011) • *Louis v British Columbia (Minister of Energy, Mines, and Petroleum Resources)* (2013) • *Chartrand v British Columbia (Forests, Lands and Natural Resources Operations)* (2015)
Internal divisions within Indigenous groups	• The consultation process cannot prioritize efficiency at the expense of ensuring that all relevant Indigenous groups are consulted, even if there are no governing bodies that unequivocally represents a nation (2011)	• *Nlaka'pamux Nation Tribal Council v British Columbia (Environmental Assessment Office)* (2011)
Assessing the adequacy of consultation and accommodation measures	• The judiciary should not decide what accommodation measures are most appropriate (2005) • Project alternatives must be considered within the specific context of the proposed project, including the anticipated goals of the proposed project (2017) • Under a standard of reasonableness, a reviewing court must consider how there can be many reasonable outcomes and should not re-weigh considerations (2019)	• *Musqueam Indian Band v British Columbia (Minister of Sustainable Resource Management)* (2005) • *Prophet River First Nation v British Columbia (Environment)* (2017) • *William v British Columbia (Attorney General)* (2019)

Conclusion

This chapter analyzed key decisions made by the BCCA between 2000 and 2020 concerning the duty to consult. The BCCA expressed some new rules that the Crown must uphold when fulfilling the duty. With regard to the procedural practices of the duty, the BCCA's decisions have followed the SCC's lead and affirmed the role of tribunals and regulatory review as viable venues and processes to fulfill the duty. Unfortunately, there is no mention that the Crown must or should include Indigenous perspectives to alter these existing processes, meaning that the Crown has the full discretion to layer consultative processes on existing state-based institutions. Moreover, the BCCA's decisions have discussed the importance of considering cumulative impacts, the provision of technical assistance to facilitate Indigenous participation, and the importance of consulting various Indigenous representatives. Although these important topics have been addressed, questions remain about how these aspects of a fair process can be consistently upheld by statutory decision-makers, particularly transparency and meaningful participation. For instance, the BCCA did not obligate the Crown to provide a strength of claim assessment nor fund Indigenous participation.

With regard to evaluating consultation and accommodation, the BCCA followed the SCC's avoidance of creating a framework to evaluate the adequacy of the Crown's accommodation measures. Indeed, the BCCA reiterated the deference afforded to tribunals and the inappropriateness of the court to intervene in the negotiation of accommodation measures. Although the BCCA's decisions incrementally addressed more specific rules of fulfilling the duty, the judiciary's standards for honourable dealing have not considered how legitimacy must also be attained from the perspective of Indigenous participants in order for consultation to meaningfully facilitate reconciliation. Perhaps unsurprisingly given the BCCA's status as a lower court, the court has continued to layer additional consultative duties onto existing state-based processes without fundamentally altering those processes to consider Indigenous expectations of good governance. Consequently, the court's decisions have not created a framework to ensure that the Crown consistently fulfills the procedural and substantive elements of the duty with good faith.

The duty-to-consult case law arguably favours the Crown's perspective in assessing impacts to Aboriginal rights and the appropriateness of accommodation measures, particularly evidenced by the BCCA's interpretation of the standard of reasonableness. But how do policy actors – Crown and Indigenous – practise the duty to consult over time and across different projects? Analyzing a specific regulatory review process can reveal how policy actors within specific institutions have chosen to interpret judicial decisions and implement consultation. A systematic analysis of environmental assessments over time can also focus attention on cases that have not been the subject of legal challenges; a broader analysis of duty-to-consult cases may more accurately reveal the strengths and weaknesses of the Crown's consultation efforts.

4

Participation in the Environmental Assessment Process in British Columbia

The duty-to-consult case law as interpreted by the Supreme Court of Canada (SCC) and the BC Court of Appeal (BCCA) reveals that the Crown exercises control over structuring consultation and accommodation processes to meet the constitutional obligations outlined by the Canadian judiciary. For instance, the SCC has ruled that the Crown can use existing regulatory review processes to meet its duty to consult; separate processes to address unique Aboriginal rights are not required. Governments have accepted this decision and have moved to layer the duty onto regulatory review processes in order to avoid duplication.[1] Regulatory review allows state agencies to ensure that specific laws and objectives are upheld and met by public or private organizations in a particular area of activity. Adding the duty to consult to regulatory review schemes means that organizations must now meet this constitutional obligation, in addition to their other legislative rules and goals.

Specifically, environmental assessment (EA) processes exist at the federal and provincial levels to evaluate whether major projects negatively impact the environment and whether mitigation measures can be taken to address those negative impacts. The EA process is a planning tool to help decision-makers decide whether to approve a major project. The Crown's duty to consult has been added to this regulatory review process. The decision-making process in an EA can be divided into three distinct phases: the application information requirements (AIR) phase, the application review phase, and the decision phase. The AIR phase is distinct because it includes negotiations to determine the scope of what the BC

Environmental Assessment Office (EAO) and relevant policy actors will review. After the AIR phase is finalized, the proponents of a major project can submit an application for review. Then, the relevant actors consider the merits of the project. Policy actors consider the various interests and concerns surrounding the project, including the protection of Aboriginal rights, within the scope of the review as determined by the AIR phase. Finally, a decision is made by the relevant decision-making minister based on the recommendation of the EAO. These different phases can be assessed based on whether they meet three aspects of legitimacy in the decision-making: input, throughput, and output legitimacy.

Background: The EA Process

The EA process is triggered when major projects are proposed that may pose negative impacts to the environment. This process, first formally created in legislation in 1994, is regarded as highly compatible with meeting the objectives of the duty to consult because of its function to inform decision-makers of project impacts.[2] In addition to identifying environmental risks, this process has been expanded to consider potential negative impacts to Aboriginal rights. Furthermore, the EAO can impose conditions when granting certification to ensure that certain mitigation measures are taken to address negative impacts to the environment and Aboriginal rights. Due to the apparent compatibility of the EA process with the objectives of the duty, the Crown has opted to use the EA process as a central way to fulfill its duty to consult.

Certain types of projects that meet a designated threshold require an EA certificate. Not all activities are subject to an EA – most notably, forestry practices and exploratory drilling or mining. These types of projects trigger the duty but do not require an EA certificate. Furthermore, only projects that meet a specified threshold are reviewable. These thresholds broadly correspond to the scope of the project and their intended output, such as the production levels or capacity. The *Reviewable Projects Regulation* details the types of projects within the scope of the *Environmental Assessment Act* and the thresholds for each type of activity.[3] Projects that are reviewable include: industrial projects, mining projects, energy projects, water management projects, waste disposal projects, food processing projects, transportation projects, and tourist destination resort projects.

After a project is deemed reviewable under the *Environmental Assessment Act,* the executive director of the EA has the discretion to determine "the scope of the required assessment" and "the procedures and methods for conducting the assessment, including for conducting a review of the proponent's application."[4] This discretionary power is significant because this one individual determines the facilities of the project that will be reviewed, the effects of the project that will be assessed, the types of information required from the proponents, and the persons or organizations that must be consulted throughout the assessment.[5] The EA director may invite Indigenous parties, public stakeholders, and other government agencies to negotiate the scope of the review.[6] Nevertheless, the final decision rests with the EA director. This initial negotiation phase is called the pre-application phase.

The result of these discussions about the scope of the required assessment culminates in the creation of the AIR. The AIR formally determines the scope and content of the proponent's application for an EA certificate. Crucially, a list of issues related to the reviewable project is identified, which helps identify valued components (VCs). VCs are "components of the natural or human environment that are considered by the proponent, public, Aboriginal groups, scientists and other technical specialists and government agencies involved in the assessment process to have scientific, ecological, economic, social, cultural, archeological, historical or other importance."[7] Once the VCs are chosen through a consultative process, then the EA director and other policy actors identify the kinds of data that are necessary to assess the impacts of the project on the identified VCs. The proponents are also expected to create a consultation plan or protocol with input from the relevant Indigenous groups. Consultation plans act as a guide to structure the consultation procedures between Indigenous groups and the proponents as they interact in subsequent phases of the EA process, such as during the application review stage.

After the AIR is approved by the EAO, the proponent must submit its application to be reviewed by the EAO and the relevant stakeholders, government agencies, and Indigenous groups. The proponent's application is under review for 180 days. During this review period, the proponent is expected to consult with Indigenous groups using their consultation plan as a guide, identify the rights of the Indigenous groups, and address any concerns or issues about the project's potential adverse impacts on those rights. The Indigenous parties are expected to communicate their concerns about any potential adverse impacts on their asserted and claimed rights. During the end of this review period, the EA director makes a recommendation to the relevant provincial minister(s) about whether the project should be approved for an EA certificate. The provincial minister(s) has forty-five days to decide; the ministerial decision-maker can approve the project, ask for further assessments, or reject the project.

The proponent can choose to withdraw or terminate their application before completing the regulatory review process. In these contexts, the proponent, the Crown, and the Indigenous parties may have interacted with one another to a significant degree, so this research includes withdrawn or terminated projects when considering input, throughput, and output legitimacy. Of the 126 projects examined in this study, 11 projects were withdrawn, and 6 were terminated. Some projects were found to not require an EA certificate or were not designated as reviewable by the EAO. As they do with terminated or withdrawn projects, the proponent, the Crown, and the Indigenous parties often still consult and negotiate with one another before deciding whether a project does not require an EA certificate, so these projects were also counted in this study. Ten projects were found to not require an EA certificate, and five were designated as not reviewable by the EAO. Where appropriate, this study will specify whether the analysis includes all 126 projects or the 94 projects that fully completed the EA process. Figure 3 summarizes the stages of the EA process.

The duty to consult is ideally fulfilled throughout the entire EA process. In the early phase of the EA, it is crucial to identify the relevant and affected

1. Application Information Requirements Stage	2. Application Review Stage	3. Decision Phase
Valued components	Consultation with actors	EAO recommendation
Consultation protocols	Scope of rights interests	Ministerial decision
	Impacts on rights interests	

Figure 3 Summary of the EA process

Indigenous parties at the earliest possible time. It is the responsibility of the Crown to inform these affected Indigenous parties whether the EA process will be relied on to fulfill the duty. The Crown must then provide reasonable opportunities for the Indigenous parties to meaningfully participate in consultation. When the scope of the proponent's application is being determined, the duty continues to be discharged as Indigenous parties express the Aboriginal rights that might be implicated; doing so helps identify the kinds of information that the proponent should provide in its application. For this reason, evaluating input and, to a certain extent, throughput legitimacy in the AIR phase is relevant as both the participatory nature of the EA process and the initial consultations occur at this stage.

The 180-day review period is the next important phase to assess how the Crown and the proponents consult with the Indigenous policy actors and address the Indigenous parties' concerns. The affected Indigenous parties are expected to participate in proportion to both the strength of their rights claims and the severity of the potential adverse impacts from the proposed project. Indigenous actors can ask the proponents any questions about the project to learn about the potential impacts and negotiate how Aboriginal rights will be accommodated with the Crown's decision-makers. Throughput legitimacy is evaluated during the application review phase to determine the quality of the interactions between the EA's participants. Finally, when the EA director makes a recommendation to the relevant provincial ministers, the Indigenous parties may make a final submission that details their own positions about the proposed project. These submissions may be an important tool for the Indigenous parties to communicate whether they believe the duty has been sufficiently fulfilled and whether their rights have been adequately accommodated. The decision phase of the review process is evaluated based on output legitimacy. In this context, output legitimacy considers whether the Crown adequately considers Indigenous peoples' concerns and rights and whether reasons and justifications are provided to explain the final decision, including any proposed accommodation measures.

In December 2019, the BC government passed a new BC *Environmental Assessment Act*.[8] This legislation brings about significant changes to the assessment process that are directed at enhancing Indigenous participants' experiences. Some of the supporting regulations to carry out provisions in the new act have not yet been detailed. Although it is outside of this book's scope to analyze the effects of these reforms, the reforms may respond to many concerns raised by Indigenous actors. Where relevant, the following analysis notes whether the new *Environmental Assessment Act* was intended to address the issues that are raised by Indigenous participants in the 2004–19 time frame. Furthermore, in November 2019, the BC government passed the *Declaration on the Rights of Indigenous Peoples Act* to implement the *United Nations Declaration on the Rights of Indigenous Peoples* (*UNDRIP*), which may also produce significant changes to the EA process.[9] Although it is noted in the following analysis whether Indigenous peoples refer to the principles outlined in *UNDRIP* throughout their consultations, this study's scope does not account for the full effects of this declaration. Chapter 7 in this book examines British Columbia's new EA provisions and details how they may be able to address some of the challenges related to obtaining the three types of legitimacy identified in this study.

Analysis of BC Environmental Assessment Reports

The duty to consult as a legal obligation has been articulated by the courts, but the way in which the Crown interprets these obligations to implement consultation must be assessed. This study evaluates the Crown's implementation of consultation and accommodation by focusing on British Columbia's EA process. As established by the case law, EAs are a key forum in which the duty to consult can be fulfilled by the Crown.[10] Moreover, EA proceedings are more formally documented, thus increasing the likelihood that a written record of consultation dynamics and outcomes is publicly available for analysis. I chose to specifically analyze British Columbia's EA process for several reasons. Many Indigenous nations in this province have not signed treaties with the Crown, and the Crown understands these Aboriginal rights claims as based on unproven rights. The duty to consult was first articulated to address this very context of unproven rights claims so it is useful to analyze the duty in a province where this situation frequently arises. Additionally, British Columbia also includes First Nations who have treaty relationships with the Crown, both historic and modern. Although there are far fewer Métis participants than First Nation participants, there are some Métis who have participated in British Columbia's

EA assessments; it is acknowledged that Inuit nations are excluded by analyzing British Columbia.

Apart from the variation of Indigenous participants that this study accounts for, British Columbia is also an important jurisdiction because a wide range of political outcomes have resulted from this province's implementation of the Crown's consultation. On the one hand, British Columbia is understood by practitioners as a leader in implementing the duty to consult in existing regulatory reviews like the EA process.[11] And, yet, this jurisdiction also shows evidence of experiencing significant conflict when practising the duty. For example, the majority of duty-to-consult challenges at the SCC level began in this province, and this province approved many major projects that produced high levels of Indigenous resistance in comparison to other regions.[12] These salient instances of political conflict when consultation fails, alongside its reputation as being a leader in implementing duty-to-consult obligations in regulatory review, indicates that British Columbia represents a wide range of duty-to-consult outcomes for study: British Columbia's record of the Crown's consultation in environmental assessment processes is not simply a reflection of a few major projects or the absence of political contestation. Therefore, the insights from British Columbia's experience also remain valuable in other jurisdictions because this province is at the forefront of implementing the duty in cases where major projects reflect varying levels of political saliency.

There is a significant existing body of scholarship that analyzes Indigenous peoples' experiences and participation in various EA processes in Canada. Much of this scholarship addresses the most common issues that Indigenous peoples face throughout the EA process and details best practices or recommendations to address their challenges.[13] In addition to detailing common problems and recommendations, other works have also focused on specific EA jurisdictions – most notably, the North[14] and the West[15] – as well as on specific instruments found in the EA process, such as the role of traditional knowledge[16] or private agreements.[17] This research helps identify the parts of the EA process that are mostly likely to be challenged by Indigenous participants. Although this literature is expansive, the EA process has yet to be analyzed as a forum for governance where issues of legitimacy are a concern, given the duty's goals to facilitate reconciliation and legitimate Crown decision-making by ensuring honourable conduct. Moreover, this literature has not systematically accounted for changes in the legal parameters of the duty-to-consult case law and how these changes may influence the way in which actors behave in the EA process. Finally, the findings of this literature generally are not directed at analyzing Indigenous peoples' experiences across projects. Most existing studies are characterized by small-N case study analyses that make it more challenging to understand the pervasiveness of the identified issues over time and across various types of projects.

To build upon this important scholarship, this book analyzes British Columbia's EA reports and recommendations from 2004 to 2019, including a total of 126 EA assessments of a possible 205 EA reports. The cases investigated here were chosen because they had a record of Indigenous peoples' participation when the duty was triggered and because Aboriginal rights were clearly engaged. This documentation means that there are records of Indigenous peoples' correspondence, submissions, or comments where they express their own perspectives themselves rather than having these ideas expressed by other actors. In each EA, there are several documents that are produced across the three main phases of the EA process itself: the AIR phase, the application review, and the decision phase. By reviewing these documents throughout the different phases of the EA process, the varying positions expressed by the Crown, the project proponent, and the Indigenous groups throughout the consultations and negotiations were uncovered. In addition to the reports for each assessment, British Columbia's EA legislation, supporting regulations, and guidelines for implementing the duty to consult were also analyzed; however, the latter document closely echoes the legal principles in the SCC's duty-to-consult case law.

When analyzing the application information requirements phase, the relevant documents included working group meetings, correspondence, and tracking tables. These documents broadly reveal if any party expressed concerns over the drafting of section 11 of the *Environmental Assessment Act*. Section 11 determines the scope of the EA and the main issues that will be reviewed throughout the EA process. The correspondence between the Indigenous actors, the proponents, and the EAO as well as the minutes of the working group meetings help identify the position of each actor. The tracking tables that are often publicly available illustrate the range of issues that may be included in section 11. Each affected Indigenous nation may add a particular issue or information requirement. The project proponent then has a chance to respond and indicate whether the issue should be included. Finally, the EAO provides input when there are disagreements over which issues should be included in section 11. The finalized section 11 document was analyzed to consider the extent to which Indigenous input was reflected in the final scope of the EA process, whether there were any outstanding issues that the EAO decided to omit, and the rationale for the omission. Unfortunately, many EAs have incomplete records of the application information requirements phase. It is not clear why there is inconsistency of information during this phase. It is possible that early deliberations were simply not documented with the same rigour as the application review phase. Alternatively, it is possible that confidential information was discussed during the early stages of the EA process and, owing to its confidentiality, was not recorded.

In the application review phase, similar types of documents – namely, correspondence, working group meetings, and tracking tables – are analyzed to identify the Indigenous peoples' perspectives of the process of consultation and accommodation. For instance, these documents can reveal whether the Indigenous participants expressed concerns about the consultations within the EA process, whether there were any requests for further action to be taken for additional consultation, whether accommodation measures to address specific potential impacts from the proposed project should be negotiated, and whether Indigenous parties expressed concerns with the actions or behaviours or other actors like the proponent or the EAO officials. Within the decision phase, I analyzed the proponent's finalized application, the EAO's findings and recommendations, any Indigenous submissions made directly to the minister apart from the EAO's report, and the minister's final decision. These decision documents were then cross-referenced with the tracking tables in the application review stage to reveal whether there were any outstanding issues brought up by the Indigenous actors that were not addressed through consultation and accommodation. The EAO often provides a rationale explaining how it reached a specific recommendation, including how it balanced competing societal interests and Aboriginal rights. The EAO also makes note of any conflicts that were present between the policy actors throughout the EA process. The proponent's application outlines the First Nation consultation protocol used to guide consultation and accommodation measures. This document is cross-referenced with the EAO and the Indigenous parties' own records of consultation and accommodation. The Indigenous parties may make their own separate submission to the minister if they disagree with the EAO's recommendation. These separate submissions can reveal any outstanding issues perceived to have been inadequately addressed by the EAO's recommendations and the Indigenous peoples' own perspectives about whether the duty to consult has been upheld. Finally, the minister also releases their decision and rationale based on the evidence provided by the EAO and any Indigenous nations' submissions. This decision further illustrates how the minister balances Aboriginal rights and other societal interests.

Any issues or concerns about the fulfillment of the duty to consult throughout the three phases of the EA process were coded in a binary fashion if they remained outstanding after consultation and accommodation were completed. If issues about consultation and accommodation were outstanding, then it demonstrates that the Indigenous peoples perceived the duty-to-consult process to have insufficiently addressed their concerns and interests. Multiple issues may be counted within a single EA, but multiple instances of the same issue within an EA were only counted once.[18] In addition to cataloguing the outstanding issues across EAs, the reasons why Indigenous peoples expressed their dissatisfaction with an aspect of legitimacy were also noted. The absence of issues expressed by Indigenous parties is treated as satisfaction with the consultative process.[19] This is a conservative indicator as the Indigenous participants may simply not have had the time or resources to explicitly communicate their positions.

Focusing on the types of issues Indigenous participants expressed throughout the EA process can help identify the limitations of this process to meet different aspects of legitimacy. As will be explained later in this chapter and in subsequent chapters, these issues were then categorized according to different dimensions of input, throughput, and output legitimacy. Legitimacy must be demonstrated by the Crown through honourable dealings, and the critiques of Indigenous parties about the Crown's performance are integral to evaluating whether this legitimacy is attained and to what degree. Counting the instances when Indigenous parties are dissatisfied with the EA process can help quantify the Crown's performance when fulfilling the duty, but there are some limitations to this approach. Assessments are counted as having an outstanding issue if at least one Indigenous nation was dissatisfied. This does not consider how various Indigenous groups have different rights at stake across projects. For instance, a project that is accepted by the Indigenous groups because no major impacts were found is qualitatively different than a project that is opposed by one Indigenous group because it believed that its rights were significantly threatened. Although the record would show that the EAO was successful at achieving legitimacy in the former instance and not in the latter, the stakes of the project are significantly different in these cases; the EAO failing to uphold legitimacy in the latter case may lead to the unjustifiable erosion of Aboriginal rights, which would not necessarily occur in the former case. This is another reason why the EAO's performance in these reports should be treated as a conservative estimate of Indigenous peoples' concerns with the EA process. Future studies may consider weighing the rights at stake for each Indigenous group in each assessment, but it should be noted that this determination is a key site of intense contestation between Indigenous and non-Indigenous perspectives.

Inconsistent access to data also presents a possible limitation to the findings. The reports of the projects that underwent an EA in British Columbia were at times incomplete. There is no assurance that the assessments contained the entire record of interactions between the policy actors. For instance, it is entirely possible that actors from the Indigenous groups, industry, and the Crown may have met confidentially to speak about Aboriginal rights. The interview data are intended to offset these types of omissions in the reports, although the interviewees were also reticent to reveal information that could affect their future bargaining positions and strategies. Moreover, although the interview data were primarily used to triangulate the findings from British Columbia's EA reports, the majority of the interviewees included in this study acted on behalf of Indigenous nations. Thus, the Crown's perspective is under-represented in the interview data collected.

There may be omissions in the data – particularly, with respect to the perspective of the Crown's side – but the available data used in the study reveal a clear picture of how the Indigenous policy actors perceived the legitimacy of British Columbia's EA process in fulfilling the duty to consult.

Since the intention of the duty is to increase the legitimacy of the Crown's decision-making, the Indigenous perspective is crucial to evaluate whether the Crown's decisions are indeed perceived with legitimacy. Moreover, the Crown's position is also prominent throughout British Columbia's EA reports as the EAO must report its recommendations throughout the decision points in the process, and the decision-making minister also reports their final decision. For these reasons, the possible limitations of the research do not undermine the robustness of the overall design to analyze the process of decision-making in the implementation of the duty to consult.

Semi-Structured Elite Interview Data

Although EAs include written documentation of the consultative proceedings between the Crown and the affected Indigenous parties, there are many instances when information and meetings are simply not disclosed. This book includes the findings from twenty-eight semi-structured interviews with key policy actors to address possible information gaps. These actors included Indigenous land planners, negotiators, and legal representatives for Indigenous nations; EAO officials; and consultants with negotiating, technical, or regulatory review expertise. Most of the interviewees have experience representing or working with Indigenous nations, including three Chiefs, seven officials, eight legal representatives, and six consultants. Only four interviewees worked for the Crown, including one lawyer, one consultant, and two EAO officials. The interview data are used to corroborate the findings from the textual analysis of the EA reports. As such, they were coded using the same indicators of input, throughput, and output legitimacy as British Columbia's EA reports. Any differences between the interview data and the reports are noted in the analysis.

The anonymity and confidentiality of the interview participants were protected, with attribution only given with their consent. No information presented in this book reveals the identity of the research participants. Before recruiting research participants, ethics approval from a university ethics board was attained. The sample of individuals that were recruited for the research is considered a low-risk group as the individuals were professional and/or political elites who could fully exercise their autonomy to understand the scope of their participation and decide the extent to which they would like to communicate their perspectives.

Coding Input Legitimacy

Input legitimacy is concerned with "the participatory quality of the process" of decision-making.[20] The three categories of participants, capacity, and forums help evaluate the quality of the actors' participation in the decision-making process.[21] The participant category captures whether the actors involved in the process of decision-making were representative of the relevant societal interests. In the context of the EA, this requirement can be understood as the timely identification of relevant Indigenous nations that would potentially be affected by the Crown's proposed action. This requirement may be difficult to achieve if there is uncertainty about the appropriate representative body of an Indigenous nation.[22] For instance, the government may recognize a band as the representative of the Indigenous group, which may be contrary to the Indigenous nation's preference to have another body represent their nation.

The capacity requirement includes any challenges that Indigenous groups face that would prevent them from effectively participating in consultative activities once they have been invited. Ensuring capacity for Indigenous parties to participate effectively in consultative forums includes three distinct dimensions. Perhaps most obviously, Indigenous parties require funding because many communities do not have extra revenue to dedicate towards fulfilling consultation requirements. Funding also ensures that Indigenous parties can hire the appropriate expertise and staff to support the identification and communication of their Aboriginal rights to the decision-makers. Since the decision-makers will only consider rights claims with supporting evidence, Indigenous groups require anthropological, ethnographic, and ecological studies to demonstrate the validity of their rights claims. Indigenous parties may also need to hire consultants and legal advisors to represent their claims in the consultative process alongside technical staff. These resources are crucial for the Indigenous parties to participate and be taken seriously by the decision-makers.

Apart from financial resources, capacity also requires allocating the Indigenous parties sufficient time to participate in the consultative processes. Indigenous parties are expected to conduct studies, review information presented by the proponents, and prepare their own findings and concerns in response to the proponent's reports. Time as a resource becomes even more significant if the Indigenous parties have limited technical staff as a smaller team of people will require more time to provide the necessary information to sustain negotiations. Timelines also become important if Indigenous parties with distinct governance processes are faced with multiple consultative obligations from several project applications occurring simultaneously. An additional dimension of capacity is the level of knowledge that Indigenous participants possess about navigating the EA process. Indigenous participants should be made aware of the various stages of consultation or the forums that the Crown will rely on to fulfill the duty within the EA process. This knowledge allows Indigenous parties to mobilize their staff and use their time most effectively.

The third category of input legitimacy is concerned with assessing whether the groups agree upon the forums and processes through which the participation should take place. In particular, any challenges experienced by the EAO and the proponent with engaging participating Indigenous nations on agreed-upon terms are significant to note. However, as stipulated by the judiciary, the Crown is not required to reach an agreement regarding what forum will be used to discharge the duty. The duty-to-consult case law may shape how the Crown perceives that it can attain this dimension of input legitimacy. The requirement for actors to agree on forums and processes during consultation is significantly curtailed as Indigenous participants cannot oppose the Crown from fulfilling the duty within the EA process. Instead, the Crown can demonstrate good faith by ensuring that Indigenous peoples agree to the terms of engagement as outlined in the consultative protocols within the broader EA process. Although the case law may alter the Crown's approach to choosing forums for implementing the duty, many Indigenous communities have developed their own consultation protocols that outline how they would like such consultations to proceed. Indigenous nations would therefore want the Crown and proponents to respect their protocols when conducting consultations, even if it must take place within the EA process. In order to maintain the emphasis on Indigenous perspectives, this study also records when the Indigenous actors contest or critique the EA process as being an inappropriate venue for the Crown to discharge the duty. Table 7 summarizes the various indicators of input legitimacy that help structure the coding of the EA reports and interview data.

Table 7: Categories of input legitimacy and corresponding indicators

Participants	*Capacity*	*Forums and processes*
Timely identification of relevant Indigenous nations	• financial resources • sufficient time • adequate knowledge	Agreement on terms of engagement within the EA process

Coding Throughput Legitimacy

Issues of throughput legitimacy are coded within the categories of inclusiveness, transparency, accountability, and effectiveness, as outlined by Vivien Schmidt.[23] These characteristics of throughput legitimacy are normative ideals,[24] and they require clearer definitions within the specific policy context in order to be effectively operationalized. In this study, inclusiveness or openness in the consultative process include the following criteria.[25] First, it will be assessed whether the Indigenous consultees were treated as constitutional rights holders throughout the consultations. As rights holders, Indigenous parties are conferred different participatory expectations and privileges than other stakeholders, such as recreational users or private landowners. Treating Indigenous parties as rights holders must be respected to uphold a robust sense of inclusiveness; it is insufficient to simply include relevant Indigenous nations in consultation without ensuring that their treatment reflects their status as self-determining nations with governing authority. Another aspect of inclusiveness is ensuring that the relevant participants with the appropriate mandates and powers are present and meeting in a timely fashion. This requirement is distinct from ensuring that the relevant Indigenous nations and actors are invited to participate in the EA process; there could be instances where the actors are officially participants of the EA process but may not be consistently participating throughout the decision-making process.

In order to uphold transparency, the Crown and the proponent should accurately identify and document the interests and concerns of the Indigenous parties throughout the EA process. An additional factor of transparency that is highly relevant to the duty to consult is ensuring that the methodologies used for assessing both the scope of interests among the affected Indigenous parties and the project's potential impacts on those interests are clearly explained. This aspect of transparency is crucial for the Crown to show the Indigenous participants how their rights have been balanced alongside other societal interests.

With regard to accountability, the EAO should ensure that each actor in the process has clearly defined responsibilities. With clear roles and responsibilities, actors know who to hold accountable in each decision point to ensure that the duty is being fulfilled. Another crucial aspect of accountability is whether the Indigenous people's feedback is included to identify the scope of their Aboriginal rights, the project's impacts on those rights, and the appropriate mitigation measures to address negative impacts on Aboriginal rights. Actors can hold one another to account when the relevant perspectives are fully included and engaged with before decisions are made.

Finally, effectiveness is achieved when Indigenous parties view participation within the EA process as being meaningful. Meaningfulness includes perceiving that participation has had an impact on the final decision. Although the duty does not mandate a specific outcome,[26] it is imperative that the Indigenous parties believe their participation has the potential to change the Crown's decision. The duty-to-consult case law emphasizes how honourable consultation entails the meaningful possibility of shaping final decisions and is not merely an opportunity for Indigenous participants to "blow off steam before [a] Minister proceeds to do what she intended to do all along."[27] This perception of meaningfulness is distinct from accepting the outcomes of consultation as it is possible that a desired outcome can be achieved without the Indigenous participants perceiving that their participation has an influence on the outcome. Due to the subjective nature of identifying effectiveness, only instances where the Indigenous parties explicitly discussed the meaningfulness of the process (or lack thereof) were included in the analysis. Table 8 summarizes these various indicators of throughput legitimacy.

Table 8: Categories of throughput legitimacy and corresponding indicators

Inclusiveness	*Transparency*	*Accountability*	*Effectiveness*
• agreement on the status of Indigenous consultees • the relevant actors are present during meetings	• accurate identification and documentation of Indigenous concerns • clear rationales are presented to explain the methodology used to assess the scope of the rights and impacts on those rights	• Indigenous knowledge and feedback are included • each participant has clear roles and responsibilities regarding the fulfillment of the duty to consult	• participation is perceived to be meaningful

Coding Output Legitimacy

Output legitimacy requires analyzing whether the substance of a decision promotes collective goals and interests.[28] In the case of the duty to consult, decisions about whether a project proceeds, whether accommodation measures are required, and the nature of accommodation measures given the potential negative impact on Aboriginal rights constitute the outputs of consultation. These outputs are legitimate if the decision reasonably and adequately addresses the Indigenous parties' concerns about the potential impact on the exercise of their rights. Since accommodation measures are the primary outputs of consultation, the mitigation plans proposed in each EA are the focus of analysis. Issues about the level of completion, the scope, and the commitment of the mitigation plans are relevant. Moreover, issues over the rationale for why certain mitigation measures are chosen over other alternatives falls within this category.

The judiciary's interpretation of the duty to consult may influence how the Crown perceives that it can attain output legitimacy. The SCC states that the duty to consult does not entail a duty to agree, so Indigenous participants cannot reject the Crown's decisions based on differing policy interests or goals.[29] Given this fact, it is unlikely that Indigenous parties will express their discontent with a decision on the grounds that their preferred policy outcome was not attained. In order to capture the Indigenous perspective for output legitimacy, close attention was paid to the Indigenous participants' perspectives on the quality of, and rationale underpinning, the Crown's accommodation measures, particularly whether accommodations are clearly linked to protect the identified Aboriginal rights at stake. Table 9 summarizes the key indicators used in this study to examine output legitimacy in the context of the duty to consult.

Table 9: Categories of output legitimacy and corresponding indicators

Accommodation
• detailed and complete mitigation plans • scope of mitigation plans proportionately addresses the expected negative impacts on Aboriginal rights • clear rationales are presented explaining why certain mitigation measures are chosen over other alternatives • sufficient commitment expressed to implement the proposed mitigation plan

Application Information Requirements Phase

Input Legitimacy: Findings

The AIR phase shows that the Crown does not meet all the qualities of input legitimacy to ensure Indigenous parties can participate in consultation. The Crown is more successful at identifying the relevant Indigenous parties that are affected and providing timely communication. Despite these successes, the Crown does not consistently provide capacity funding and structuring timelines that are sufficient for Indigenous groups to participate meaningfully.

As recorded in British Columbia's EA reports, there were no complaints from the affected Indigenous parties about the timeliness of the EA's initial communication that an EA process would be underway. Instead, some concerns were expressed over the EAO's identification of the relevant affected Indigenous parties. There are eight instances out of 126 assessments (6 percent) when the Indigenous parties expressed disagreement with the EAO's decision to either exclude or include certain groups from deep consultation or various stages of the EA process. Of these eight instances, three involved disagreements over the representative status of bands and traditional governance bodies, which is a growing area of concern.[30] Indeed, one of these three cases involved an Indigenous nation petitioning the BC Supreme Court to include representatives of a nation apart from the identified band.[31] In the end, the BC Supreme Court rejected the Indigenous nation's claims and stated that it was reasonable for the EAO to take different consultative approaches with bands and the tribal council given the disagreements within the Indigenous nation over their appropriate representative.[32] These reports show that there does not appear to be overt bias on the part of the EAO to contact certain Indigenous groups over others, apart from some confusion over which Indigenous authority is representative of, or responsible for protecting, a community's Aboriginal rights.

Interestingly, apart from these eight cases, there were six additional instances of the EAO itself recording that the affected Indigenous parties faced internal divisions over the appropriate representative to participate in consultation. In one of these six cases, the EAO detailed that the Tahltan Band Council and Iskut First Nation governments were divided over the "acceptability and pace of development within their asserted traditional territory and with who should represent each First Nation in regard to this development."[33] The issue in this case was resolved by the Iskut First Nation advising the EAO that they should be consulted separately from the Tahltan Central Council.[34] It may be difficult to consistently evaluate the EAO's efforts to maintain inclusivity because there may be internal disputes within the Indigenous nations when choosing a legitimate and appropriate representative. In these instances, the EAO often opts to include as many entities as possible and is open to including additional groups as the assessment unfolds.[35] This prudent approach to consulting would also meet the expectations outlined in the duty-to-consult case law as the BCCA ruled in the *Nlaka'pamux Nation Tribal Council* case that the Crown can fail to discharge the duty despite questions surrounding the appropriate Indigenous representative.[36]

The other five instances when the EAO noted Indigenous groups disputing the inclusion or exclusion of nations from the EA process are related to issues with the Crown's strength-of-claim assessments. As outlined in the case law, a strength-of-claim assessment helps determine the appropriate scope of consultation with the affected Indigenous groups: a strong Aboriginal rights claim entitles an Indigenous group to more opportunities for "deep" consultation and accommodation. Groups with weaker claims have fewer opportunities to engage with the proponent and the Crown. The EAO uses the strength-of-claim assessments from the Crown, which were developed using government data on Indigenous peoples' historical land use. However, many Indigenous groups, drawing from their own knowledges and histories, contest the Crown's determination of the strength of claims and, thus, dispute the EAO's initial scoping of consultation activities. Nevertheless, one official from the EAO stated that their office displays flexibility in including Indigenous groups in deeper forms of consultation if there is an obvious conflict between the Crown and the Indigenous group over a strength-of-claim assessment.[37] Instead, the strength of claim is even more concerning when it is used to guide subsequent consultative interactions with the Crown. For example, negotiations with the Crown and the proponent to determine adverse impacts or appropriate accommodation may be influenced by a particular interpretation of the strength of claim. Overall, strength-of-claim issues are disclosed infrequently throughout the EA reports due to the concern that this information can negatively influence future Indigenous-state negotiations.

Another barrier to achieving input legitimacy from the perspective of Indigenous parties is the inability to change the terms of Indigenous participation within the EA process. The duty to consult can be fulfilled using existing regulatory frameworks,[38] so there is no requirement to provide a new process to fulfill the Crown's constitutional obligations that reflects Indigenous world views or values. As long as Aboriginal rights are identified separately from other types of impacts and risks, and there are opportunities to adequately address and accommodate Aboriginal rights, the duty can be discharged within the EA process.

Although Indigenous peoples are unable to change the structure of the EA process, they can shape consultative procedures by collaborating with the proponent to create consultation engagement protocols. The proponent is required to outline a consultation protocol, allowing Indigenous groups to influence and shape how they are to be approached by the proponent. These protocols are presented during the pre-application phase, and their content can vary depending on the project and the type of Indigenous groups involved. The protocols typically detail how the proponent intends to engage with Indigenous parties throughout the application review process and details a summary of past consultative activities to date. The EAO approves the protocol agreements after consulting with the relevant Indigenous groups. Depending on the Indigenous groups' feedback, the EAO may request the proponent to adjust its consultative engagement with the relevant Indigenous parties. There are only four instances (3 percent) when the Indigenous parties expressed that the proponent did not establish a suitable Indigenous consultation protocol. Due to this low number of recorded instances of this problem, this aspect of Indigenous participation exhibits very few issues. Nevertheless, the fact that Indigenous peoples are forced to participate in an EA process contributes to the perception that Indigenous peoples cannot represent themselves and their rights on their own terms.[39] Across the 126 assessments, Indigenous parties stated in thirty-three cases (26 percent) that they were concerned with the efficacy and suitability of the regulatory review process to address Indigenous concerns and Aboriginal rights. This much higher number of cases reveals that Indigenous participants contest the Crown's ability to rely on the EA process to fulfill the duty to consult without including Indigenous-led assessments or processes.

There are considerably more issues concerning Indigenous parties' capacity to participate meaningfully in consultation. The EAO is not solely responsible for providing funding to participating Indigenous parties; they have some funds to support participation, but proponents are often relied on to negotiate with Indigenous parties over the terms of funding for studies and personnel. Section 32 of the 2002 *Environmental Assessment Act* states that the EAO director can order the proponent to pay fees or charges incurred by the EAO, but funding for participants is not outlined. Apart from financial resources, Indigenous participants also require sufficient time to review the proponent's application. The EAO can control the timelines of the review process, but it is under some pressure to ensure that the assessment is performed in a timely manner. Efficiency must also be balanced with the flexibility to provide additional time if actors cannot adequately review the proponent's application. Apart from adequate resources and time, a legitimate consultative process also entails ensuring that participants understand how to navigate the process. It is the role of the EAO to provide information about the EA process and Indigenous parties' roles and expectations throughout the assessment. Out of the 126 assessments, there are seventy-four instances (59 percent) when the Indigenous parties stated in the documentation that they faced capacity issues, including a lack of financial support (25 percent), insufficient timelines to review relevant information (28 percent), or, relatedly, a high workload that prevented them from fully participating (6 percent).

Evaluating input legitimacy requires analyzing the participatory aspect of decision-making. In the context of the EA process, input legitimacy can be attained if the relevant Indigenous nations are invited in a timely fashion to participate, if the Indigenous nations that are participating have the appropriate capacity and resources to effectively participate, and if the terms of participation are accepted by the Indigenous nations. Table 10 highlights the percentages of projects that exhibit problems across each indicator of input legitimacy.

Table 10: Percentages of projects with problems across each indicator of input legitimacy during the AIR phase

Participants		*Capacity*		*Forums and processes*	
Identification of relevant Indigenous nations	6%	Financial resources	25%	Agreement on terms of engagement within EAs	3%
Timeliness of communication	0%	Sufficient time	28%	Appropriateness of EAs to fulfill the duty	26%
		Adequate knowledge	4%		

Although the percentage of projects that exhibit each input legitimacy problem can be considered low, the same project can contain multiple issues. Sixty-two projects (49 percent) had at least one input legitimacy issue, and twenty-seven projects (21 percent) have more than one input legitimacy issue. As this is only one phase of the decision-making process, it is concerning that almost half of the total projects begin with at least one input legitimacy problem from the perspective of Indigenous participants.

Input Legitimacy during the AIR Phase: Indigenous Participants with Little Capacity

Overall, the EAO has managed to invite affected Indigenous parties to participate in EAs in a timely manner, as indicated by the relatively low number of documented issues that arose between 2004 and 2019. However, the issue of which organization or governing body represents a rights-bearing Indigenous nation did lead to a judicial challenge during one EA, indicating that the stakes on this issue can be high. The rules about how the Crown should identify the correct governing body to consult remains unclear,[40] particularly when the Indigenous nation itself is divided. The BCCA has somewhat engaged with this issue more directly than the SCC. Recall that the BCCA stated in the 2017 case of *Spookw v Gitxsan Treaty Society* that it is inappropriate for the state to interfere in the internal affairs of Indigenous governments as that would violate the principles of self-government.[41] Moreover, in the 2011 case of *Nlaka'pamux Nation Tribal Council v British Columbia (Environmental Assessment Office)*, the BCCA found that the duty was not discharged because the EAO did not adjust the scope of consultation as it became clear that additional Indigenous groups were coming forward that expressed their intention to participate in the EA process.[42] Although it may be prudent for the Crown to simply consult as many groups as possible to avoid litigation, it is also unwise for the Crown to increase internal divisions by seeming to legitimate certain groups over others or only to consult organizations that more closely align with the goals of the Crown.

This type of internal conflict is precisely what triggered the Wet'suwet'en protests in the beginning of 2020 over the Coastal Gaslink Pipeline that received an EA certificate in 2014. When the project was approved against the recommendation of the Office of the Wet'suwe'ten, the proponent moved to secure agreements with members of the elected band council but failed to meet with the Hereditary Chiefs.[43] Despite the project successfully attaining an EA certificate, the Wet'suwe'ten Hereditary Chiefs and other community members blocked construction.[44] The attempt by the Royal Canadian Mounted Police to enforce the BC Supreme Court's injunction by arresting land defenders sparked solidarity protests across the country with repercussions affecting transit and the national economy.[45] Although this issue emerged outside of the EA process and was triggered by proponent-led negotiations, the EAO may be faced with a similar situation in future assessments. With the legitimacy of band councils being challenged in certain Indigenous communities, this issue may become more prominent within the EA process.

The fact that the EAO prioritizes the inclusion of relevant Indigenous actors means that an important aspect of input legitimacy has been attained, thus demonstrating an element of honourable behaviour on the part of the Crown. But since the EA process is already structured to invite relevant stakeholders to review a proposed project, the constitutional requirement to invite affected Indigenous nations is not a drastic departure from the existing processes. This may explain why the EAO is effective at upholding this aspect of input legitimacy; the duty to consult's requirement to include relevant Indigenous groups does not impose sweeping changes to the EAO's mandate to recruit stakeholders to review the proponent's application. The other aspects of input legitimacy are more difficult for the EAO to uphold precisely because they would entail extensive changes to the existing practices. However, these changes are necessary to help address the negative consequences of Canada's colonial legacy.

For example, the most prominent barrier to achieving input legitimacy is the capacity issues faced by many Indigenous nations – particularly, a lack of finances, personnel, and time. Indigenous policy actors consistently expressed throughout the EA process that they face capacity challenges that prevent them from participating effectively to express and defend their rights. Because there is "no legal obligation on the part of the Crown to fund consultation," the Crown can exercise discretion in determining how much funding is appropriate for Indigenous nations to receive.[46] Moreover, the duty-to-consult case law emphasizes the fairness of the decision-making process but is silent on the reality that the state's assimilatory policies and genocide have rendered many Indigenous governments with fragile governing capacity. The promise of the duty to promote procedural fairness is compromised without additional measures to bolster Indigenous governments' capacities and independence throughout consultation.

Rather than using its own resources to increase funding to Indigenous participants, the state relies on proponents to supply funding, but this source is neither consistent nor guaranteed. Although it is commonplace for the proponent to supply some funding, the amount that Indigenous nations receive depends on negotiations,[47] the results of which are more successful when an Indigenous nation has skilled negotiating personnel. The consequences of failing to acquire adequate funding and capacity for participation can lead to highly disadvantageous positions throughout the consultation and accommodation phases. For instance, a lack of capacity may compromise the ability of Indigenous groups to produce high-quality studies or carefully review the proponent's application. This may mean that Indigenous actors cannot effectively hold the proponent to account when the proponent presents its findings and assessments of the project's potential impacts and mitigation plans. Furthermore, the Crown may interpret delayed, incomplete, or rudimentary studies as insufficient evidence to support Indigenous nations' positions about the impact of a project on lands that are central for the exercise of their rights.[48] Indeed, if Indigenous actors do not fully raise concerns within the allotted time frame, it is assumed that the participating nations do not have any concerns with the project.

Compounding this issue is the lack of trust Indigenous nations have towards other actors – most notably, proponents – to conduct studies about Indigenous land use and rights. One consultant who has experience with both the Crown and Indigenous nations stated that they "would always recommend to an [Indigenous] client [to] never let the proponent have the pen on a study. It's a bit of a dangerous thing, because [the] proponent will never give you enough money to conduct a credible study."[49] Similarly, a First Nations Chief stated that proponents "have their own consultant, but we like our own consultant, also. We negotiate on who's going to do the study itself ... to make sure it's done right."[50] Indigenous nations feel pressure to conduct their own studies, but they can lack the capacity to do this crucial work. Moreover, not all proponents can provide Indigenous nations with adequate funding. Junior companies may lack the resources to fully support Indigenous nations throughout the EA process.[51] There are some instances when even larger companies will resist providing adequate funding,[52] although there is a much higher likelihood that fully resourced companies can provide financial support.[53] Finally, failing to fully participate in available consultation activities means that Indigenous parties are foreclosing the possibility of mounting a legal challenge against the Crown if they perceive the duty has not been adequately discharged; as one individual expressed about the SCC's 2013 decision in *Behn*, a lack of Indigenous participation, such as a lack of timeliness to communicate concerns, is understood as acting without good faith in consultative activities.[54] For example, as one lawyer working with Indigenous groups explained, "if your client doesn't participate in [EAs], it's going to be used against you."[55]

The frequency with which Indigenous parties stated that they face capacity issues demonstrates that the quality of Indigenous peoples' participation is highly variable across assessments.[56] This finding is corroborated by the experiences of Indigenous participants and their staff. Policy actors on the side of Indigenous nations stated that having adequate resources is crucial to sustaining effective negotiations with proponents and the Crown.[57] As one First Nation leader explained, "I had to negotiate with every industry or company that came, capacity money. So, you negotiate a capacity funding agreement and then you agree on what studies have to be done ... all of that you have to negotiate, all of it."[58] Yet there are barriers to ensuring that Indigenous parties receive or build this capacity. The sheer volume of consultative activities that Indigenous nations may face at a given time also reduces the likelihood that Indigenous nations can be effective negotiators during all the consultative activities.[59] One consultant for Indigenous nations suggested that even "well-resourced First Nations have to pick and choose what they are going to get involved in. There's just no way with all the referrals coming in ... they don't have the staff to process them, they just don't."[60] Allowing discretion and negotiations to determine an integral reality of participating in an EA process fundamentally undermines the pursuit of input legitimacy.

The fact that Indigenous peoples cannot demand alternative forums to consult with the Crown directly compromises the Crown's ability to attain this aspect of input legitimacy from the perspective of Indigenous peoples. However, the Crown is permitted to use the EA process as stipulated by the case law. Since the Crown can follow the court's standard of legitimate conduct rather than engage with Indigenous-led processes, the Crown has not moved to alter its reliance on regulatory review to discharge the duty. The EAO is highly vigilant in ensuring that the proponent consults with Indigenous parties about their consultation plans, but Indigenous peoples contest the imposition of the EA process itself.[61] A First Nations representative identified that a major flaw with the EA process is its disconnect with Indigenous governance as they note how "we always have outsiders I guess, so to speak, doing the assessments where there's no cultural knowledge from the people who are doing the environmental assessments."[62]

The state's colonial relationship with Indigenous peoples makes Indigenous peoples' demands for a new process that is established through collaboration urgent. The court's approach to simply layer Indigenous actors and the instruments of consultation onto a process that is primarily structured by the colonial state and is imbued with its logics has been shown to insufficiently provide appropriate space for Indigenous perspectives to be understood and valued. When British Columbia's EA process underwent reform, the province adopted a more collaborative approach, establishing several forums and roundtables to solicit the perspectives of Indigenous groups. Although Indigenous perspectives were sought, the overall structure of the EA process continues to be accepted as the appropriate venue to fulfill the duty to consult, foreclosing the possibility of a process that would exhibit Indigenous world views and values. The possibility of performing Indigenous-led assessments alongside the EA process may be a pathway forward to meaningfully engage Indigenous perspectives in the regulatory review of constitutional rights.

British Columbia's EA process during the application information requirements phase upholds a key aspect of input legitimacy – that is, ensuring that the relevant participants are included. But the EA process does not ensure that the Indigenous parties have the adequate capacity to participate meaningfully, and the Indigenous parties cannot contest the EA process itself as an appropriate forum for consultation and accommodation. This is not a strong foundation for Indigenous-Crown relations as decision-making continues into the application review phase.

5

Assessment of Impacts in the Application Review Phase

This chapter continues the examination of the application information requirements (AIR) phase and analyzes the next phase of British Columbia's environmental assessment (EA) process, the application review phase. The application review phase is the stage when the proponent's application for an environmental assessment certificate is closely reviewed by the relevant parties, including the affected Indigenous nations. It is during this stage that the bulk of the consultation and accommodation measures are pursued. These two stages of the process are analyzed to determine whether the four aspects of throughput legitimacy – inclusiveness, transparency, accountability, and effectiveness – are attained. Throughput legitimacy aims to assess the quality of the interactions between the actors as they negotiate key policy choices. Such interactions provide a crucial insight to assessing the overall quality of the Crown's consultation and accommodation efforts.

As the AIR phase is the initial step in the EA process, a comprehensive determination of whether the Crown is upholding the various characteristics of throughput legitimacy cannot be made. Yet, in this initial phase, there are signs that point to the Crown's mixed performance in upholding accountability and transparency in decision-making. Specifically, when deciding key aspects of the EA review's scope, it may be unclear how the BC Environmental Assessment Office (EAO) reached its final decision when the proponent and Indigenous groups have had conflicting views. This lack of transparency is coupled with the inconsistent ability of Indigenous groups to hold the proponent to account when disagreements arise over the appropriate methodology with which to evaluate the adverse impacts. The proponent may seem to be accepting of Indigenous feedback when it does not risk significantly increasing the length of time for the application review. The proponent's and the EAO's acceptance of Indigenous feedback when those suggested changes do not incur a lengthy review process or change methodologies to assess negative impacts may indicate the Indigenous participants' overall lack of power to hold the proponent to account.

The issues found in the AIR phase come into sharp focus during the application review phase. Throughout the application review phase, the Crown does not consistently attain key aspects of throughput legitimacy, particularly accountability, transparency, and effectiveness. This result is highly concerning considering that the purpose of the application review phase is for Indigenous participants to express how the final decision can affect the exercise of their constitutional Aboriginal rights and how best those rights can be protected. The EAO itself determines how transparently it communicates its decisions to include or exclude the Indigenous participants' feedback. Moreover, heavy burdens are placed on Indigenous parties to contest and revisit studies and decisions made by the proponent, weakening the ways in which the Indigenous policy actors can hold the proponent accountable. Due to these significant shortcomings, the process may be perceived by the Indigenous parties as lacking effectiveness.

These problems in British Columbia's EA process are directly linked to the problems identified within the duty-to-consult case law in previous chapters – mainly, the Supreme Court of Canada's (SCC) inconsistent emphasis on crafting a fair process for consultation. Additionally, the government has not dramatically altered the EAO's statutory mandates to enable them to engage with Indigenous concerns and issues. As a result of both the case law and the lack of statutory guidance, the EAO's actors are not empowered to act discretionarily for fear of undermining the government's political and legal position vis-à-vis Indigenous rights and land governance; instead, they hew closely to the court's arguably low threshold for adequate consultation. As a result, Indigenous parties perceive the process as opaque and unmeaningful.

Application Information Requirements Phase

Although the AIR phase significantly shapes the subsequent stages of the EA process, only twenty-three projects out of the total 126 projects (18 percent) had comprehensive records of the deliberations, meetings, and interactions that comprised the pre-application phase. A possibility why there is a dearth of information during this phase is that record-keeping is only done consistently once the proponent has submitted its application for review by the EAO and the other relevant decision-makers. As a result, it is difficult to generalize whether the Indigenous parties were regularly consulted and if they participated in the decision-making at this stage. Nevertheless, the findings from these cases can help illustrate the nature of the participation by Indigenous groups and the kinds of issues that were contested during the drafting of the AIR.

Most of the projects that documented the pre-application phase revealed that the Indigenous groups participated in the drafting of the AIR by detailing their comments through letters, participating in working group meetings, and meeting directly with the proponent. In the earlier years – from 2006 to 2010 – the Indigenous groups appeared to participate mainly in working group meetings and through letters detailing their positions about the draft AIR. After 2010, the proponent and the EAO used tracking tables that detail the comments from the Indigenous groups, the proponent's responses to those comments, and the EAO's evaluation of the adequacy of the proponent's responses. In the available records, the proponent frequently engaged early with the Indigenous parties, although the quality of those early interactions is difficult to assess. Early engagement can simply entail the proponent giving notice to the affected Indigenous parties, while more robust forms of early engagement involve the proponent allocating funding for Indigenous groups to complete initial studies that help identify the full range of Indigenous interests, like traditional use studies. The information from initial land use studies is also relied upon by the EAO to conduct a preliminary assessment of the appropriate scope of consultation based on both the Indigenous group's strength of claim and the potential negative effects of the project. This preliminary assessment is directly drawn from the SCC's ruling in *Haida Nation v British Columbia (Ministry of Forests)*, wherein the court outlined that the content and scope of the Crown's duty depends on the Indigenous party's strength of claim and the proposed project's adverse impacts.[1] Although Indigenous groups fully participated in these forums to express their opinions on the draft AIR, the feedback from the Indigenous parties that led to changes in the

AIR is low. Only six assessments have records of a full tracking table that shows which Indigenous nations' comments are adopted, and, at most, half of all comments made by Indigenous parties are added by the proponent.

The aspects of the AIR that are more likely to be accepted by the proponent for change include explicit commitments to incorporate more input from Indigenous groups such as requiring studies to include their traditional knowledge or Indigenous representation in future studies. Other feedback from Indigenous groups that proponents are more likely to adopt include adjusting the scope of studies that measure impacts to the valued components (VCs) or changing the indicators used in those studies. Recall that VCs are aspects of the natural or human world that are determined to have value and should be protected from negative impacts resulting from the proposed project.

In contrast, other types of feedback from Indigenous groups are more likely to be met with resistance from proponents. In particular, the requirement for the proponent to detail alternative project designs or mitigation measures was treated as premature in the pre-application phase. Proponents also often disagreed with the Indigenous groups' understandings of how to assess the threshold for significant impacts to VCs. A related point of contention lies in Indigenous peoples' concerns that the proponent relies too heavily on existing studies or information about the environment or region instead of committing to conducting additional studies. The proponents justified their decisions to reject Indigenous groups' comments to change the draft AIR in two main ways. First, they asserted that Indigenous groups' requests for additional information about the project or its effects would be part of the larger assessment beyond the AIR phase. For instance, cumulative effects assessments and the detailing of mitigation measures or project alternatives would be part of the assessment but not outlined in the AIR. The proponents also responded that additional studies were unnecessary since the available information is deemed sufficient by the EAO. Second, the proponents stressed that they were willing to continue their engagement with the affected Indigenous groups, such as continuing negotiations either in other stages of the EA or beyond the EA process, to address the ongoing concerns. This response was often given to Indigenous groups' requests for specific mitigation measures such as compensation or revitalization plans. Most of the time, the proponents appeared to defer the Indigenous actors' questions by stating that it could be revisited at another point in the EA process. Although some questions may not be possible to address without additional information and studies, the refusal of the proponents to change their methodology regarding the threshold to assess significant impacts or to collect new data is the most concerning issue and is not clearly justified. Including additional studies and Indigenous perspectives are less likely to change the assessments of decision-makers if the method by which negative impacts are understood and evaluated do not reflect Indigenous perceptions of risk.

The EAO largely facilitated working group meetings by clarifying the EA process, such as how it can be used to fulfill the duty to consult, and evaluating whether the proponents' responses to the concerns of Indigenous groups were adequate. In the earlier projects, the EAO clarified that neither the proponents nor the Crown required the consent of the affected Indigenous groups to proceed with a project and that the EA process could fulfill both consultation and accommodation requirements under the law. The EAO, when assessing the actions of the proponents, was vigilant about ensuring that Indigenous groups were consulted about the proponents' future consultation plans throughout the EA process; that a rationale was provided detailing why certain VCs and indicators to measure the impacts to VCs were chosen over others; and that an explanation about the relationship between the project's effects on a VC was provided.

Once the AIR is finalized and approved by the EAO, the EAO passes an order under section 11 of the *Environmental Assessment Act*.[2] This order confirms "(a) the scope of the required assessment of the reviewable project, and (b) the procedures and methods for conducting the assessment."[3] The scope and content of the section 11 order has changed over time. From 2006 to 2010, the section 11 orders outlined the proponent's responsibility to Indigenous parties in more limited ways, such as specifying that proponents only need to identify Indigenous interests related to asserted rights and title claims. Moreover, proponents only need to make reasonable efforts to engage with affected Indigenous parties. After 2010, the section 11 orders became more expansive and provided more detail about the responsibilities of both the proponent and the EAO regarding consultation. For instance, proponents are expected to consult Indigenous groups with regard to their rights, which reflects more robust language than interests related to asserted rights and title claims. Proponents are also expected to display adequate effort to engage with Indigenous parties rather than just reasonable efforts. The EAO clarified its own role as a vehicle to facilitate government-to-government negotiations when requested by an Indigenous party. The EAO also began to state that Indigenous groups can make their own submissions in addition to the final assessment report and that Indigenous participants require sufficient information and reasonable time frames to prepare comments. This shift in the content of section 11 suggests that the EAO itself has become more vigilant to identify in more detail the various measures within the EA process that can facilitate the fulfillment of the duty to consult.

During the pre-application review phase, the principles of throughput legitimacy – in particular, effectiveness – cannot be fully assessed because this phase is only one stage of the consultation and accommodation process. However, the data suggest that this stage exhibits mixed results concerning whether policy actors can hold one another to account. On the one hand, proponents are often willing to change the studies that inform the assessment, such as increasing Indigenous peoples' participation in studies and adding or changing the scope of the studies and the indicators used to assess impacts to the VCs. Indigenous parties' concerns over conducting additional studies are more likely to be dismissed. The proponents also often reject Indigenous peoples' perspectives about the thresholds to determine significant impacts on VCs. There were no reported issues with the parties meeting and engaging with one another, indicating that the process at this stage at least upheld inclusiveness. With regard to transparency, the EAO ensures that the proponent provides rationales to explain the choice of VCs and their measurement of alternatives. Other decisions, such as the proponent's decision to reject other methodologies to assess significant impacts, were not clearly explained. Record-keeping also became more sophisticated with the use of tracking tables over time. Thus, upholding transparency was uneven during this phase of the EA process, particularly earlier in the time span under investigation.

The proponents did not provide a reason why certain changes to the AIR, as requested by Indigenous participants, were accepted over others. However, the proponents have a clear interest in rejecting methodological changes that would lengthen the EA process or increase the potential of a refusal. For example, changing the significant impact thresholds could make the project's potential negative impacts look more significant. In contrast, the proponents' openness to adding more Indigenous participation in studies and data collection is relatively less likely to dramatically increase the length of the regulatory review process. These interests could explain why a proponent is more likely to reject certain Indigenous groups' demands over others. Although these rationales correspond to the proponents' interests in advancing their project, they would not be suitable reasons to justify the exclusion of Indigenous participants' recommendations. The EAO's decision to accept the proponents' decisions without a clear justification in these instances is puzzling.

This initial stage of the decision-making process reveals limitations in terms of upholding accountability and transparency as the proponents can pick and choose which demands from Indigenous parties to accept without a clear rationale. Inclusiveness appears to be upheld consistently as policy actors seem willing and able to meet.

Application Review Phase

Throughput Legitimacy: Findings on Inclusiveness[4]

Once the AIR is approved by the EAO, the proponent submits its application for an EA certificate. The proponent's application undergoes review for 180 days. During this time, the project's effects on the VCs, including Aboriginal rights, are assessed, and mitigation measures to address the potential negative effects of the project are negotiated. To begin evaluating throughput legitimacy, the characteristics of inclusiveness will be examined first. The first indicator to help measure inclusiveness is whether the Indigenous parties were treated as constitutional rights holders. Recognizing Indigenous consultees as holding a unique status throughout the consultations means that the Crown and the proponent understands their obligations to the Indigenous parties as distinct from other interested parties and stakeholders. There are only twelve instances of the 126 cases examined (9 percent) when the Indigenous parties explicitly expressed concern that their status as rights holders was not being respected. In these instances, the Indigenous groups stressed that they were not to be treated like other interest groups or members of the general public. For example, in the 2011 Kokish River Hydroelectric project, the Namgis First Nation voiced their concern that uninformed recreational land users should not influence the application review process at the expense of primary land users like Indigenous nations.[5]

Proponents were also identified as sometimes demonstrating an unwillingness to follow appropriate protocols when engaging with the Indigenous leadership or officials, revealing a lack of knowledge and sensitivity to Indigenous groups and their nation status. A prominent instance of this issue can be found during the 2009 assessment for the Northern Rockies Secure Landfill project. The Fort Nelson First Nation characterized their interactions with the proponent as amounting to "sharp dealings" because the proponent "has a history of contacting Elders 'just to chat' and coming into Lands offices unannounced and uninvited."[6] These problems may be especially pertinent in the case of international proponents as it is widely known among Indigenous policy actors and representatives that proponents outside of Canada are unfamiliar with protocols for respectful interactions with Indigenous nations.[7] Other than these cases, it appears that Indigenous peoples are largely treated as having distinct status in the EA process, which is a key element of inclusiveness.

Another indicator of inclusiveness is ensuring that all the relevant parties, including the proponents and the Crown's actors, are available to exchange information and negotiate accommodation measures. Based on the EAO's reports, Indigenous parties were concerned with the level of inclusiveness of actors in sixteen of the 126 projects (13 percent) that underwent a full assessment. Although this is a small minority of cases, there are some stark examples where crucial provincial or federal representatives from agencies and departments were not always present, even though they may have been better positioned than the EAO and the proponent to negotiate meaningful accommodation measures. This problem is especially pertinent with respect to federal government representatives as these actors can change legislation or practices in response to Indigenous peoples' interests beyond a specific project.[8] A related issue is the concern that the Crown's actors who are present in the EA process do not have the mandate to negotiate responsive accommodation measures.[9]

In the 2008 Port Mann Highway 1 project, the Kwantlen First Nation stated that its interactions with government officials were mostly technical in nature because these officials had no mandate to address issues related to Aboriginal rights and title.[10] Similarly, in the 2011 Northwest Transmission Line project, the Tahltan Nation also stated that EA officials and government actors with whom they were in contact had a "lack of mandates or willingness to discuss elements of appropriate accommodation."[11] The Federal Court of Appeal objected to the "note-taker" approach to consultation in *Tsleil-Waututh Nation v Canada (Attorney General)*, stating that "Canada [is] obliged to do more than passively hear and receive the real concerns of the Indigenous applicants."[12] Regardless of this rejection by the Federal Court of Appeal, interviewees also recounted that the Crown sends passive note takers or actors who lack knowledge of the project and the overall region. In the context of the Coastal Gaslink Pipeline project, an Indigenous political representative recounted the following scenario: "We were [in] meetings with the crown, with the actual EAO people ... the project lead didn't know nothing ... when I was talking about – I read the whole 7,000-page application, I could tell that guy stuff about the project, he had no clue. The poor guy had no clue."[13]

These experiences reveal how the Crown's actors in consultation processes can be poorly informed or lack mandates to address the substantive concerns of Indigenous groups. When inclusiveness is lost, it may lead to hostile interactions between policy actors that are not conducive to productive negotiations. Overall, challenges relating to the attainment of inclusiveness were not numerous across the EA reports as most projects did not show that the Crown or the proponent had neglected the constitutional rights holder status of the Indigenous participants or failed to attend key meetings. Although not numerous, the Crown's actors who do not have mandates to negotiate accommodation measures negatively affects the ability of the Crown to discharge the duty to consult.

Throughput Legitimacy: Findings on Transparency

In addition to having the relevant parties present and interacting with one another, it is also important that the proponent and the EAO are reliably and accurately documenting the positions and concerns of the Indigenous parties. If this aspect of transparency is not met, the degree to which other aspects of throughput legitimacy are attained is undermined. For instance, a lack of documentation could decrease the ability of the actors to effectively hold each other to account. There are only ten instances (8 percent) among the 126 assessments where the Indigenous parties expressed concerns about the accurate record-keeping of Indigenous peoples' comments. This low number indicates that the proponent and the EAO have been quite successful at documenting the positions of Indigenous groups.

Once the relevant information is gathered, the project's potential effects on Aboriginal rights are assessed. Ensuring that the methodologies to assess both the Indigenous group's strength of claim and the significance of the impacts on Indigenous peoples' interests are transparently communicated can help avoid disagreements. The scope of Aboriginal rights is ideally assessed before the project's impacts are evaluated to ensure that the assessment of the impacts is connected to the affected Indigenous nations' rights. In the drafting of the AIR, the EAO makes a preliminary determination of the scope of consultation owed to various Indigenous parties with different strengths of claim. The EAO may change this preliminary assessment if additional information is brought forward that demonstrates that an Indigenous nation has a strong strength of claim to rights or title and/or the project's potential impacts are more severe than anticipated. However, the SCC does not require administrative tribunals to give a full *Haida Nation* analysis in their decision-making,[14] meaning that tribunals are not required to explicitly explain the scope of Aboriginal rights affected when explaining the impacts on those rights. It may not be legally required for the EAO to provide this specific form of justification in its decision-making, but the lack of transparency in this part of the assessment appears to decrease the overall perception of throughput legitimacy for the Indigenous participants.

In the application review stage, the EAO should transparently communicate the rationale underpinning the assessment of both the Indigenous groups' strength of claim and the significance of impacts on the Indigenous peoples' rights. Yet there are fifty-five reported instances out of 126 completed assessments (44 percent) where at least one Indigenous party was concerned with the EAO's level of transparency when it interpreted the proposed project's impacts on Aboriginal rights. These instances are also spread out over time, indicating that this issue has persisted regardless of changes in the duty-to-consult case law. For instance, in the 2018 application for the Revelstoke Unit 6 project from BC Hydro, the Syilx Okanagan Nation stated that "the criteria used by the EAO to reach its conclusions on Project effects to our title and rights are still not clear."[15] This statement was in response to the EAO's recommendation to approve the project for an EA certification; although the EAO's decision-making was not transparent to the Syilx Okanagan Nation, the nation could not directly hold the EAO to account for its decision. The 2015 assessment over the Woodfibre LNG (liquified natural gas) project also displayed similar issues. The Tsleil-Waututh First Nation stated in their separate submission to the decision-making ministers that "the EAO ... unjustifiably interprets what it does not know or understand to mean that the information does not exist or there will be no impact."[16] When problems arise with the EAO's reasoning, the only recourse available at the later stages of the process is to share its perspective with the decision-making minister rather than reopen negotiations.

Indigenous parties are concerned with how the EAO explains its interpretation of impacts on rights and its overall decision-making when it is concluded that Aboriginal rights will not be significantly impacted. In terms of fulfilling the duty to consult, this lack of transparency is harmful because the SCC has stated that the Crown, as part of its honourable dealings, must provide "written reasons to show that Indigenous concerns were considered and to reveal the impact they had on their decision."[17] Explaining the rationale underlying the determination of the project's effects is a key area where the Crown should show how Indigenous concerns shape the final decision. Although the importance of written reasons is established by the case law, the SCC has not extensively commented on what the Crown's written reasons should entail. In *Chippewas of the Thames First Nation v Enbridge Pipelines*, the SCC appeared to defer to the tribunal's expertise over assessing impacts to Aboriginal rights. The court only stated that the National Energy Board (NEB) had "assessed the risks that the project posed to those rights and interests and concluded that the risks were minimal."[18] There was no further comment on the substance of the NEB's justification.

Throughput Legitimacy: Findings on Accountability

The next main principle of throughput legitimacy is accountability. In the context of the EA process, accountability requires the incorporation of feedback from Indigenous participants, such as knowledge about the technical aspects of the proposed project and the nature of the Aboriginal rights at stake. The perspectives of Indigenous participants help hold the proponent to account for a project's potential impacts on Aboriginal rights, so it is imperative that Indigenous feedback and questions are answered and addressed by the proponent. Out of the completed 126 assessments, seventy-two of those assessments (57 percent) revealed that at least one Indigenous party did not believe their concerns regarding the project and/or project data were adequately incorporated. Common issues include omissions of important information about the project and issues with the quality of the data being used by the proponent, such as its accuracy, whether it is up to date, and its credibility.[19] The prevalence of this issue is highly troubling, considering that a primary function of the EA process and the duty to consult is to identify and consider Indigenous parties' views on the proposed project's impacts. Since this goal to collect various perspectives through regulatory review is consistent with the EAO's functions before the duty to consult was added, it is surprising that issues of data being omitted or being unreliable are pervasive across the assessments.

Indigenous participants perceive that their perspectives are being ignored because their knowledge is typically not systematically used to inform the entire assessment.[20] In the 2006 Deltaport Third Berth project, the EAO acknowledged in its recommendation to the minister that the Tsawwassen First Nation, the Sencot'en Alliance, and the Hul'qumi'num Treaty Group raised concerns about the use of traditional knowledge during the review.[21] However, the EAO did not comment on how these concerns were addressed. In another example, the 2015 Woodfibre LNG project also reveals the same problem, with the Tsleil-Waututh First Nation stating that the EAO did not clearly incorporate the First Nation's traditional use studies to assess the project's impacts on Aboriginal rights.[22] Even the completeness of the traditional use studies is variable – for example, in a 2006 assessment for the Brule Mine project, a representative from the West Moberly First Nation stated that the study did not speak to "hunters, fishers, and trappers with respect to the Hunting Rights, Fishing Rights, and Trapping Rights."[23] It appears that the EAO has the discretion to decide the degree to which Indigenous feedback and perspectives are included in the assessment. The exercise of this discretion may constrain the ability of Indigenous peoples to hold other actors – notably, the proponent – to account on a wide range of issues that may be caused by a project's potential impacts.

Related to the issue of incorporating Indigenous feedback is the timing of when that knowledge is included in the assessment. Indigenous parties expressed the concern that the collection of relevant missing data should not be a project condition after the EA certification is granted; rather, such data need to be collected beforehand to accurately assess the project's impacts.[24] Otherwise, the collected information cannot be effectively used to limit or avoid negative impacts. In the 2018 Red Mountain Underground Gold project, this concern was expressed by the Nisga'a Lisims government. The Nisga'a Lisims government was "concerned that more detailed information on ... potential impacts would come later in the life of the project (i.e., during permitting) when it may be more challenging to change aspects of the Project."[25] Moreover, information that is collected beyond the time frames set out in the EA process may be unfairly dismissed or overlooked due to the preference of the proponent to complete the EA process in a timely fashion.[26]

Accountability-related concerns also arise when the EAO determines the scope of Aboriginal rights that are at stake with the project. The EAO makes the initial determination of an Indigenous group's strength of claim but then places the onus on Indigenous actors to provide data if the Indigenous parties disagree with that determination.[27] There are sixteen instances out of the 126 assessments (13 percent) where the Indigenous parties explicitly challenged the EAO's strength-of-claim analysis. This is expected to be a significant underestimation as sensitive evidence to support Indigenous peoples' rights and title claims would not be documented in the EA process for confidentiality reasons. Disagreements may have been communicated to the EAO and other government actors in private discussions. In the sixteen cases (13 percent) where the strength-of-claim assessment was contested, the Indigenous parties expressed that the EAO had relied on inaccurate ethnographic, archeological, and historical data. The Indigenous groups perceived that there were data inaccuracies because the government largely used Western sources and literature that prioritize written accounts of Indigenous land use patterns and activities.[28]

In interviews, lawyers, officials, and consultants expressed frustration with how the Crown's strength-of-claim assessment is incomplete or rudimentary.[29] The Crown typically relies on its own internal data that detail the various Indigenous nations that claim territory in the province. A First Nation political representative stated that "those maps – what do they call them – statement of interest maps [do not] even match any strength of claim. And I'm just annoyed because the BC government keep taking these crazy maps that people just make up, it's not even evidentiary and make it to be so."[30] Corroborating this account, a consultant noted that "the material upon which strength of claims are based are extremely limited and this limitation ... does not temper their decisions."[31] Moreover, this consultant observed that the strength of claim is not only based upon contested information, but its determination is "done by people who are not qualified to do them ... the task is being delegated to clerks and First Nation liaisons who may not have [an appropriate] background at all."[32]

Prioritizing certain historical accounts is not a defensible way to establish strength-of-claim assessments, especially since many First Nations in the province may claim the same territory as part of their Aboriginal right or title in British Columbia. The Semiahmoo First Nation, in the context of the 2013 Vancouver Airport Fuel Delivery project, explained how all Indigenous nations can point to different archeological or historical sources to "make similar statements and formulate similar arguments" to demonstrate a rights or title claim; therefore, given that this kind of data do not help distinguish which group(s) may have a stronger claim to a territory over others, the EAO should not be permitted to use this data to justify prioritizing certain Indigenous nations in consultation and accommodation negotiations.[33]

If Indigenous parties seek to change the Crown's strength-of-claim assessment, they are faced with a high burden of proof. This burden is the result of the EAO basing its assessment of rights and title on legal tests established by the SCC's decisions in cases such as *R v Van der Peet* and *Delgamuukw v British Columbia*.[34] These tests are critiqued for characterizing rights, land use, and occupation from a Eurocentric perspective.[35] For instance, Aboriginal rights are arbitrarily limited as rights that must be distinctive and integral to the culture of the Indigenous group at the time of first contact with Europeans,[36] and title claims must demonstrate exclusive occupation.[37] The more recent case of *Tsilhqot'in v British Columbia* changed how title claims should be assessed; the SCC granted the Tsilhqot'in Nation title over land that did not have permanent settlements.[38] Nevertheless, the Tsilhqot'in Nation could demonstrate their exclusive use of the land, something that may not be applicable to all Indigenous peoples' land use patterns.

The responsibility of Indigenous nations to provide specific data to change the strength-of-claim assessment even before formal legal recognition is pursued shifts accountability away from the Crown. Crucially, the case law does not stipulate that Indigenous groups must prove rights claims following the distinctive culture test to be entitled to meaningful consultation. Moreover, the nations that suffer most from the effects of colonialism are also the least well positioned to have the resources and evidence to present adequate proof to substantiate rights claims based on a *Van der Peet* standard. One First Nations political representative even asserted that governments assume that, if a community is "badly managed, then their strength of claim is probably low."[39] Applying the distinctive culture test raises an additional barrier to Indigenous peoples' ability to hold the Crown's actors to account and change the course of the assessment. This onus is especially inappropriate within the context of the duty to consult where proving rights and title is not the objective.

It is unclear why the Crown unilaterally decides the scope of rights. Although the case law clarifies that the scope of consultation and accommodation should be proportionate to the scope of Aboriginal rights or rights claims,[40] there is no indication that this determination is made solely by the Crown. Also recall that the EAO is not required to present a *Haida Nation* analysis, adding transparency issues alongside a lack of accountability in this process. Disagreements over the strength-of-claim assessment may then influence the acceptance of the accommodation measures at the decision phase as the Indigenous participants may be more likely to reject the mitigation plans premised on the Crown's unilateral assessment of the strength-of-rights claims.

The final dimension of accountability involves the roles and responsibilities of each party to fulfill the duty to consult. Only two instances out of 126 assessments (2 percent) mentioned this issue. In contrast, five interviewees representing Indigenous groups spoke about the challenges with identifying the responsibilities of the Crown and the proponent. The case law states that the Crown can delegate procedural aspects of the duty to proponents.[41] However, the interview data suggest that the Crown exhibits an over-reliance on proponents to reach agreements with Indigenous groups rather than just completing procedural aspects like information sharing because the duty can be more easily discharged when Indigenous nations support the project.[42] For example, a consultant noted that proponents, especially large companies, are open to "sit down and negotiate and not talk like petty cash, but, you know, fairly substantial things."[43] These payments are negotiated in exchange for Indigenous groups waiving their right to pursue litigation against the project and its outputs.

However, this approach does not respect the governing authority of Indigenous peoples as "First Nations want to be owners of companies, not just bystanders or getting paid off a little bit on the side."[44] This statement indicates the possible shortcomings with proponents fulfilling more than simply the procedural elements of Crown consultation. Proponents are not positioned to negotiate shared governance over policy areas or territory; an absent Crown in accommodation negotiations limits how the duty can foster reconciliation between the Crown and Indigenous governance.[45] A consultant for Indigenous groups expressed that the Crown is "doing a really terrible job at accommodation, and it's stuff that simply the proponents shouldn't be stepping up on. And it's not that they're over-delegating, it's that they're ... underachieving their own mandate; they could do way more, and they're just simply not."[46]

In contrast, representatives from the EAO dispute this charge. They state that the EAO ensures that the proponent fulfills its part of the consultation because one of the Crown's priorities is to avoid litigation.[47] Nevertheless, this statement also reveals that the Crown is motivated to use proponents to fulfill many aspects of the duty to consult as it can help them meet their legal obligations set out in the case law, even if the proponent's attempts at accommodation are insufficient from the perspective of the Indigenous participants. The different roles of the EAO and proponent to fulfill the duty may be a source of frustration on the part of the Indigenous parties, but the low number of recorded instances in the assessments suggests that it may not be a significant point of contention for the attainment of accountability.

It should be noted that there are exemptions under the *Environmental Assessment Act* to account for Indigenous nations with recognized treaty rights, giving treaty nations potentially more power to influence the EA process. According to section 29.1(1) of the *Environmental Assessment Act,* the EAO may be required to negotiate with a treaty nation to harmonize the EA process with the treaty nation's procedures for evaluating proposed development if it is outlined in the final agreement. This provision protects Indigenous-created assessment requirements, although final agreements may stipulate that provincial and federal laws apply if there is a conflict between the Indigenous laws and the Canadian law.[48] Extending the protection of Indigenous-led assessments to non-treaty Indigenous groups may increase accountability as Indigenous groups would have more oversight powers to ensure that the proponent and the EAO are including Indigenous perspectives throughout the assessment. Despite this ability to harmonize EA processes with Indigenous-led assessments, the participation of treaty nations in the EA process does not appear more positive than non-treaty nations, as expressed in the EA reports. Although treaty nations are more likely to be categorized by the Crown as requiring "deep" consultation, the concerns that the EAO selectively incorporates Indigenous perspectives or does not provide adequate explanations is shared across Indigenous groups with or without formal agreements.

Throughput Legitimacy: Findings on Effectiveness

The final principle of throughput legitimacy is effectiveness. Effectiveness refers to whether the Indigenous parties perceive the consultations and the process of negotiating accommodation measures as meaningful exercises to identify and protect Aboriginal rights. Without a sense of meaningfulness, the act of consultation becomes hollow and simply "an opportunity to blow off steam before the Minister proceeds to do what she intended to do all along."[49] As such, evaluating the perception of meaningfulness is a good representation of whether the Indigenous parties perceive consultation as being effective. Indigenous parties explicitly stated forty times (32 percent) in the EA reports that they were dissatisfied with the meaningfulness of consultation. This negative sentiment was expressed either throughout the review process or in the Indigenous peoples' separate submissions to the decision-making minister. This number is likely a highly conservative estimate as only explicit statements using the term "meaningfulness" were counted.[50] For instance, Indigenous parties may state that the Crown did not uphold the duty due to other throughput legitimacy issues, such as having a lack of accountability or transparency, but these were not counted as instances where Indigenous peoples were concerned with the effectiveness of the process.[51]

Some recurring sentiments that demonstrate Indigenous groups' concerns with the meaningfulness of consultation include: the perception that outcomes were pre-determined; that the Crown places more emphasis on the procedural aspects of consultation than on the negotiation of adequate accommodation measures; and that, overall, interacting with the proponent, the Crown, or both was a frustrating experience. For instance, in the 2008 assessment for the Hermann Mine project, the West Moberly First Nations perceived the EAO to be prioritizing the interests of the proponent, leading the First Nation group to believe that its participation was "more about a display of tokenism rather than respectful engagement indicative of meaningful consultation."[52] When the EA process is perceived to lack meaningfulness, Indigenous parties may turn to judicial intervention to change the process. The Carrier Sekani Tribal Council issued a warning to the EAO during the assessment of the 2014 Coastal Gaslink Pipeline project, stating that failing to discharge the duty "plac[es] the future of the Pipelines and the LNG industry in the Province at risk, and detrimentally harming [to] its important ongoing relationship with us."[53] An Indigenous official working in their government's natural resource department described the typical duty-to-consult process as the following: "First Nations provide their information. A clerk records it, and files it away."[54] Projects with major economic and political stakes may produce more substantive negotiations,[55] but, overall, the duty to consult is viewed by some as merely a procedural exercise that does not meaningfully change the Crown's decision-making to protect Aboriginal rights.

Throughout the process of engaging Indigenous groups in consultation, the EA process is susceptible to a lack of transparency, accountability, and effectiveness. During the application review phase, many Indigenous groups perceive that the EAO does not transparently explain why a certain methodology is employed to assess Indigenous peoples' strength of claim and the impacts on Aboriginal rights. There are several accountability issues – most notably, the inconsistency with which Indigenous feedback in multiple stages of the application review phase informs the assessment. Finally, Indigenous parties perceive the EA process to lack effectiveness precisely because their participation does not appear to meaningfully shape the Crown's final decision. Table 11 summarizes the percentages of projects that exhibit problems across each indicator of throughput legitimacy in the application review stage.

This chapter has evaluated the application information requirements and the application review phases of British Columbia's EA process to examine whether the Crown upholds the key elements of throughput legitimacy. The EA process reveals shortcomings in three out of four key characteristics of throughput legitimacy: accountability, transparency, and effectiveness. In contrast, inclusiveness is more consistently upheld throughout the EA process as Indigenous parties' status as distinct constitutional rights holders is respected and relevant policy actors are generally available throughout the consultations and accommodation negotiations. The other deficiencies in the EA process are the result of the Crown's narrow

Table 11: Percentages of projects with problems across each indicator of throughput legitimacy during the application review stage

Inclusiveness		*Transparency*		*Accountability*		*Effectiveness*	
Agreement on the status of Indigenous consultees	9%	Accurate identification and documentation of Indigenous concerns	8%	Indigenous knowledge and feedback are included	57%	Participation is perceived to be meaningful	32%
Relevant actors are present during meetings	13%	Clear rationales are presented explaining the methodology to assess scope of rights and impacts on rights	44%	Each participant has clear roles and responsibilities regarding the fulfillment of the duty to consult	2%		

interpretation of the duty-to-consult case law. The SCC has presented inconsistent or vague rules about how decision-making should be structured to uphold transparency and accountability. As a result, tribunals like the EAO can determine their own level of transparency when communicating their reasons in their decision-making. Moreover, the EAO remains closely aligned with the scope of its planning mandate, leaving other obligations of the duty, such as the negotiation of accommodation measures, to be handled outside of the EA process without clear accountability mechanisms. Due to poor throughput legitimacy outcomes, Indigenous participants' dissatisfaction will clearly influence their perceptions towards the outputs of the EA process.

6

Accommodations in the Decision Phase

Once the proponent's application is reviewed by the relevant policy actors, the BC Environmental Assessment Office (EAO) decides whether to recommend an environmental assessment (EA) certificate. The positions of the EAO and the Indigenous parties are made explicit at this stage, which helps determine whether the process yields output legitimacy. The duty does not require that the Indigenous participants obtain their preferred policy outcome, but it is still expected that consultation yields appropriate accommodation measures that protect Aboriginal rights. The EA process exhibits issues with regard to obtaining output legitimacy because the Indigenous parties are often dissatisfied with the adequacy of the accommodation measures. Specifically, the EAO does not adequately explain why certain accommodations, such as mitigation measures, are chosen over alternatives and does not provide adequate assurances that the mitigation measures will be implemented and maintained throughout the life of the proposed project. Furthermore, the Crown displays an over-reliance on the proponents to negotiate benefits from the project in the place of accommodation measures to address project impacts on the exercise of Aboriginal rights.

A key reason why these shortcomings persist lies in the Supreme Court of Canada's (SCC) consistent reticence to evaluate the substance of the Crown's accommodation measures.[1] The BC Court of Appeal (BCCA) confirmed this approach by emphasizing that it is inappropriate for the judiciary to intervene in the substance of political negotiations.[2] In the event where the Crown takes a contrary position than an Indigenous party, the

BCCA provided some additional guidance on how the Crown must explain why the Indigenous party's position is unreasonable,[3] such as presenting positions without alternatives that are consistent with the Crown's policy objectives.[4] The judiciary has arguably made it easier for the Crown's actors to justify the prioritization of the Crown's objectives when evaluating accommodation measures, and, yet, the EAO's opaque and arguably unresponsive decision-making persists in the final stage of the EA process.

Output Legitimacy in the Decision Phase

The outputs of the EA process include, foremost, the EAO's recommendations to the relevant minister once the application review has concluded. The EAO's recommendation includes an assessment report that describes the various stages of the EA process and the assessment's results. Indigenous parties can present a separate submission to the decision-making minister, outlining their own conclusions of the assessment if they disagree with the EAO's conclusions. Accordingly, the mitigation measures detailed during the assessment, the EAO's final assessment report, and the Indigenous parties' submissions are relevant in analyzing output legitimacy.

The negotiated accommodation measures that are proposed vary depending on the projected impacts of the project on Aboriginal rights. They primarily involve mitigation measures to avoid or minimize negative impacts and monitoring activities after the project's approval to identify and manage future impacts. Thus, all projects that have some potential to impact Aboriginal rights will include accommodation measures. Of the total ninety-six completed projects, only two projects – the Kemess North Copper-Gold Mine project in 2008 and the Ajax Mine project in 2017 – were rejected by the EAO due in part to the severity of the impacts on Aboriginal rights. This indicates that the vast majority of projects receive an EA certificate. The EAO typically justifies its decision to approve a project for an EA certification by stating that varying societal interests have been reasonably balanced. Of the ninety-three assessments that were approved by the EAO, Indigenous groups were explicitly dissatisfied with the mitigation measures detailed by the proponents and accepted by the EAO sixty-seven times (72 percent). The Indigenous parties' dissatisfaction with the accommodation phase of the consultations persists across the projects and even appears to increase over time.

Some recurring issues include dissatisfaction with the mitigation plans themselves. For instance, Indigenous groups claimed a total of fifty times (54 percent) that mitigation measures lacked detail or completeness and asserted thirty times (32 percent) that accommodations were insufficient in scope given the potential negative impacts on rights. The plans were also critiqued thirty-eight times (41 percent) for insufficient commitment from the proponent to assure Indigenous groups that the plans would be implemented as outlined after certification or that they would produce the intended results. This critique was expressed when mitigation plans entailed monitoring for potential impacts without further explaining how negative impacts would then be addressed given the results of the monitoring programs. This very issue arose during the application review for the Pacific Northwest LNG (liquified natural gas) project that was finalized in 2014. The Kitsumkalum Indian Band stated that "the consequences (to the Proponent/Holder) should the ... required ... monitoring programs prove project (or cumulative) effects to be more significant than predicted in the EA Application" were unclear.[5] The Kitsumkalum Indian Band added that "simply requiring further compensation or offsetting is not the appropriate solution."[6] Furthermore, these various concerns about the mitigation plans often overlapped. For instance, the Musqueam Indian Band during the assessment of the 2017 George Massey Tunnel Replacement project stated that the EAO cannot "conclude that yet-to-be developed mitigation measures will be appropriate or successful," particularly without specific commitments.[7] Thus, without a clear, detailed mitigation plan and a firm commitment to implement it, the EAO cannot assure Indigenous groups that the plans will effectively address potential impacts on Aboriginal rights.

Other concerns over the mitigation plans were related to the formulation of the plans. As recorded in the EA reports, Indigenous groups asserted that alternatives to conduct the project were inadequately considered thirty times (32 percent). The Indigenous parties also insisted that the proponents include Indigenous participation in designing and implementing mitigation plans thirty-nine times (42 percent), such as integrating Indigenous land management plans and practices. In the case of the Line Creek Operations Phase II mining project assessed in 2013, the Ktunaxa Nation was concerned that the project would negatively impact the "exercise of

Ktunaxa stewardship authority and responsibilities in the Elk Valley."[8] However, the proponent only committed to "confirm land and water use planning objectives for the Elk Valley" and did not provide other assurances that existing Indigenous governance over the land and water would be respected.[9] The EAO responded that this issue was under negotiation through an impact benefit agreement because this type of accommodation measure was deemed to be outside the scope of the project-specific assessment.[10] This case exemplifies how mitigation plans within the EA process fail to meet Indigenous parties' governance practices and can be offloaded to forums that are not guided by the honour of the Crown, such as private negotiations with the proponent.

Although a majority of Indigenous groups explicitly opposed projects forty-one times out of 126 assessments (33 percent), the EAO agreed that a project should be declined only three times.[11] Since the EAO denied one of these projects for reasons that were unrelated to the potential impacts to Aboriginal rights, the EAO only sided with the Indigenous group's majority position to reject a project two times. Thus, Indigenous groups unequivocally opposed 33 percent of projects, while the EAO only opposed 2 percent of proposed projects. The EA process is intended to address outstanding issues before proposals are brought forward to the decision-making minister; therefore, projects are not typically advanced if there is a high likelihood that a certification cannot be granted.[12] It is concerning that, from the perspective of Indigenous participants, a sizable number of projects are exhibiting outstanding problems even though the EAO's perspective is that the issues have been resolved to its satisfaction.

The reports show a persistence of conflicting interpretations between the EAO and the Indigenous parties over the suitability of the accommodation measures, with Indigenous groups appearing to justify their position more recently in ways that depart from the duty to consult. Across the duty-to-consult case law, the courts have expressed that Indigenous peoples do not exercise a veto to demand a particular accommodation measure. However, in *Tsilhqot'in Nation v British Columbia* in 2014, the court opened the possibility that the Crown may be obligated to seek consent under certain conditions, such as when an Indigenous group has a strong title claim.[13] The earliest mention of an Indigenous nation demanding consent in the EA reports was in 2011, and, by 2017, the consequences of the

Tsilhqot'in decision and other legal developments such as the introduction of the *United Nations Declaration on the Rights of Indigenous Peoples* (*UNDRIP*) appear to have resonated: the demand for the Crown to obtain free, prior, and informed consent was brought up eleven times out of the forty-one instances (27 percent) where Indigenous parties opposed a proposed project.[14] Moreover, after 2016, Indigenous groups also began to explicitly refer to *UNDRIP* in their written submissions. Indeed, the reforms to British Columbia's EA process that have recently passed seek to incorporate more consensus-based decision-making processes,[15] although Indigenous consent is still not required to approve a project.

Based on the 126 assessments, output legitimacy is not being attained. The accommodation measures negotiated throughout the EA process – mainly, mitigation measures to avoid or offset potential negative impacts to Aboriginal rights – are often considered inadequate by the Indigenous participants. This inadequacy can be the result of incomplete mitigation plans, a lack of commitment to implement plans, or a lack of Indigenous input and perspectives in the formulation and future implementation of plans. Table 12 details the percentage of projects that exhibited problems across each indicator of output legitimacy.

Accommodations Shaped by Private Interests and Power

The concerns expressed by Indigenous parties about the Crown's mitigation plans do not show that the Indigenous participants are dissatisfied simply because they did not obtain their preferred accommodation measures. The findings show that the Indigenous groups perceived the mitigation plans to be lacking clarity, commitment, and/or justification.

Table 12: Percentages of projects with problems across each indicator of output legitimacy during the decision stage

Output legitimacy	
Detailed and complete mitigation plans are provided.	54%
Scope of mitigation plans proportionately addresses expected negative impacts on Aboriginal rights.	32%
Clear rationales are presented explaining why certain mitigation measures are preferred over other alternatives.	32%
Sufficient commitment expressed to implement the proposed mitigation plan.	41%

The Indigenous participants were also dissatisfied about how the EAO explains why it chose certain mitigation plans over others, despite the reservations expressed by the Indigenous groups. These findings suggest that the Crown's obligation to produce appropriate accommodation measures that address Indigenous interests and concerns in decision-making is not consistently upheld.

Mitigation plans detailed within the EA process are intended to address the project's potential negative impacts on Aboriginal rights. However, there is growing frustration among Indigenous peoples that certain accommodation measures are easily dismissed by the EAO as falling outside the EA's scope or are not necessary to consider for the Crown to discharge its constitutional duties. For instance, the co-management of lands by Indigenous peoples and the Crown's agencies, as well as the implementation of Indigenous land management plans, can extend Indigenous nations' control over their ancestral territories. However, the SCC's stipulation that Indigenous parties cannot assert a right to a preferred accommodation,[16] and the Crown's insistence that Indigenous nations must prove their rights before the Crown gives space to Indigenous jurisdictional authority, can prevent these arrangements from being considered as mitigation measures. An Indigenous lawyer expressed his opinion that meaningful consultation, which transforms unilateral Crown decision-making, must be premised on respecting Aboriginal rights: "True reconciliation requires that within the duty to consult ... the Crown ... sometimes has to actually recognize the rights before they're proven. There's still a huge reluctance to do so."[17]

Some interviewees stated that, in certain contexts, the Crown is learning to take the initiative to approach Indigenous peoples to collaborate in land management, either as a robust way to fulfill the duty or as a separate initiative.[18] For example, one Indigenous consultant observed that, over time, there are more instances when settler governments "are asking us how to do things better, whether it's regulation, development policy legislation, planning ... we're starting to see that they realize they can't just ignore us ... and that it's beneficial to them to have these conversations."[19] Although these initiatives are promising, they are not mandated by the constitutional obligations flowing from the duty-to-consult case law. Furthermore, the Crown may assume that, within these partnerships, its power and authority remain unfettered and paramount, despite a relationship of joint decision-making with an Indigenous nation.[20] Without constitutional obligations or statutory protection, partnerships run the risk of devolving back to the Crown's unilateral decision-making.

The duty-to-consult case law arguably also presents a low threshold for the Crown to fulfill its obligation to present accommodation measures, thus rendering Indigenous parties unable to make additional demands for the outputs of decision-making to reflect their interests. In addition to clarifying that Indigenous parties cannot claim a certain type of accommodation measure, the SCC has shown a disinclination to guide the Crown's policy choices. And, yet, even if the court displays an aversion to influencing policy outputs, its silence on providing any rules to evaluating the adequacy of accommodation measures is striking. The perceived absence of explanations to clarify why certain mitigation measures are chosen over others, as well as weak demonstrations of commitment to mitigation plans being implemented throughout the life of the project, are shortcomings in British Columbia's EA process. Legally mandating the Crown to provide a clearer rationale for its choices would not necessarily invite judicial interference into the Crown's decision-making powers.

Moreover, creating more judicial safeguards throughout the life of a project to ensure that mitigation measures are implemented would also help ensure that Aboriginal rights are protected even when Indigenous groups initially agree with the proposed project. Although the SCC has specified that strategic, higher-level decisions can trigger the duty to consult,[21] the question of whether unfulfilled actions would constitute a breach of the Crown's honour remains unknown. The duty to consult before project approval appears to constitute the bulk of the court's attention, but the issue of how to uphold the Crown's honour after the project is approved is also of concern to Indigenous peoples when they negotiate accommodation measures with the Crown. Including the commitment to implement accommodation measures as a factor of the Crown's honour can ensure that the relationship between Indigenous peoples and the Crown remains honourable over time. Thus, stipulating that the honour of the Crown must guide the negotiation *and* implementation of accommodation measures would also be more consistent with the court's vision of reconciliation as an ongoing process.

The unspecified role of proponents to implement accommodation measures further compounds concerns about upholding the honour of the Crown over time. Industry actors do not have any legal obligations to carry out consultations, yet they may be relied upon to provide accommodation measures. Indigenous parties are often approached by established proponents to sign impact benefit agreements, which stipulate in a private contract the benefits that Indigenous nations can gain for their support of a proposed project. Although these agreements may detail measures that are akin to accommodation measures that address the anticipated negative impacts to Aboriginal rights, such as changing aspects of the project's design, they can be negotiated before the full scope of the potential negative impacts are known. As such, Indigenous parties may be agreeing to a project and its accompanying accommodation measures that do not address the full range of negative impacts.

Moreover, the content of the agreements may not necessarily support the Indigenous communities' governing capacity but, rather, detail compensation for the project's negative effects. Due to the private nature of the contracts, the content of these agreements is rarely known by the Crown. Indeed, the fact that the Crown encourages proponents to reach agreements with Indigenous parties demonstrates that the Crown is open to delegating its responsibility to negotiate accommodation measures with Indigenous nations.[22] Certain desired accommodation measures can only be attained with the cooperation of the Crown, such as collaborative land management arrangements, but this option is not available if the Crown chooses to delegate accommodation negotiations to other proponents. If an agreement is signed, the EAO may treat its completion as an indicator that the Indigenous nation approves of the project, regardless of the accommodation measures that have been negotiated. However, it may be concerning to the EAO's actors that these agreements can end conversations about the potential impacts that are uncovered throughout the EA process, which may negatively impact the transparency and rigour of their own review.[23] Due to the judiciary's silence on how accommodation measures should be reached, the Crown's reliance on proponents remains unchecked.

Although proponents do not have a legal obligation to provide accommodation measures to address Aboriginal rights, having a direct relationship between the proponent and the Indigenous nation can be advantageous. For instance, these interactions can be perceived by the Indigenous side as exercising jurisdictional control and autonomy because they can negotiate directly with the industry actors with little interference from the Crown.[24] Moreover, proponents are often more willing to acknowledge Indigenous rights over territory because, unlike settler governments, they are not competing to assert jurisdictional control. Recall in the previous chapter concerning throughput legitimacy that negotiating with the Crown's actors may be challenging if those actors lack mandates beyond a specific project under review or authority to promise funds. This problem particularly arises when a project exhibits cumulative effects from the presence of existing projects or when compensation is discussed as a potential accommodation measure; questions surrounding these issues are often beyond the scope of the statutory decision-makers.[25] Furthermore, the Crown's absence is especially problematic in smaller-scale projects that are less politically important to governments,[26] making it sometimes more worthwhile for Indigenous parties to approach proponents for accommodation measures. These shortcomings in attaining the accountability dimension of throughput legitimacy thus negatively shape the outputs of consultation and unduly implicate proponents in the accommodation phase.

The Crown's tendency to delegate accommodation negotiations to proponents also arises due to the Crown's own structure. The Crown, particularly at the federal level, does not have a uniform policy or approach to the duty to consult. Apart from broad guidelines in each jurisdiction, the Crown has opted to take a case-by-case approach and address each accommodation request as it appears. This approach is meant to provide flexibility over how the Crown implements the duty in highly variable situations. A shortcoming to this case-by-case approach is that various departments and agencies within and across orders of government that may be involved in a single project do not have a uniform consultative process with Indigenous nations.[27] One Indigenous official observed that "part of the challenge with consultation is that it seems every ministry and even districts within that ministry operate quite differently. So, it is a challenge to ... learn how different staff basically manage consultation."[28] Similarly, a lawyer explained that, for their

Indigenous clients, it is challenging especially when the federal government is involved because "the federal government is highly siloed. … The difficulty is … that in any major project where there [are] multiple … federal agencies involved, the government doesn't speak with one voice. And, of course, the federal approach to that situation is to not speak."[29] Consequently, the Crown's relevant actors may not regularly meet with Indigenous nations to negotiate accommodation measures because a united position is often not easily reached.[30] A First Nations representative corroborated this experience by sharing that "anytime there's a duty to consult in which the federal government needs to be involved, it's an empty chair, an empty space."[31]

Indigenous parties must navigate and interact with a variety of actors throughout consultation to try to attain acceptable accommodation measures. Due to the lack of rules prescribed by the courts to evaluate the adequacy of accommodation, the quality of accommodations depends on the individuals involved in each project, particularly whether the proponent is open to negotiating accommodation measures. The EAO can do little to resolve disagreements over mitigation plans when the Crown's actors themselves may be divided, siloed, or absent, but it can urge Indigenous parties to deal directly with the proponent to secure agreements. Since accommodation measures are the primary means by which Aboriginal rights can be protected, leaving the outcome of accommodation negotiations to the proponent in each project leads to highly uneven outputs, threatening the perception that the Crown's decision-making is legitimate. Although the duty to consult has a substantive dimension that must be fulfilled by the Crown, the outputs of the EA process are highly influenced by the power of the private actors, making it more challenging for Indigenous groups to hold the Crown accountable to ensure that Aboriginal rights are respected.

The EA reports and interviews demonstrate that the EA process does not consistently uphold the key aspects of output legitimacy since decisions are not explained thoroughly and the Crown appears to be offloading its obligations to negotiate accommodation measures to proponents who are not always equipped to fully address the potential impacts on the exercise of Aboriginal rights. This issue persists partly because the SCC has not devised any clear framework to evaluate the Crown's accommodation measures. Without clear legal rules, it appears that any effort, regardless of the scope of the Aboriginal rights claims at stake, can be justified by the Crown as adequate and reasonable.

An Opaque and Unilateral Consultation Process

The duty-to-consult case law directly shapes how the Crown implements and practises the duty. Unfortunately for those hoping that the duty would transform the Crown's decision-making to reflect Indigenous forms of governance, the duty has mainly redirected the Crown's power to manage legal risk. This result occurs because the case law permits the Crown to simply layer consultative duties onto the Crown's existing decision-making processes. Without Indigenous nations co-creating a new decision-making process that imbues their understandings of legitimacy and a fair process, the state can claim legitimacy for its decisions by only following the judiciary's standards of meaningful consultation. The duty-to-consult case law's flexible rules regarding how the Crown should fulfill the procedural and substantive obligations within the duty also help facilitate the Crown's dominance in decision-making as state actors can control the extent to which Indigenous feedback and perspectives are incorporated. The state's goal to manage legal risk by meeting the court's incremental interpretation of the duty, which has maintained the primacy of the state to structure decision-making processes over time, helps explain why the state continues to produce decisions that appear illegitimate from the perspective of the Indigenous participants.

The SCC has emphasized that the duty to consult can facilitate reconciliation by legitimating the Crown's decisions through honourable conduct and the inclusion of Indigenous perspectives. Indigenous participants are now mandated to be included in specific consultative processes, but few other additional instruments, or adjustments to British Columbia's EA process, have been produced to facilitate a thorough engagement with Indigenous viewpoints. As such, the actors within the EAO are not empowered to act beyond their narrow and unchanged mandates to address the various concerns of Indigenous participants. Given this limitation, the EAO's actors simply ensure that their agency will not land the Crown in a legal dispute by focusing on meeting the court's rules on the meaningful duty to consult. This interest is corroborated by the interview data and other studies.[32] Crown representatives contend that the risk of litigation ensures that the Crown does its due diligence to uphold the law.[33] Some lawyers representing Indigenous clients agree with this perspective and affirm that governments have changed their behaviour to avoid and manage litigation risk. One lawyer explained the changing relationship between Indigenous nations and the Crown in the following way:

> It didn't start from a change of mindset from government, it didn't start from the honour of the Crown concept that the Court hopefully expressed; it started from the cold, cruel reality that if you didn't go through the motions of consulting your project wasn't going to proceed. And that, though, has had its own momentum. So over time, that evolving and strengthening government policy to consult for quite pragmatic reasons has increased the power of First Nations, and as that power has increased ... the relationship has necessarily changed. So that today ... we pay more lip service to First Nations. But I still think if governments and companies had their way, they'd ... like it all to go away.[34]

Another lawyer expressed a similar sentiment by explaining that, even if the case law permits the Crown to structure consultation processes without Indigenous input, there is still an incentive to obtain Indigenous approval for a project. They noted that, "if [proponents] want to de-risk or garner certainty about their projects they should be trying to get to 'yes'. ... Who comes to the table ... saying 'I have this switchblade under the table and – I'll use it if I want to, now please tell me what your perspective is.' That is not consent – it's like stupid negotiations 101."[35] Like the Crown, litigation risk can force proponents to listen to Indigenous demands even if the case law arguably sets a lower standard for acceptable Indigenous engagement.

The threat of litigation is a powerful source of motivation to change the state's and the proponent's behaviour, but it does not guarantee the creation of new relationships or patterns of governance with Indigenous peoples, as shown in the frequency of legitimacy issues across various projects. Litigation risk is best leveraged by Indigenous nations with the capacity to negotiate more equally alongside the proponent and the Crown and helps explain why litigation over consultation persists despite the

Crown's efforts to manage it. The most egregious forms of arbitrary decision-making may be avoided, but litigation risk alone produces highly uneven results in terms of upholding legitimate decision-making. The Crown closely follows the law to avoid litigation, while Indigenous parties build their own record for a possible legal challenge, which creates an adversarial environment that can make it challenging to negotiate accommodation agreements or engage in collaborative decision-making across projects.[36] A First Nations political representative affirmed the inconsistency with consultation by observing that "we're always dealing with different individuals on different processes all the time. So, there's really no consistency on who you're dealing with."[37]

The Crown focuses on managing legal risk as its main policy objective when implementing the duty to consult rather than legitimating its decisions from the perspective of the Indigenous participants. With this policy goal in mind, it is not surprising that the Crown has not supplemented consultation with additional policy guidance that transform how the EAO's actors engage with the range of concerns brought forward by Indigenous policy actors. The EA process was reformed once during the period under study – in 2002 – yet these reforms arguably have made it easier for projects to attain a certification because the discretionary power of the minister and executive director of the EAO were enhanced.[38] The EAO's actors may ensure that a wide range of interested Indigenous nations are included in the review, that their interests are recorded separately, and that they are provided with a distinct evaluation of the project's impacts on their rights, but there are no statutory changes to transform how the EAO evaluates the project's impacts.

To start, the EAO's members are typically not accustomed nor trained to understand Indigenous world views and knowledge about Aboriginal rights. Additional training or adding rules about requiring expertise in Aboriginal law in the EAO could help facilitate its responsibility to evaluate the scope of Aboriginal rights at stake. Instead, a lawyer representing Indigenous clients stated the following about the expertise of the EAO's actors:

> The main issue in most regulatory bodies is that the person who [is] in charge of assessing the impact and reviewing the information from the

> First Nations are not really trained in doing that. So, we're often confronted [with] people who are experts in engineering or other areas that are really like relevant to the technical aspects of the project ... but not so much in the ... First Nations and cultural aspects of the project.[39]

Without relevant knowledge or experience with Indigenous world views of their rights, the EAO's determination of an Indigenous group's strength of claim and impacts to those claimed rights may be misinformed and incomplete. The EAO's actors are expected to engage with Indigenous perspectives but have few instruments or processes to rely on to help fulfill this task.

Another key area that illustrates the limitations of the existing EA process to engage with Indigenous participants' perspectives is in the scoping of the assessment, which first begins in the application information requirements (AIR) phase. The EAO directs its assessment of impacts to the area where the project will be developed. In contrast, Indigenous peoples tend to consider the overall patterns of development in the region as well as the fact that the exercise of their rights have already been degraded or taken away due to the continuation of colonial policies.[40] Statutory changes targeting the scope of review in the EA process could help align impact assessments with Indigenous perspectives regarding the appropriate pace and nature of development on land. Instead, consultation is added without any significant changes to how the EAO conducts its assessment. One consultant explained how the cumulative effects assessment can be highly limited or scoped out of the EA process altogether:

> In most EA processes, the current state of the landscape, the current state of like, fish and wildlife that supports the meaningful exercise of rights is not considered, it's not considered whatsoever. So that whole thing about [how] a First Nation may actually not be able to, at present, go out and exercise a right because of the state of their landscape and industrial development, etc., that doesn't get ... scoped into the assessment of First Nations' interest at all.[41]

The case law has distinguished past infringements from cumulative effects,[42] but some confusion remains about how these issues should be dealt with in practice.[43] In *Rio Tinto Alcan Inc. v Carrier Sekani,* the SCC stated that, since the duty to consult is forward looking, it cannot be invoked to address past infringements to rights; other remedies like compensation are more suitable.[44] The BC Court of Appeal's 2011 decision in *West Moberly First Nations v British Columbia (Chief Inspector of Mines)* also displays division over the extent to which past developments should inform the scope of the Crown's consultation, although the majority asserted that past developments provide an important context to understanding current project impacts.[45] Similarly, six years later, in *Chippewas of the Thames First Nation v Enbridge Pipelines,* the SCC asserted that project impacts cannot be fully understood without considering the larger context, such as ongoing projects and the historical context.[46]

In the EAO's reports, it reiterates, consistent with the case law, that the EA process cannot compensate for past infringements. But, in the context of cumulative effects, the EAO can unilaterally decide the scope of these assessments and avoid being held accountable when Indigenous parties disagree with this scope. For example, during the 2014 assessment of the Seabridge Gold's KSM mine project, a consultant for the Gitanyow Hereditary Chiefs disagreed with the proponent's approach to assessing cumulative effects because past, present, and reasonably foreseeable future projects were inadequately included.[47] In response, the EAO acknowledged the different opinion from the Gitanyow Hereditary Chiefs but asserted that the proponent's narrower approach was suitable.[48] Compounding this problem of competing interpretations of data is the fact that Indigenous perspectives and studies are often presented late in the EA process, such as after the proponent has presented its completed project application.[49] As a result, the Indigenous-led studies are not thoroughly engaged with by other actors, preventing Indigenous participants from effectively dialoguing with the Crown and proponent to resolve competing positions.

A potentially more fruitful avenue to consider the cumulative effects of resource projects on Indigenous territory is regional planning.[50] Regional planning is a process to help determine the type and pace of industrial development in a larger region apart from project-specific areas. A drawback is that regional planning processes are beyond the scope of the EA process. Any issue that is considered best addressed in external processes has no clear accountability mechanisms to ensure that discussions take place with the relevant government entities before the EA process ends. In the case of the 2014 KSM mine project, the EAO stated that the broader issues are "more appropriately managed by the Province as opposed to an individual Proponent."[51] In response, the EAO helped organize an advisory group, of which the Gitanyow Hereditary Chiefs were a part.[52] However, the results of the advisory group's meetings fell outside the scope of an EA with no legal mechanisms to ensure that external negotiations were incorporated in the final decision. Although it is beyond the EAO's organizational capacity to negotiate broader land planning initiatives with Indigenous nations, it is a flaw on the Crown's part that there is weak coordination among the Crown's relevant departments and agencies to negotiate with Indigenous nations when Aboriginal rights are affected beyond a project-specific assessment. The Crown's policy actors could provide more opportunities to negotiate the scope of cumulative effects in each project since the court has given the state flexibility over how these issues can be resolved in regulatory review. However, these differences are not addressed consistently as the EAO can point to their mandates and assert that the concerns of Indigenous nations regarding cumulative effects from ongoing resource extraction fall outside of the scope of an EA.

Without an explicit statutory reform to adjust the various stages of the EA process, such as how assessments are scoped, the EAO will not change how it conducts assessments, particularly if those existing practices will not be subject to litigation. For example, when assessing whether accommodation measures that address potential impacts to Aboriginal rights are appropriate, an actor from the EAO asserted that a project will not proceed if there is the potential that the accommodation measure will be the subject of a legal challenge.[53] However, the EAO official also reiterated that the standard to evaluate accommodation measures is reasonableness, as outlined in the existing case law:

> Regulatory processes have to be reasonable. If they're not reasonable, then you get sued. Nobody wants that. So, there's a lot of pressure to be very, very reasonable. And really, if there are concerns, really consider those. And there's a lot of support that's provided by our, you know, our legal counsel and our technical experts ... to ensure that those regulatory decisions are reasonable. They're procedurally fair, they meet the principle

> of natural justice, and all of those things, because it is a regulatory process. It's fundamental to what we do.[54]

Although it is likely that British Columbia's EA actors genuinely seek to understand and address Indigenous concerns about the exercise of their rights, this assessment occurs within the confines of the existing regulatory review process. The reasonableness standard employed in regulatory review contexts may not adequately address the substantive nature of the Indigenous parties' concerns because substantial deference is given to statutory decision-maker's interpretation of a reasonable outcome, which may overlook the constitutional status of Aboriginal rights.

In the interview data, there are some limited accounts of Crown and Indigenous policy actors using consultation to negotiate new agreements that depart from the existing decision-making processes. But, even when collaborative governance occurs, one First Nation official warned that actors can default to law or existing statutes to undermine an agreement. For instance, they stated the following about the constraints of existing legislation:

> What we often face is that the default always comes back to, "well it's not legislated." Or "this is how it's legislated." So, I told you about our collaboration agreement and ... the communities came to an agreement on what the permit ... conditions should be. Those conditions were drafted up, they were given to the proponent, [and] the proponent basically was able to ask for an exception because that exists in the legislation. So, all that work done between the First Nation, BC and the OGC [BC oil and gas commission] and the EAO office was basically ignored because there's legislative requirements that allow them to get an exception.[55]

Unique agreements between Indigenous and Crown actors that arise from consultation negotiations are few and can be contested by existing statutory and legal rules. It is more likely that consultation is performed to avoid legal challenges. Unfortunately, litigation risk does not necessarily motivate actors to improve the most crucial legitimacy deficits as the actors mainly follow the court's standards of fair consultation and reasonable accommodation. Interactions between state and Indigenous actors thus remain transactional rather than transformative towards a new relationship. This flaw is also significant given the fact that the SCC itself conceived of the duty as an alternative to litigation since political negotiations were considered more productive to advancing reconciliation.[56]

Ironically, although the duty to consult mandates a meaningful process to legitimate the Crown's decision-making from the perspective of Indigenous peoples, the implementation of the duty has not resulted in Indigenous peoples feeling they are consistently in a fair process. The content and presence of the law itself may hinder transformative interactions between the policy actors, resulting in highly uneven consultative experiences across various cases involving Indigenous participants. The duty-to-consult case law permits the Crown to simply layer consultative obligations without disturbing the existing regulatory review processes, such as British Columbia's EA process. This layering has only redirected the Crown's policy goals to manage legal risk rather than transform its governance practices to align with Indigenous expectations of a legitimate process. Without additional legal or statutory changes, the EAO appears reluctant to alter how it conducts its assessments, including its scoping, how Aboriginal rights are identified and assessed, and how accommodation measures are evaluated, particularly since these practices can currently be defended under the court's interpretation of a fair duty to consult. The legitimacy deficits throughout British Columbia's EA process also enhance the perception among Indigenous parties and their representatives that the EAO, although it presents itself as an impartial body,[57] represents the Crown's interests in advancing certain projects.[58] If the EAO is perceived to be acting in the interests of the Crown, then the entire EA process may also risk being discredited as disadvantageous towards Indigenous participants with constitutional rights at stake.

7

UNDRIP and the Duty to Consult

Due to the perception among Indigenous peoples that the duty to consult is not being practised in a legitimate way or meaningfully advancing reconciliation, there is a movement to altogether reject the duty-to-consult framework. The principles of free, prior, and informed consent found in the *United Nations Declaration of Rights for Indigenous Peoples* (*UNDRIP*) are considered to be a more robust form of protection against the Crown's potential encroachment of Indigenous rights that can facilitate nation-to-nation decision-making between the state and Indigenous nations.[1] Importantly, these principles are informed by international law as a result of global Indigenous mobilization rather than Canadian constitutional law. *UNDRIP* was first presented in the United Nations in 2007, but it was not until 2016 that Canada formally signed it. The BC government passed legislation committing itself to align existing legislation to the principles of *UNDRIP* in 2019,[2] with the federal government also committing to align federal laws with *UNDRIP* in 2021.[3] The government of Canada released a 2023–28 Action Plan that was developed in cooperation with First Nations, Inuit, and Métis peoples, which outlines a broad, all-encompassing government roadmap for implementing the principles of *UNDRIP*.[4] The category of "shared priorities" reflects commitments that are of interest to all Indigenous peoples and are cross-cutting priorities.[5] It states that the *Impact Assessment Act,* which governs the federal Impact Assessment Agency, will "carr[y] out impact assessments in a manner that emphasizes the need to seek free, prior, and informed consent."[6] How the agency structures its process to seek the free, prior, and informed consent of

Indigenous participants when reviewing major projects is undergoing reform. The federal government remains in the early phases of reforming the federal Impact Assessment Agency.

In contrast, the BC government approved significant reforms to the province's environmental assessment (EA) process on December 16, 2019, only one month after the province passed the *Declaration on the Rights of Indigenous Peoples Act*, which established *UNDRIP* as the province's framework for reconciliation.[7] The "revitalization" process to draft changes to British Columbia's EA process began in March 2018. One of the main goals was to ensure that the new EA process enhanced its reconciliatory impact by ensuring the process supported the implementation of *UNDRIP*.[8] This goal demonstrates a clear intention by the BC government to adopt a new approach to dealings with Indigenous peoples in the area of regulatory review.

The EA Reform Process

The BC government began the EA reform process with a view to increase the process's legitimacy from the perspective of the relevant stakeholders and Indigenous nations. The engagement with these relevant groups was aimed at supporting both the development of a new EA legislative act and supporting policies and regulations. To develop the new act, the BC Environmental Assessment Office (EAO) sought feedback from various groups in direct engagement settings, four regional workshops, and two province-wide forums. Afterwards, the EAO directly engaged with Indigenous nations in the crafting of supporting policies and regulations. Forty-four direct engagement meetings occurred with over seventy-five Indigenous nations. Apart from these direct meetings, an Indigenous Implementation Committee was also created in June 2019. In terms of membership, the First Nations Leadership Council was invited to nominate three representatives, with the aim of obtaining individuals representing different regions in the province.

The committee's mandate was to provide technical advice on the development of supporting regulations and policies – particularly, to ensure that the new act would positively contribute to reconciliation efforts. This technical advice included providing feedback on best practices or instruments in the new EA process, such as capacity funding, including Indigenous feedback, seeking consensus at key decision points, and developing a new dispute resolution entity. British Columbia's previous EA process reflected the province's unilateral layering of consultative processes onto existing regimes. In contrast, the new reforms were the result of significant Indigenous participation, which possibly signals more co-creation over the terms of how the Crown can demonstrate legitimate conduct. These new measures or practices in the EA process will now be assessed to uncover whether they may improve the state's attainment of input, throughput, and output legitimacy based on the deficiencies of the process outlined in the previous chapters.

Input Legitimacy

The key characteristics of input legitimacy in the EA process relate to the timely identification of the relevant Indigenous nations; the capacity of Indigenous nations to effectively participate in the EA process; and the ability of Indigenous nations to agree to the terms of engagement within the EA process. Each of these characteristics of input legitimacy will be considered in light of the new reforms.

Timely Identification and Inclusion of Indigenous Nations

The new rules surrounding how Indigenous nations become participants in an EA process can reveal whether the timely identification of the relevant Indigenous nations will be improved. In the previous process, the EA reports reveal that the EAO typically includes Indigenous groups in the EA process in a timely fashion and is generally open to including additional groups interested in participating even as the assessment process is underway. This approach reflected the EAO's goal of managing legal risk by ensuring that no Indigenous group was completely excluded from the Crown's consultation.[9] However, there were some instances in the reports that showed that some Indigenous groups disputed the EAO's decision to include or exclude groups based on a strength-of-claim assessment. The main issue in these instances was that the Crown's strength-of-claim assessment was done unilaterally, and the onus was placed on Indigenous groups to show how their rights may be affected in order to request participation in the EA process.

Under the new *Environmental Assessment Act,* Indigenous nations have up to eighty days after the proponent's initial project description is publicly posted to give notice to the EAO about their request to participate in the EA process.[10] In this request, the Indigenous nation is meant to describe the group's interests at stake and how it could be affected by the proposed project.[11] The EAO can only deny an Indigenous group's request to participate if "the chief executive assessment officer has determined that there is no reasonable possibility the Indigenous nation or its rights recognized and affirmed by section 35 of the *Constitution Act, 1982,* will be adversely affected by the project."[12] These reasons must also be accompanied by a denial for participation.[13] It appears that the EAO is no longer relying on an initial strength-of-claim assessment to determine which Indigenous groups will participate in each assessment. Instead, inclusion appears to be based on the proponent's initial project description, which should detail the Indigenous nations whose traditional territories or section 35 rights under the *Constitution Act, 1982,* may be affected by the proposed project,[14] and the EAO's own determination of what constitutes a reasonable possibility for impacts.[15]

The standard by which the EAO determines a reasonable possibility for impacts is not detailed in the legislation or in the guiding policy documents. However, the guiding policy document on early engagement states that, if the chief executive assessment officer (CEAO) has concerns about the rationale in an Indigenous group's request for participation, the Indigenous group has an opportunity to respond to these concerns.[16] Additional time may also be allocated in these instances where clarification is needed.[17] If a consensus is not reached about the inclusion of an Indigenous nation, the EAO or Indigenous nation can trigger the involvement of dispute resolution facilitators.[18] The addition of an exchange between the EAO and the Indigenous groups concerning requests for participation and the ability to bring disagreements to a dispute resolution body shows a departure from previous practices. The strength-of-claim process is not explicitly used to determine inclusion, and the EAO's discretion to unilaterally decide Indigenous participation requests has been limited. In particular, the dispute resolution body and additional time allocation are measures to help ensure that Indigenous perspectives on their requests are seriously considered by the EAO. The procedures and outputs of the dispute resolution body will be discussed in more detail later in this chapter, but it is worth noting that the outputs of the dispute resolution process are not binding on the CEAO or the ministerial decision-maker.[19] Therefore, the CEAO still ultimately decides which Indigenous groups participate. Recall that under the previous *Environmental Assessment Act,* the EAO had more unilateral powers but consistently attained this aspect of input legitimacy.[20] It is likely that the EAO will continue its positive record for including relevant Indigenous groups given these additional measures to include Indigenous perspectives in this determination.

Capacity to Effectively Participate

Another key indicator of input legitimacy, but one that the Crown was not found to sufficiently uphold under the previous *Environmental Assessment Act,* is ensuring that Indigenous participants have the necessary capacity and resources to participate in consultative activities. The capacity funding provided to Indigenous participants was not standardized, and the proponent was relied upon to provide financial resources to support Indigenous groups. Under the new reforms, a capacity-funding tariff is currently being developed. This tariff would establish the "required amounts, funding sources, timing and distribution of capacity funding to support Indigenous consultation in EA Process."[21] This new measure would ensure that Indigenous participants are guaranteed supports to effectively participate, although it remains unknown whether the amount of capacity funding will be adequate from the perspective of Indigenous nations. In the new *Environmental Assessment Act,* the CEAO maintains the ability to establish a tariff of costs to be paid by the proponent to financially support participating Indigenous nations in the assessment process.[22] This indicates that the proponent may remain a key resource for Indigenous peoples to access necessary funds.

There are some encouraging signs that the EAO has a renewed understanding of the importance of developing Indigenous nations' capacity to effectively participate in assessments. A key principle of *UNDRIP* is ensuring that Indigenous participants can express their free, prior, and informed consent in key decision points throughout the assessment. The EAO has defined informed consent as requiring that "information provided should be sufficient, objective and accurate, and supported by adequate resources and capacity."[23] Therefore, in order to ensure that Indigenous peoples have sufficient information to make an informed decision, the EAO is committed to supporting this objective with resources and capacity. It is the hope that the goal of informed consent will ensure that the EAO sufficiently and consistently provides financial supports to Indigenous participants.

Shared Terms of Engagement

The third aspect of input legitimacy that the EAO could not sufficiently uphold is ensuring that Indigenous nations agree to the terms of an EA process to fulfill the duty to consult. Under the current case law, the Crown is not legally obliged to create additional processes to discharge the duty. Indigenous nations must participate in the EA process to exercise their right to be consulted if the Crown has communicated that an EA will be relied upon to fulfill the duty. And, yet, a recurring issue has been that Indigenous groups have contested the use of the EA process to identify and address negative impacts to Aboriginal rights, despite the case law. Interestingly, the reformed EA process may improve this aspect of input legitimacy despite the continued lack of legal obligations on the part of the Crown to seek Indigenous approval for using an EA process to fulfill the duty. Under the new process, a process planning phase must occur after the EAO has decided to review a project through an EA and before the proponent submits their application for review.

The purpose of this process planning phase is to formalize the information requirements of the proponent's application, including detailing how this information must be gathered, who must be involved in the EA, and the timing of subsequent phases.[24] At this point, it must be clarified how the EA process will assess impacts to section 35 rights. The assessment of impacts to Aboriginal rights can be led by the EAO, the participating Indigenous nation, or a combination of these actors. In other words, an Indigenous nation can lead the assessment of the impacts to their section 35 rights and will collaborate with the EAO about how to incorporate the results of the separate assessment into the broader EA process.[25] Although the results must be incorporated back into the EA, the Indigenous nation can conduct parts of the assessment using their own methods and processes. This choice gives Indigenous participants more autonomy to conduct parts of the assessment according to their own governance customs, practices, and methodologies. Including Indigenous-led assessments represents a key departure from the duty-to-consult case law requirements and may signal a significant change within the EAO's core rules and operations. Much depends on how the results of an Indigenous-led assessment is treated by the EAO in key decision points.

The process planning phase is aimed at determining the scope of the EA and how it will be carried out. Because it occurs before the assessment takes place, the new requirements and actions taken therein may positively improve the EAO's attainment of input legitimacy. However, the planning phase entails additional actions that may influence how the EAO will also attain throughput legitimacy. For these reasons, the planning phase will also be considered in the next section.

Throughput Legitimacy

Throughput legitimacy aims to evaluate the quality of interactions between the participants throughout the decision-making process.

Inclusiveness

Inclusiveness ensures that the relevant actors who are responsible for decision-making are present and available to negotiate and discuss key issues with one another. This includes ensuring that officials representing various bodies or departments have the powers and authorities to carry out decisions during important deliberations. Another important factor for inclusiveness that is more specific to Indigenous-Crown relations in decision-making is ensuring that Indigenous participants are treated and recognized as distinct constitutional rights holders. Due to this distinct status, Indigenous actors have a unique relationship with the Crown that should reflect intergovernmental interactions.

In the EA reports completed under the previous *Environmental Assessment Act,* the EAO typically ensured that the Indigenous actors were treated as constitutional rights holders. This issue is unlikely to worsen, particularly as the EAO has strongly signalled its commitment to enhancing Indigenous participation to maintain its commitments outlined in *UNDRIP*. However, the new process does not explicitly address the issue expressed by Indigenous participants that decision-makers have not always had the mandate to negotiate accommodation measures during consultations. In particular, Indigenous groups have been concerned that discussions with government representatives were only technical in nature, while concerns about Aboriginal rights and title remained unanswered. A possible reason why the reforms did not specifically address this issue may be because other reforms could help avoid this problem by indirect means, such as the EAO's stance on seeking consensus with Indigenous groups throughout the EA process. The EAO's guidance on seeking consensus will be covered in subsequent sections outlining how the new process may improve the Crown's attainment of accountability. However, it should be noted at this point that consensus-seeking behaviours can improve inclusiveness indirectly because the imperative to seek consensus before moving onto subsequent decision-making phases can prevent Indigenous concerns from being neglected by absent policy actors.

Transparency

Transparency entails actors behaving in ways that are clearly understood by others. Clear record-keeping of each participant's position and providing rationales for key decisions points in the EA process are measures to uphold transparency in decision-making. One of the EAO's greatest strengths in the previous EA process was keeping a clear and accurate record of all participants' positions in each decision phase. In contrast, the EAO often did not clearly communicate its decisions when assessing the significance of impacts to Aboriginal rights. This problem arose in part because the EAO and the Indigenous nations came to different conclusions about the thresholds that constitute severe or marginal impacts that could be effectively mitigated.

The process planning phase, which occurs before the application is reviewed, may help alleviate this issue of conflicting methodologies. In the process planning phase, the EAO and the participating Indigenous nations aim to seek consensus on the methods used to assess the impacts to section 35 rights. Assessment methods can be "culturally specific or custom methods provided by the participating Indigenous nation."[26] The goal is "to ensure all parties are aware of and understand how the assessment will be conducted, what the inputs of the assessment are and how conclusions are reached."[27] If this commitment is followed, then it is possible that the EAO will improve its communication of the potential impacts to Aboriginal rights since those methods are agreed upon before the assessment takes place. This reform is a highly promising one and may address a significant issue that was experienced by many Indigenous groups. The potential of this measure to substantially improve transparency depends on the EAO's ability to hold actors, including itself, to account if disagreements over the appropriate methodology arise in the process planning phase.

Accountability

Accountability is a key characteristic of throughput legitimacy because it ensures that the participants in decision-making are answerable to each other through clear justifications of their decisions. A key aspect of being able to hold other participants to account is having the knowledge about the roles and responsibilities of each party. With this knowledge, participants know to whom to communicate concerns or problems, which in turn leads to those problems being resolved efficiently and effectively. Another crucial way in which accountability is upheld is ensuring that all participants' feedback and perspectives are appropriately included in the decision-making. The inclusion and consideration of Indigenous knowledge and perspectives is a crucial way in which Indigenous actors can seek more clarity in the decision-making process about matters that are most important to them. In the reports, it was found that the EAO did not consistently incorporate Indigenous views by taking unilateral action in deciding when Indigenous perspectives would inform the assessment. Furthermore, there was often conflict between the EAO and the Indigenous participants' opinions on the acceptability and usefulness of information provided by the proponent about the proposed project.

The new *Environmental Assessment Act* includes additional guidelines about how to include Indigenous knowledge. These new guidelines show a radical departure from the previous practices, whereby Indigenous studies and knowledge were included seemingly arbitrarily or narrowly throughout the assessment. To begin, the EAO outlines that Indigenous knowledge is to be treated with respect, including the recognition that Indigenous knowledge systems are as equally valid as Western forms of knowledge.[28] The EAO also asserts that Indigenous knowledge should be applied throughout the EA process, including "how to conduct an EA process, how to evaluate impacts, and how decisions are made by Indigenous nations."[29] This statement demonstrates that Indigenous knowledge is intended to inform the entire EA process, including its scope, the assessment of impacts, and how the process itself is carried out. The importance of ensuring proper permissions for using Indigenous knowledge and how to best understand it are also detailed.[30]

A significant challenge when adopting various forms of knowledge into a process is how to evaluate competing information that may emerge from those different knowledge systems. The EAO's guidelines state that, in the event of a difference between Indigenous knowledge and Western knowledge, "the EAO will engage the Proponent and the Indigenous nation to better understand the difference and where possible, reconcile the different through a collaborative process."[31] It is not detailed what this collaborative process will entail or how different knowledges will be reconciled fairly by the EAO, a body that ostensibly has significantly more training in Western forms of knowledge. Furthermore, it is stated that the "differences between knowledge could be an opportunity for establishing adaptive management approaches."[32] Adaptive management is an iterative approach to management in contexts with high uncertainty. Plans are established to collect information and monitor the effects of a project; management over a resource or project is then adjusted in light of incoming information.[33] The cycle between planning, monitoring, and adjusting continues throughout the life of the project. Therefore, the EAO's statement about using adaptive management to reconcile Indigenous and Western knowledges may suggest a preference for addressing differences through monitoring programs and the subsequent follow-up or adjustments to management plans. However, the establishment of monitoring programs and adjustments to the project's management assumes that the project will be approved by the EAO. It is troubling that the EAO's statement about reconciling knowledges in the context of mitigation measures seems to ignore the possibility that uncertainties around a project's effects could mean that the project should not be approved for an EA certificate. Moreover, adaptive management processes may be less effective when different parties approach the task with different goals and priorities in mind.[34] Nevertheless, the EAO's new guidelines indicate a stronger, explicit commitment to include Indigenous perspectives throughout the assessment, but it remains to be seen whether this commitment is matched by a change in how the EAO evaluates various knowledge.

Apart from the incorporation of Indigenous knowledge, Indigenous peoples have also been concerned with the previous EA process because of the Crown's unilateral strength-of-claim assessment. It is notable that the new EA guiding documents do not mention the strength-of-claim assessment at all. Although this assessment was established by the courts to identify the appropriate scope and content of consultation, it appears that the EAO is departing from this legal standard. This is likely a positive development as a significant hurdle for Indigenous groups was providing evidence to the Crown that they were entitled to certain consultation and accommodation measures based on the strength of their rights or rights claims. It appears that the EAO's new approach is simply to assume that the Indigenous groups in the EA process have rights that may be affected by the project. The issue of competing rights between Indigenous groups is not outlined, but it can be assumed that the strength-of-claim determination will remain a factor in helping sort and prioritize certain groups' interests over others. There has yet to be any guiding documents about how the strength-of-claim assessment is integrated, if at all, into the new EA process.

Also relevant to issues of accountability is the narrow focus on the project-specific impacts of previous EA processes on claimed or recognized Aboriginal rights. The overall patterns of development in a region were often dismissed by the EAO as falling outside the scope of a specific EA. As a result, Indigenous participants could not effectively hold the EAO or the Crown's other actors to account over the scope of the EA. The new *Environmental Assessment Act* may be more responsive to this issue. Under section 35(1) of the act, the CEAO may undertake a regional assessment that is broader in scope than the project-specific assessment.[35] The CEAO must also seek to achieve consensus with the affected Indigenous nations on the direction and scope of the regional assessment.[36] Guiding policies about how these assessments are triggered and their scope are still being negotiated. The BC Supreme Court's 2021 decision in *Yahey v British Columbia* regarding the importance of evaluating cumulative effects, particularly from the perspective of Indigenous peoples, may also influence how the CEAO triggers and uses regional assessments.[37] It remains to be seen whether CEAOs will be willing to initiate a regional assessment in response to Indigenous concerns about the impacts of broader resource development and extraction in a region.

Apart from regional assessments, the EAO is also taking on a stronger coordinative role to ensure that issues raised in an EA that cannot be addressed within this process will be communicated to the relevant regulatory processes or agencies with appropriate follow-up. In the process planning phase, the EAO is required to create a regulatory coordination plan. The objective of the regulatory coordination plan is to identify the required permits for a project and "ensure that issues raised in the EA are broadly understood and managed by appropriate agencies."[38] Therefore, the plan will explain how issues raised in the EA process will be addressed either "through the EA, subsequent permitting or other regulatory processes or government initiatives."[39] This new requirement will help ensure that issues outside the scope of the EAO's competency will be addressed by other actors as the project moves through additional approval processes. This measure will help the Crown attain accountability because Indigenous feedback can no longer be dismissed only because it is not appropriate to address it within the EA process; Indigenous groups now have clearer recourse to have their issues revisited.

These new measures appear to be promising avenues to improve the Crown's performance in attaining accountability from the perspective of Indigenous participants. But perhaps the most significant change is the EAO's commitment to seek consensus with Indigenous nations throughout the EA process. This behavioural change appears to be one of the most direct ways in which the EA process is incorporating the principles of *UNDRIP* – particularly, the goal of acquiring Indigenous groups' free, prior, and informed consent. According to the EAO, consensus seeking helps meet the objectives of obtaining prior consent because consent must be sought before subsequent decisions are made or allowed to proceed.[40] On a broader level, the EAO's commitment to consensus seeking also acknowledges the "inherent jurisdiction and authority [of] Indigenous leaders ... over their communities concerning major projects."[41] Seeking consensus is consistent with the attainment of accountability because the practice ensures that actors must take responsibility and address disagreements before the final decision.

Consensus seeking throughout the EA process may entail meetings or collaborative working groups, tracking tables that document areas of consensus and non-consensus, and reviewing these points of contention at the end of each EA phase.[42] Apart from the opportunity to revisit points of contention after each EA phase, the working groups, meetings, and tracking tables resemble former practices that the EAO uses to facilitate interactions between Indigenous peoples, the Crown, and the proponent. Although all parties' positions are documented and reviewed after each phase of the EA process, a lack of consensus on certain issues in previous EA stages "should not deter the EAO and participating Indigenous nation from seeking consensus on other matters at later stages."[43] This statement indicates that the EA process will not be stopped if consensus is not reached. It is understandable that the process may become inefficient if disagreements with certain groups can stall an EA entirely. However, also letting the process continue when there are outstanding concerns may appear to Indigenous groups as permitting the EAO and the proponent to push a project through the EA. This outcome would clearly demonstrate a continued lack of accountability to hold actors responsible for addressing outstanding issues.

Whether or not points of contention will be meaningfully addressed throughout the EA process also depends on the quality of the proposed dispute resolution that is available in certain key stages of the EA process. Dispute resolution is aimed at supporting Indigenous groups and the EAO to reach a consensus.[44] The *Environmental Assessment Act* describes the role of the dispute resolution facilitator and how dispute resolution can be initiated within an EA. The minister may appoint individuals to act as facilitators to resolve disputes in the EA process after considering a recommendation from any Indigenous participant.[45] Either the CEAO or the participating Indigenous nation may refer matters to a dispute resolution facilitator.[46] This option is available during several phases of the renewed EA process, including in early engagement, the EA readiness decision, process planning, effects assessment, and when the EAO prepares a recommendation. The executive can regulate the powers and duties of a dispute resolution facilitator such as their qualifications, the issues that must be considered before they issue a report, and the time in which a report must be produced.[47] Most significantly, the report produced by the dispute resolution facilitator "is not taken as guiding (a) the chief executive assessment officer or minister respecting a project not addressed in the report, or (b) a decision maker under another enactment."[48] In other words, the dispute resolution facilitator cannot compel the EAO or minister to adopt any particular action. If dispute resolution is used but issues remain outstanding, "the EAO and Indigenous nation should document the issue and include reasons for why the issue remains unresolved."[49]

In preparation for finalizing the supporting regulations, the EAO solicited opinions from First Nations in the summer of 2023. The Lake Babine Nation, the Tsleil-Waututh Nation, and the First Nations Leadership Council expressed concern that the proposed dispute resolution process is contained within the architecture of the *Environmental Assessment Act*, which only requires the Crown to seek consensus rather than obtain consent from participating Indigenous nations. The submissions from these groups explain that a dispute resolution process that does not compel the decision-making minister to obtain the consent of Indigenous parties fails to respect *UNDRIP*'s principles and further entrenches decision-making power solely with the Crown.[50] These concerns show that the new EA process may already be dampening the possibility of transforming the Crown's decision-making.

If disagreements remain up to the point when the EAO must provide the minister with a recommendation, the EAO "should clearly articulate the outstanding issues, each party's views on the issue, and the steps taken to resolve the issues" in the referral package.[51] Although the reporting requirement is explicit, the process to outline points of disagreement between the parties does not appear to significantly depart from previous practices. Under the previous EA process, the EAO's recommendations would often include outstanding issues among Indigenous participants – particularly, those issues that conflict with the EAO's own conclusions. Moreover, the EAO has consistently used working group meetings and tracking tables to identify points of agreement and disagreement between participants. Since these procedural measures remain largely unchanged, whether consensus seeking improves the EAO's attainment of accountability will likely depend on whether the EAO's officials and the Crown's actors have adopted a new policy goal to obtain the free, prior, and informed consent of Indigenous participants or whether the new instruments serve to preserve the Crown's decision-making power. The dispute resolution body's inability to compel the EAO or decision-making minister may point to a maintenance of state control over decision-making.

Effectiveness

Effectiveness is understood as ensuring that Indigenous participation in the EA is meaningful. Indigenous participants should perceive that their input throughout the consultations influences the decision-making and is not simply a means to blow off steam. The previous EA process did not reflect a meaningful process because other key throughput legitimacy factors, such as transparency and accountability, were not consistently upheld. It remains premature to evaluate the effectiveness of the new EA process for this reason; a sense of meaningfulness is a subjective measure that is best appraised once the Indigenous participants have experienced the new process.

It can be tentatively suggested that attaining effectiveness under the new process will also depend on how the new process upholds transparency and accountability. The new EA process appears to have stronger measures in place to attain higher levels of transparency, such as establishing agreement on the methodologies used to assess impacts. Accountability may be improved as well depending on whether the EAO's consensus seeking genuinely departs from previous practices of simply recording points of agreement and disagreement. Based on the reforms alone, there is a good possibility that Indigenous peoples will view the new process more favourably. Given that Canada has committed to implement *UNDRIP*, the new process will be measured against whether Indigenous peoples' understandings of the key principles of *UNDRIP* are adequately practised. For instance, the new EA process is intended to obtain Indigenous people's free, prior, and informed consent, but there may be differences between the state's understanding of these principles and the understanding of Indigenous nations. Indeed, the concerns expressed by First Nations regarding the dispute resolution process thus far show that there are serious reservations about whether the reforms to British Columbia's EA process will align with *UNDRIP*. Moreover, this conflict over what *UNDRIP* entails may be exacerbated, as the federal court's 2025 decision in *Kebaowek v Canadian Nuclear Laboratories* illustrates that the court interprets the standard of free, prior, and informed consent as a right to a robust process of decision-making.[52] It will be more important than ever for the Crown to clearly demonstrate how Indigenous input is shaping the final decision now that commitments to *UNDRIP* have been formally adopted. Similar to the duty to consult, if Indigenous expectations of free, prior, and informed consent are not shared by the Crown, the renewed process is likely to continue exhibiting legitimacy deficits.

Output Legitimacy

Output legitimacy is obtained when the outputs of decision-making reflect the interests and demands of the governed. The law on the duty to consult does not give Indigenous peoples a veto to ensure that the Crown's decisions must reflect their interests. As a result, output legitimacy was evaluated under the previous *Environmental Assessment Act* by considering whether the accommodation measures negotiated were communicated transparently and whether the measures appropriately addressed the prospective impacts to Aboriginal rights. The previous EA process did not adequately uphold output legitimacy because mitigation measures were often not deemed by Indigenous parties as complete or appropriate given the prospective impacts. Under the new *Environmental Assessment Act,* Indigenous participants can give or withhold their consent in two decision points in the EA process. The first point is at the EA readiness decision. At this stage, the EAO, with input from the Indigenous parties, must make a recommendation about whether the project proposal should proceed through the formal EA process, proceed to the permitting process without an EA process, halt the process to obtain more engagement, or leave the EA process.[53] When the relevant minister makes a decision, they must balance protecting the environment, fostering a sound economy, and reconciliation.[54] The balancing of these objectives is not different than in previous practice. If the minister's decision is contrary to the position of an Indigenous group, the minister must hold a meeting with that Indigenous group and give reasons to explain why their decision was made.[55] The second point where Indigenous peoples can give or withhold consent is before the minister decides whether or not to issue an EA certificate, based on the EAO's recommendation. Similarly, a decision taken in opposition to an Indigenous group's stance must be accompanied with reasons.

Under the new EA process, Indigenous parties are given a formal opportunity to express their consent or lack of consent.[56] However, the minster's decision-making powers remain largely undisturbed. Under the previous EA process, the minister also balanced reconciliation with other objectives such as environmental sustainability and the province's economic interests. More significantly, the minister can proceed with their decision even if it is contrary to the position expressed by Indigenous peoples. Under the previous EA process, the minister often provided reasons as to why they acted against the interests of the Indigenous parties as well. The issue was that the reasons were too vague to show how the minister could conclude that negative impacts to Aboriginal rights would be sufficiently mitigated or addressed. Based on the supporting guidelines, it does not appear like the minister's report must be more thorough or comprehensive when a decision is contrary to the positions of the Indigenous participants. Therefore, the formal ability given to Indigenous nations to express or withhold consent may be meaningless if this expression does not meaningfully influence the minister's final decision.

It remains to be seen whether a minister acting against the position of Indigenous nations in this context will produce significant political backlash, given the province's commitment to *UNDRIP*. The political costs of such a decision may act as an informal constraint on the minister, even if the new *Environmental Assessment Act* gives them the power to override the Indigenous nations' positions. Similarly, it also remains to be seen whether a minister in opposition to the Indigenous parties will face more legal risks if judicial review is sought for such a decision. The Supreme Court of Canada (SCC) has yet to rule on the duty based on Canada's adoption of *UNDRIP*.[57] If *UNDRIP* supplants or influences the court's understanding of section 35 and the duty to consult, then the minister's behaviour in the decision phase may change from previous practices. At the time of writing, the federal court's 2025 *Kebaowek* ruling suggests that *UNDRIP* is not replacing the duty-to-consult framework, but it may encourage the incorporation of Indigenous perceptions of a fair process in existing decision-making processes.[58] As such, litigation risk may only produce more legitimate decision-making if future court decisions fundamentally reconceptualize the duty to consult to align with *UNDRIP*, such as clarifying how Indigenous perspectives regarding procedural rights can inform or transform Crown decision-making processes.

Overall, the new EA process may improve key elements of input and throughput legitimacy. Consistent capacity funding, the option of Indigenous-led assessments, agreement over the methodology to assess impacts, and consensus seeking are some examples of significant improvements from the previous EA process. Output legitimacy may remain insufficiently upheld because of the minister's continued ability to act against the positions of Indigenous peoples. The new *Environmental Assessment Act* may strengthen the EA process to try and attain the free, prior, and informed consent of the Indigenous participants, but if that consent is not respected, then the decision-making process will remain illegitimate from the perspective of Indigenous peoples. It remains to be seen whether the statutory changes reflect the adoption of new policy goals by the EAO and the Crown. These new instruments may show that the Crown intends to take seriously the positions of Indigenous participants throughout the EA process, but there is also evidence to suggest that these statutory changes serve to protect the Crown's power by giving Indigenous participants more formal opportunities to participate but maintaining discretion to disregard that participation in key decision points.

There remain many outstanding questions regarding the efficacy of British Columbia's EA reforms, and the input, throughput, and output legitimacy framework can continue to be a useful framework to measure the state's implementation of *UNDRIP*. The framework can be adjusted to adopt Indigenous peoples' expectations for legitimate state governance given the new standards set out by *UNDRIP*, as demonstrated by this chapter's assessment of British Columbia's new *Environmental Assessment Act*. Although some key supporting regulatory measures remain unknown, the new *Environmental Assessment Act* appears to address some significant legitimacy deficits, perhaps because Indigenous actors were directly involved in the crafting of the reforms. Nevertheless, some crucial legitimacy gaps remain – mainly, in the attainment of throughput and output legitimacies. Consensus-seeking measures must influence the EAO's and Crown actors' behaviours rather than merely redirecting them to simply record points of agreement and disagreement. Especially concerning are the minister's powers to override Indigenous participants' consent or lack of consent, which is contrary to *UNDRIP*'s principles.

Based on the experience with the implementation of the duty to consult under British Columbia's previous EA regime, litigation risk does not consistently ensure the Crown's legitimate decision-making, and much depends on the Indigenous participants' ability to use that legal leverage to extract favourable accommodation measures from the state. However, in the context of the new reforms, there is a lack of judicial guidance on how the principles of *UNDRIP* must be upheld by the state's actors and processes. Although the state may be less focused on managing litigation risk and may adopt a new policy goal that exceeds the arguably low threshold of the duty to consult, there is a possibility that the Crown can default back to the formal legal standards in the duty when disagreements arise. It is the hope that the political commitments to *UNDRIP* signify a change in the state's policy goals so that the new policy instruments will serve to respect Indigenous consent rather than preserving the Crown's decision-making power. The input, throughput, and output legitimacy framework can help assess whether the proposed statutory changes are layered onto British Columbia's EA process in a manner that facilitates long-term transformative changes that alter the core rules and institutions or simply preserves the settler-colonial status quo.

Conclusion

This book has shown how constitutional rights are implemented in the policy process by examining the duty to consult's implementation by the Crown through British Columbia's environmental assessment (EA) process. The duty to consult is intended to legitimize the Crown's decision-making when Aboriginal rights are at stake by facilitating honourable and good faith negotiations. The framework of input, throughput, and output legitimacy is employed to evaluate the Crown's conduct during its various decision-making phases when major projects are reviewed by the BC Environmental Assessment Office (EAO). By detailing how the Crown performs in consultation, it becomes clear why the Crown is perceived by Indigenous parties as failing to attain key aspects of legitimacy. Due to the Supreme Court of Canada's (SCC) interpretation of the duty to consult, consultation with Indigenous peoples has been layered onto existing state institutions and processes, such as British Columbia's EA process. However, this layering is not sufficient to weave together Indigenous perspectives of legitimate conduct at the agency level. Without statutory changes to alter how the EAO conducts assessments, the EAO's main policy goal with consultation is to meet the expectations set out in the case law and manage litigation risk; it does not facilitate broader negotiations about how Indigenous and state governance should interface. In addition, the judiciary's evolving standards of legitimate conduct in the Crown's consultations further preserve the core of state decision-making authority, turning the duty into a mainly procedural process that suffers from key legitimacy deficits.

To substantiate this explanation, the research has analyzed legal decisions from the SCC and the BC Court of Appeal (BCCA) to demonstrate how the legal parameters and characteristics of the duty to consult shape its implementation and affect the results of consultation. In total, 126 EA decisions from British Columbia's EA process from 2004 to 2019 were analyzed, alongside twenty-eight semi-structured elite interviews, to show how policy actors implement the duty based on the standards outlined in the case law. Scholarship on the duty to consult usually focuses the analysis exclusively on either judicial decision-making or the implementation phase. In contrast, this book has investigated the degree to which judicial decisions can make an impact on policy actors and their decision-making. In doing so, the research has identified the nature and scope of judicial influence on public policy processes, explaining how policy actors respond to legal obligations and the effects of their choices when they implement constitutional obligations.

This book has examined British Columbia's EA process to understand how the duty to consult has been implemented. Major projects that are likely to impact claimed and recognized Aboriginal rights must undergo regulatory review, such as an EA. Most First Nations in British Columbia have not signed historic or modern treaties with the Crown, with the result that their rights and title claims are not yet recognized by the state. The duty to consult was first established to consider contexts where rights and title claims are not yet recognized, so it was important to choose a jurisdiction where this situation frequently arises in addition to including nations with historic and modern treaty relations. Although few, some Métis nations have also participated in British Columbia's EA processes, leaving Inuit experiences excluded from this study. Moreover, British Columbia's EA process is considered by practitioners to provide one of the most robust considerations of Indigenous interests, so it is expected that any challenges with implementation in this context will manifest in other jurisdictions.[1]

In terms of the projects themselves, British Columbia's EA process not only addresses various infrastructure and extractive industries, but there is also variation on its political saliency, with many projects attracting Indigenous resistance and overt political contestation.[2] The shortcomings and strengths of British Columbia's EA experience can thus be valuable to other jurisdictions because there is a wide range of consultation outcomes to explore. As of 2024, British Columbia is the only province that has adopted the *United Nations Declaration on the Rights of Indigenous Peoples* (*UNDRIP*), which further enforces it as an important case to examine the promise and perils of reforms to the EA process: using the input, throughput, and output legitimacy framework, it can be tentatively suggested which statutory changes can help meet the principles of *UNDRIP* and which types of policy change might fall short of transforming the Crown's decision-making powers.[3]

The Limitations of Court-Mandated Policy Change

This book has demonstrated the limits of solely relying on courts to facilitate more legitimate processes of decision-making and relationship building between Indigenous peoples and the state. The SCC's and BCCA's duty-to-consult jurisprudence incrementally outlines some of the ways in which the Crown can fulfill its legal obligations and the goals that should be achieved when fulfilling the duty to consult. Mainly, the Crown is expected to act honourably towards Indigenous peoples as the duty itself emerges from the obligation of honourable conduct.[4] Other aspects of honourable conduct include negotiating in good faith, which requires "[effort] to understand each other's concerns and move to address them."[5] There is a clear signal from the courts that honourable conduct can demonstrate the Crown's legitimacy to Indigenous peoples with section 35 rights under the *Constitution Act, 1982*.[6] In contrast, the court does not provide guidance over how policy actors should structure consultation or benchmarks to evaluate the adequacy of the accommodation measures that mitigate negative impacts to the exercise of section 35 rights.

The threat of litigation from failing to meet the duty to consult is managed by state actors and is insufficient to provoke changes in governance that reflect Indigenous perspectives. Litigation risk will ensure that the Crown takes seriously its responsibility to fulfill the duty but only insofar as its actions can be defended before the courts. As such, the Crown is mainly interested in achieving the state's own standard of legitimacy rather than correcting its legitimacy deficit that arises from its unilateral assertions of sovereignty. Additionally, the flexibility afforded to the Crown in subsequent duty-to-consult case law has permitted the state to largely preserve how regulatory review, like the EA process, scopes assessments, assesses impacts to rights, and evaluates the adequacy of accommodation measures. In contrast, Indigenous parties emphasize the normative goals of the duty as presented by the SCC, which is to understand consultation as a tool to advance reconciliation by adjusting the Crown's decision-making and taking seriously the legitimacy of Indigenous perspectives.[7] Since Indigenous and Crown actors focus on different aspects of the duty-to-consult case law, the Crown's aim of meeting the legal requirements outlined by the judiciary may not be perceived by the Indigenous parties as acting honourably or with good faith to transform colonial decision-making. In other words, Indigenous parties may still perceive their rights as being inadequately incorporated and see the EA process as lacking legitimacy even when the Crown meets the minimum legal obligations outlined by the courts. This outcome is antithetical to the promise of the duty to garner legitimacy for the Crown's decision-making that may affect section 35 rights.

The Crown's implementation of the duty to consult shows that the courts alone may not drive transformative institutional change. The judiciary themselves face strong institutional constraints as they generally avoid being perceived as dictating policy goals. It is understandable that the court is reluctant to impose its own ideas of a fair process onto governments. Nevertheless, the court could have urged governments to collaborate with Indigenous peoples to co-create honourable decision-making processes while affirming the importance of upholding the exercise of section 35 rights in both the consultation and negotiation of accommodation measures.[8] The degree of discretion that the judiciary – particularly, the SCC – affords to the Crown's decision-makers to structure its consultation and accommodation processes does not ensure that Indigenous perspectives will consistently inform and shape the Crown's decisions. Those using the courts as a venue for institutional change must consider that the courts may not produce decisions that sufficiently alter the government's policy goals. Similar to the context of rights under the *Canadian Charter of Rights and Freedoms*, governments can pass their preferred legislative agenda and manage litigation risk, even with increased judicial scrutiny.[9]

The government's management of legal risk in this instance is facilitated by the development of the duty-to-consult case law itself, which provides governments with unilateral powers to design and implement consultation and accommodation processes. As one lawyer representing Indigenous clients explained, subsequent decisions on the parameters of the duty can be advantageous to governments seeking to manage legal risk:

> What happens is you have a wonderful decision at the beginning which has broad brush strokes that the court articulates and – helps them resolve the fact patterns that they have before them in that case. And then what you naturally have by the development of the common law is ... the courts starting to curtail [the law]. ... I think it's just a natural way of how the common law develops and sometimes having uncertainty or lack of answers on some of these things, it's helpful because then our clients just say, "well of course [the law] means this," and we don't have a case that says ... "no it doesn't mean that."[10]

Although the judiciary can change the government's incentives through litigation risk, some legal uncertainty can also help policy actors encourage collaborative negotiations that could produce more substantial institutional change. Under the current duty-to-consult case law, the state can more easily manage litigation risk, defend its record of consultation, and protect its decision-making powers. As *UNDRIP* is being adopted in British Columbia and at the federal level, the court's limitations may once again shape *UNDRIP*'s implementation to frustrate institutional change if the judiciary maintains the primacy of section 35's consultative framework. However, given the statutory commitment made by British Columbia and the federal government to align laws with *UNDRIP*, the courts may be moved to respect these policy goals and ultimately help hold these governments accountable for those statutory commitments. Thus, securing political commitment to *UNDRIP* may lead to more transformative changes to the policy process than only favourable court decisions.

Institutional Layering as a Source of Change and Stability

This book has found that the implementation of the duty to consult demonstrates how institutional layering can be a method to preserve institutions rather than change them. The literature on settler-colonial systems is attuned to the many ways in which settler-colonial institutions and logics can be reproduced to continue dispossessing and eliminating Indigenous ways of life. I have found that institutional layering can be a method to sustain state control over decision-making authority. The concept of institutional layering helps explain how institutions can change incrementally over time by adding new rules or institutions that exist alongside the previous sets of rules or institutions.[11] This type of change is more likely to occur when the political system has strong veto points and when political actors exercise only a low level of discretion in interpreting or enforcing rules.[12] Within such a context, actors seeking institutional change are unlikely to completely dismantle the existing rules and must work alongside them to try and bring about change.[13] Since this concept was introduced, other scholars have used it to explain the policy effects of adding new actors and instruments in existing institutions.[14]

Indigenous actors in Canada seeking institutional change face similar challenges as the state exhibits strong veto points across key institutions, and negotiations for self-government or the exercise of Aboriginal rights must closely meet the legal requirements and tests that are outlined in past section 35 cases. And, yet, the Haida Nation's legal victory at the SCC in 2004, where the Crown's duty to consult was confirmed, showed how a key veto point – the courts – could be a site for radical change.[15] Unfortunately, this 2004 case, and subsequent duty-to-consult decisions, did not completely overhaul the Crown's existing decision-making. Interestingly, it was a state institution – the courts – that maintained the old rules, such as the structure of the Crown's decision-making, and then these constitutional duties to consult Indigenous peoples were added onto this existing structure. The fact that institutional layering was driven by the courts rather than by the constrained Indigenous policy actors is an interesting departure from the literature's expectations. Although layering is identified as having the potential to produce profound changes over time in highly constrained contexts, the duty to consult may show that layering can also contain institutional changes that may threaten the existing rules.

This insight is consistent with an interpretation of layering as a tool used by the state to design the institutional arrangement of a specific policy field given strong contextual constraints.[16] According to this view, the purpose and effects of institutional layering can be variable, as policy-makers can use layering to maintain institutional stability such as by adding actors and instruments to help legitimate a specific institutional arrangement.[17] Institutional stability appears to be the main goal in the duty to consult's implementation as guided by the judiciary. Institutional layering may have produced more transformative change if the new rules were co-created between Indigenous and state policy actors. Under these circumstances, the way in which consultation is practised by the Crown could have been informed by Indigenous views of legitimate conduct. Instead, the courts permitted the Crown to largely maintain existing decision-making processes and granted itself the position as the sole interpreter of a fair and meaningful consultative process. Thus, not only can the Crown maintain its decision-making structure, but also the addition of new consultative processes and their effects need only conform to the court's standards of legitimate conduct rather than to the perspectives of the Indigenous participants.

When the duty to consult was obligated by the courts, the state did not change the statutory mandates of the agency actors tasked with conducting the duty. In particular, no specific statutory direction was given to the EAO that empowers them to thoroughly engage with Indigenous perspectives and world views. As a result, the EAO's officials did not carry out actions that fell outside of their existing practices, even if it may improve the legitimacy of the process for Indigenous participants and make consultation more meaningful. Without more direct statutory guidance, the EAO's officials perceive that they do not have the appropriate capacity to address the full range of demands from Indigenous participants.[18] Moreover, acting beyond the statutory mandates may disadvantage the Crown's other policy actors in future negotiations involving Indigenous groups by creating unfavourable precedents or expectations. This issue is further compounded by the duty-to-consult case law, which does not include any benchmark to assess the quality of the Crown's accommodation measures when negative impacts to Aboriginal rights are suspected. This judicial avoidance to devise any framework to evaluate accommodation measures permits the EAO to focus on fulfilling the procedural aspects of consultation and more easily meet the lower threshold for the substantive dimension of the duty to consult.

My findings have shown several instances where the frustrations of the Indigenous participants with British Columbia's EA process have derived from the simple layering of additional actors and instruments onto the existing processes. For example, the EAO sometimes delegates certain consultation and accommodation negotiations to actors and forums outside of the EA process if those concerns are deemed beyond the scope of project-specific impacts. However, this delegation occurs without any corresponding accountability measures to ensure that these negotiations are resolved before the projects are granted environmental certificates. Consultation and accommodation processes in project-specific contexts could be used to identify broader shortcomings in the Crown's governance over land and water resources that have an impact on Aboriginal rights. Even if the EA process is inappropriate to manage these conflicts, the EAO could still help facilitate and coordinate actors to negotiate on those matters before moving project applications forward. However, neither the duty-to-consult case law nor the statutory mandates of the EAO necessitate a change or rethink of the EA process, such as its impact on broader governance over land and water.

Moreover, when the EAO communicates its decision-making, there is a consistent perception among Indigenous participants that the rationale provided does not clearly explain how the consideration of Aboriginal rights has influenced the final decision or how the EAO can conclude that the impacts are not significant given the range of concerns expressed by the affected Indigenous groups. In contrast, the EAO is more effective at conducting procedural tasks, such as inviting the relevant Indigenous parties in a timely manner and documenting the concerns of various parties throughout the application review process. The EAO may claim that these actions constitute "deep" consultation, or show a commitment to act beyond the minimal legal requirements, because they are performed regardless of an Indigenous group's strength-of-rights claims.[19] However, the problems expressed by Indigenous participants across various EAs show that including more Indigenous peoples in the application review phase alone does not improve or change the quality of the interactions within the review process or the EAO's decision-making. Layering policy actors and additional instruments like consultation can introduce incremental institutional change,[20] but the duty-to-consult experience shows that layering can also serve to protect the institutional status quo. Based on the numerous legitimacy deficits throughout British Columbia's EA process, the duty's primary goal to demonstrate good faith reconciliation efforts appears inconsistent with the powers and interests laden in the old institutions and the new, layered institutional arrangement.[21]

The perceived lack of legitimacy of British Columbia's EA process has precipitated the newest sets of reforms to align the process with *UNDRIP* – particularly, the principles of free, prior, and informed consent. It is an important question for future research and practitioners to consider whether the BC government's public commitment to *UNDRIP* and the new reforms will produce a sufficient institutional shift to direct the EAO's actors to seek more legitimacy from the perspective of Indigenous participants. The input, throughput, and output legitimacy framework can be adopted to assess the efficacy of the new reforms to British Columbia's EA process and other reforms that may be proposed in other jurisdictions. The BC reforms aim to align regulatory review with the principles of *UNDRIP* – particularly, the requirement to attain the free, prior, and informed consent of relevant Indigenous groups. The legitimacy framework can assess whether these reforms meet Indigenous peoples' expectations about how free, prior, and informed consent can be upheld in the various decision-making stages.

For instance, the participatory characteristics of input legitimacy can account for the conditions under which Indigenous groups can participate free of material and external constraints. Throughput legitimacy captures the interaction dynamics between participants and can evaluate whether the input of Indigenous parties is being sought prior to key decision points and whether they are able to make informed decisions throughout the process. And, finally, output legitimacy depicts whether the outputs of decision-making reflect the preferences of the governed. How Indigenous parties' consent is attained and treated in key decision points will show the degree to which Indigenous consent is changing the Crown's actions. These reforms have significantly altered certain aspects of the EA process, such as recognizing Indigenous-led processes of impact assessments, while maintaining other aspects that are of concern to Indigenous parties. These concerns mainly centre on the continued discretionary power of the decision-making minister to grant certification or exemption from the EA process altogether.[22] Projects undergoing the new review process are still underway; since reviewing applications can take several years, it will be some time before there are enough cases to evaluate British Columbia's EA's new process.

This book described many promising changes that could prompt the EAO to take on a proactive role in consultation – particularly, the option to include Indigenous-led assessments and a commitment to attain consensus throughout the decision-making process. And, yet, some key issues remain. The decision-making minister continues to retain the sole authority to determine whether a project proceeds and attains an EA certificate, even if Indigenous parties withhold their consent. Without a clear position by the government regarding whether *UNDRIP* supersedes the duty to consult, the EAO's officials and the government may continue to fall back on the legal requirements of the duty in section 35 as a backstop to inform these new practices, even though *UNDRIP* posits a more robust standard of engagement with Indigenous peoples. This result, although likely disappointing for Indigenous peoples, may occur because the Canadian government has been careful to communicate that *UNDRIP* does not immediately change the Crown's duty to consult.[23] Indeed, the Canadian government expressed that *UNDRIP* is a set of normative ideals that exceed the legal requirements of honourable conduct, which is guaranteed under section 35.[24] *UNDRIP*'s potential may be hindered if the state can continue to layer *UNDRIP*'s principles onto state-centric understandings of legitimate decision-making, as was done with the duty to consult. Institutional layering may jeopardize reconciliation if Indigenous perceptions of legitimate conduct continue to be excluded.

The federal court's 2025 ruling in *Kebaowek* presents a mixed picture with regard to whether *UNDRIP* can fundamentally alter Crown decision-making.[25] The standard of free, prior, and informed consent (FPIC) was interpreted as a right to a robust process, which arguably does not reflect Indigenous perceptions of FPIC. However, the decision also asserts that Indigenous perspectives of a robust process must be considered. This statement may suggest a firmer assertion that Indigenous understandings of legitimate conduct and good governance should inform and change Crown decision-making processes. Based on how the state reacted to the duty-to-consult jurisprudence, it will likely take more forceful legal rules, or steadfast political leadership, to significantly shift how the Crown evaluates the desirability of major projects.

The state may try to minimize and control the extent to which its governance practices must change in light of *UNDRIP*. But, just like Indigenous groups' eventual rejection of the duty to consult, Indigenous groups will also persist in resisting state dominance and asserting jurisdictional control over their territory if the state continues to contain Indigenous demands for decision-making reforms. It is the hope that state actors learn that their legitimacy to govern will never be accepted by Indigenous peoples unless Indigenous perspectives on legitimate governance are respected. If actors such as the EAO want to maintain their legitimacy from the perspective of Indigenous participants, it may be a sounder long-term strategy to begin respecting Indigenous governance rather than continue with the status quo, which may be altogether discarded for failing to meet the expectations of reconciliation. To that end, employing the input, throughput, and output legitimacy framework can help assess whether statutory reforms are on the path to adopting Indigenous standards of honourable and legitimate conduct in the Crown's decision-making.

Based on these developments, it appears that the duty to consult and past approaches to Indigenous consultation will continue to play a role in guiding how the Crown structures decision-making processes to account for Aboriginal rights as they are recognized under section 35. The Crown may treat its legal obligations in a restrictive manner, but the content of the duty is sufficiently flexible to promote a different approach, one that could be consistent with *UNDRIP*. The Crown should alter how new legal obligations and political commitments to Indigenous peoples are implemented; rather than simply manage legal risk, state legitimacy is better protected by making space for Indigenous governance in the decision-making structures themselves. Understanding the honour of the Crown and good faith negotiations as a question of legitimacy can reveal the kinds of institutional changes required to meaningfully advance a new relationship. Attaining more aspects of legitimacy on a consistent basis would uphold the honour of the Crown from the perspective of Indigenous peoples and demonstrate that reconciliation is being advanced with good faith. By governing with legitimacy, an honourable political society can steadfastly reject and dismantle settler-colonial governance.

Notes

Introduction

1 See Stuart Scheingold, *The Politics of Rights: Lawyers, Public Policy, and Political Change* (Ann Arbor: University of Michigan Press, 1974); Gerald Rosenberg, *The Hallow Hope: Can Courts Bring About Social Change?* (Chicago: University of Chicago Press, 1991); Joel Bakan, "Constitutional Interpretation and Social Change: You Can't Always Get What You Want (Nor What You Need)," *Canadian Bar Review* 70, 2 (1991): 307–29; Charles Epp, *The Rights Revolution: Lawyers, Activists, and Supreme Courts in Comparative Perspective* (Chicago: University of Chicago Press, 1998); and Matthew E.K. Hall, *The Nature of Supreme Court Power* (New York: Cambridge University Press, 2011).

2 *Canadian Charter of Rights and Freedoms,* Part 1 of the *Constitution Act, 1982,* being Schedule B to the *Canada Act 1982* (UK), 1982, c. 11.

3 See, for example, James Kelly, *Governing with the Charter: Legislative and Judicial Activism* (Vancouver: UBC Press, 2005); Janet Hiebert, *Charter Conflicts: What Is Parliament's Role?* (Montreal and Kingston: McGill-Queen's University Press, 2002); and Matthew Hennigar, "Why Does the Federal Government Appeal to the Supreme Court of Canada in Charter of Rights Cases? A Strategic Explanation," *Law and Society Review* 41, 1 (2007): 225–50.

4 I will use the term "Aboriginal" when referencing the legal category of "Aboriginal peoples" as defined in the *Constitution Act, 1982,* being Schedule B to the *Canada Act 1982* (UK), 1982, c. 11, under section 35, which includes First Nations, Métis, and Inuit peoples. Otherwise, the term "Indigenous" is used when referencing the original inhabitants of the land that is now called Canada.

5 Christa Scholtz, *Negotiating Claims: The Emergence of Indigenous Land Claim Negotiation Policies in Australia, Canada, New Zealand, and the United States* (Oxford: Routledge, 2006); Christopher Alcantara, *Negotiating the Deal:*

Comprehensive Land Claims Agreements in Canada (Toronto: University of Toronto Press, 2013).

6 The concept of a duty to consult was addressed by the Supreme Court of Canada, prior to the 2004 *Haida Nation* case, as part of the *Sparrow* test that the Crown must follow to justifiably infringe section 35 rights outlined in *R v Sparrow,* [1990] 1 SCR 1075 [*Sparrow*]. Apart from proving a valid legislative objective (*Sparrow,* 1113), the Crown's infringement must be consistent with the honour of the Crown (*Sparrow,* 1114). As part of this honourable dealing and depending on the circumstances of the situation, the court stated that an Aboriginal group whose rights may be infringed should be consulted with respect to the Crown's intended action (*Sparrow,* 1119). The 2004 *Haida Nation* case is unique because it affirms a duty to consult beyond the *Sparrow* test and applies it proactively to situations where an Aboriginal group asserts a right, regardless of whether it has been recognized by the state. *Haida Nation v British Columbia (Ministry of Forests),* 2004 SCC 73.

7 "The Crown" refers to the federal and provincial orders of government in Canada.

8 *Haida Nation.*

9 See Kiera Ladner, "Treaty Federalism: An Indigenous Vision of Canadian Federalisms," in *New Trends in Canadian Federalism,* 2nd ed., ed. Francois Rocher and Miriam Smith, (Peterborough, ON: Broadview Press, 2003), 167–94; and James Youngblood Henderson, "Empowering Treaty Federalism," *Saskatchewan Law Review* 58, 2 (1994): 241–330.

10 See Courtney Fidler, "Increasing the Sustainability of a Resource Development: Aboriginal Engagement and Negotiated Agreements," *Environment Development Sustainability* 12, 2 (2010): 233–44; and Ciaran O'Faircheallaigh, "Extractive Industries and Indigenous Peoples: A Changing Dynamic?" *Journal of Rural Studies* 30 (2013): 20–30.

11 For example, Gordon Christie, "Developing Case Law: The Future of Consultation and Accommodation," *UBC Law Review* 39, 1 (2006): 139–84.

12 *United Nations Declaration on the Rights of Indigenous Peoples,* GA Resolution 61/295, UNGAOR, 61st Sess., Supp. no. 49, UN Doc. A/61/49, September 13, 2007 [*UNDRIP*].

13 United Nations General Assembly, *United Nations Declaration on the Rights of Indigenous Peoples: Resolution Adopted by the General Assembly, Article 19,* Doc. A/RES/61/295, October 2, 2007.

14 Sheryl Lightfoot, "Adopting and Implementing the United Nations Declaration on the Rights of Indigenous Peoples: Canada's Existential Crisis," in *Surviving Canada: Indigenous Peoples Celebrate 150 Years of Betrayal,* ed. Kiera Ladner and Myra J. Tait (Winnipeg: ARP Books, 2017), 453.

15 Crown-Indigenous Relations and Northern Affairs Canada, "Government of Canada and the Duty to Consult," *Government of Canada*, last modified November 29, 2024, https://www.rcaanc-cirnac.gc.ca/eng/1331832510888/1609421255810.

16 Crown-Indigenous Relations and Northern Affairs Canada, "Government of Canada."

17 Minh Do, "Ask About Policy Change First, Courts Second," in *Policy Change, Courts, and the Canadian Constitution*, ed. Emmett Macfarlane (Toronto: University of Toronto Press, 2018), 21.

18 See Fritz Scharpf, *Governing in Europe: Effective and Democratic?* (Oxford: Oxford University Press, 1999); and Vivien Schmidt, "Democracy and Legitimacy in the European Union Revisited: Input, Output and 'Throughput,'" *Political Studies* 61, 1 (2013): 2–22.

19 Métis people have been identified as largely being excluded from duty-to-consult processes. See Christopher Gall and Brodie Douglas, "Shifting the Status Quo: The Duty to Consult and the Métis of British Columbia," in *Bead by Bead: Constitutional Rights and Métis Community*, ed. Yvonne Boyer and Larry Chartrand (Vancouver: UBC Press, 2021), 52–70.

20 Interview with anonymous legal representative for Indigenous nations, September 19, 2018; interview with anonymous consultant for Indigenous nations, October 2, 2018; interview with anonymous consultant for Indigenous nations, December 21, 2018.

21 Minh Do, "Salient Indigenous Acts of Resistance in Canada, 2010–2020: Current Trends," *Canadian Journal of Political Science* 56, 4 (2023): 936–49.

22 Glen Coulthard, *Red Skin, White Masks: Rejecting the Colonial Politics of Recognition* (Minneapolis: University of Minnesota Press, 2014).

23 See Wolfgang Streeck and Kathleen Thelen, "Introduction: Institutional Change in Advanced Political Economies," in *Beyond Continuity: Institutional Change in Advanced Political Economies*, ed. Wolfgang Streeck and Kathleen Thelen (Oxford: Oxford University Press, 2005), 1–39; and James Mahoney and Katheleen Thelen, "Introduction: A Theory of Gradual Institutional Change," in *Explaining Institutional Change: Ambiguity, Agency, and Power*, ed. James Mahoney and Kathleen Thelen (Cambridge, UK: Cambridge University Press, 2009), 1–37.

24 Kathleen Thelen, "Institutional Change in Advanced Political Economies," *British Journal of Industrial Relations* 47, 3 (2009): 489.

25 Interview and discussion with anonymous legal representative for Indigenous nations, December 2017.

26 Robert Hamilton and Joshua Nichols, "The Tin Ear of the Court: Ktunaxa Nation and the Foundations of the Duty to Consult," *Alberta Law Review* 56, 3 (2019): 729–60.

27 See, for example, John Borrows, "Sovereignty's Alchemy: An Analysis of *Delgamuukw v. British Columbia*," *Osgoode Hall Law Journal* 37, 3 (1999): 537–96; Kiera Ladner, "Up the Creek: Fishing for a New Constitutional Order," *Canadian Journal of Political Science* 38, 4 (2005): 923–53; and Gordon Christie, *Canadian Law and Indigenous Self-Determination: A Naturalist Analysis* (Toronto: University of Toronto Press, 2019).

28 *Kemess North Mine Joint Review Panel Report*, September 17, 2007, 236 (on file with author).

29 Minister of Environment and Climate Change Strategy and the Minister of Energy, Mines and Petroleum Resources, *Ministers' Reasons for Decision: Ajax Mine Project*, December 13, 2017, 7 (on file with author).

30 Projects were counted if more than 50 percent of participating Indigenous nations in an assessment explicitly opposed a project receiving an environmental assessment certificate. This count does not consider how certain nations have higher stakes in certain projects compared to others.

Chapter 1: Legitimacy Deficits in Settler-Colonial Canada

1 Alain-G. Gagnon, *The Legitimacy Clash: Challenges to Democracy in Multinational States* (Toronto: University of Toronto Press, 2022).

2 Peter Russell, *Sovereignty: The Biography of a Claim* (Toronto: University of Toronto Press, 2021).

3 Peter Russell, *Recognizing Aboriginal Title: The Mabo Case and Indigenous Resistance to English-Settler Colonialism* (Toronto: University of Toronto Press, 2006).

4 Gina Starblanket, "The Numbered Treaties and the Politics of Incoherency," *Canadian Journal of Political Science* 52, 3 (2019): 443–59.

5 Audra Simpson, *Mohawk Interruptus: Political Life across the Borders of Settler States* (Durham, NC: Duke University Press, 2014).

6 Glen Coulthard, *Red Skin, White Masks: Rejecting the Colonial Politics of Recognition* (Minneapolis: University of Minnesota Press, 2014).

7 Corey Snelgrove and Matthew Wildcat, "Political Action in the Time of Reconciliation," in *Indigenous Resurgence in an Age of Reconciliation,* ed. Heidi Kiiwetinepinesiik Stark, Aimée Craft, and Hōkūlani K. Aikau (Toronto: University of Toronto Press, 2023), 157–75.

8 Heidi Kiiwetinepinesiik Stark, "Generating a Critical Resurgence Together," in Stark, Craft, and Aikau, *Indigenous Resurgence,* 3–20.

9 Michael Asch, "Confederation Treaties and Reconciliation: Stepping Back into the Future," in *Resurgence and Reconciliation: Indigenous-Settler Relations and Earth Teachings,* ed. Michael Asch, John Borrows, and James Tully (Toronto: University of Toronto Press, 2018), 29–48.

10 See Jon Pierre, *Debating Governance: Authority, Steering, and Democracy* (Oxford: Oxford University Press, 2000); Jon Pierre and B. Guy Peters, *Governance, Politics and the State* (London: Macmillan Press, 2000); Lester M. Salamon, "The New Governance and the Tools of Public Action: An Introduction," in *The Tools of Government: A Guide to the New Governance*, ed. Lester M. Salamon (Oxford: Oxford University Press, 2002), 1–47; Mark Moore and Jean Hartley, "Innovations in Governance," *Public Management Review* 10, 1 (2008): 3–20; Stephen P. Osborne, ed., *The New Public Governance? Emerging Perspectives on the Theory and Practice of Public Governance* (London: Routledge, 2010); Jean Hartley, Eva Sørenson, and Jacob Torfing, "Collaborative Innovation: A Viable Alternative to Market Competition and Organizational Entrepreneurship," *Public Administration Review* 73, 6 (2013): 821–30; Douglas F. Morgan and Craig W. Shinn, "The Foundations of New Public Governance," in *New Public Governance: A Regime-Centred Perspective*, ed. Douglas F. Morgan and Brian J. Cook (London: M.E. Sharpe, 2014), 6; and Pearl Eliadis, Margaret M. Hill, and Michael Howlett, "Introduction," in *Designing Government: From Instruments to Governance*, ed. Pearl Eliadis, Margaret M. Hill, and Michael Howlett (Montreal and Kingston: McGill-Queen's University Press, 2005), 5.

11 See Jon Pierre, *Debating Governance: Authority, Steering, and Democracy* (Oxford: Oxford University Press, 2000); and Grace Skogstad, "Who Governs? Who Should Govern?: Political Authority and Legitimacy in Canada in the Twenty-First Century," *Canadian Journal of Political Science* 36, 5 (2003): 955–73.

12 Michael Howlett, "Managing the 'Hollow State': Procedural Policy Instruments and Modern Governance," *Canadian Public Administration* 43, 4 (2000): 422; see also Renate Mayntz, "Legitimacy and the Directive Capacity of the Political System," in *Stress and Contradiction in Modern Capitalism*, ed. Leon N. Lindberg et al. (Lexington, KY: Lexington Books, 1975), 261–27; and Jürgen Habermas, *The Legitimation Crisis* (Boston: Beacon Press, 1975).

13 See Martin Papillon, "Canadian Federalism and the Emerging Mosaic of Aboriginal Multilevel Governance," in *Canadian Federalism: Performance, Effectiveness and Legitimacy*, ed. Herman Bakvis and Grace Skogstad (Toronto: Oxford University Press 2008), 291–313; Gabrielle Slowey, *Navigating Neoliberalism: Self-Determination in an Era of Globalization* (Vancouver: UBC Press, 2007); Kiera Ladner, "Colonialism Isn't the Only Obstacle: Indigenous Peoples and Multilevel Government in Canada," in *Federalism, Feminism and Multilevel Governance*, ed. Marian Sawer Hausmann and Jill Vickers (London: Ashgate, 2010), 83–96; Martin Papillon, "Adapting Federalism: Indigenous Multilevel Governance in Canada and the United States," *Publius: The Journal of Federalism* 42, 2 (2012): 289–312; Christopher Alcantara and Jen Nelles, "Indigenous Peoples and the State in Settler Societies: Toward a More Robust

Definition of Multilevel Governance," *Publius: The Journal of Federalism* 44, 1 (2014): 183–204; and Martin Papillon and André Juneau, *Canada: The State of the Federation, 2013: Aboriginal Multilevel Governance* (Montreal and Kingston: McGill-Queen's University Press, 2015).

14 See Sari Graben, "The Nisga'a Final Agreement: Negotiating Federalism," *Indigenous Law Journal* 6, 2 (2007): 63–94.

15 Herman Bakvis, "In the Shadows of Hierarchy: Intergovernmental Governance in Canada and the European Union," *Canadian Public Administration* 56, 2 (2013): 203–18.

16 Alex Latta, "Indigenous Rights and Multilevel Governance: Learning from the Northwest Territories Water Stewardship Strategy," *International Indigenous Policy Journal* 9, 2 (2018): 1–22.

17 The *Recognition and Reconciliation of Rights Policy for Treaty Negotiations in British Columbia*, September 4, 2019, stipulates that treaties and agreements do not extinguish rights in form or result (s. 9.c). Without any new agreements passed since this new framework, it is difficult to assess how rights and title interface with the Crown's asserted sovereignty in modern treaties.

18 *Calder et al v British Columbia (Attorney General),* [1973] SCR 313; *Royal Proclamation* (UK), October 7, 1763.

19 Patrick Macklem and Douglas Sanderson, "Introduction: Recognition and Reconciliation in Indigenous-Settler Societies," in *From Recognition to Reconciliation: Essays on the Constitutional Entrenchment of Aboriginal and Treaty Rights,* ed. Patrick Macklem and Douglas Sanderson (Toronto: University of Toronto Press, 2016), 5–6.

20 Brian Slattery, "The Generative Structure of Aboriginal Rights," in *Moving toward Justice: Legal Traditions and Aboriginal Justice,* ed. John Whyte (Saskatoon: Purich Publishing, 2008), 16.

21 *R v Sparrow,* [1990] 1 SCR 1075, 1105; *Constitution Act, 1982,* being Schedule B to the *Canada Act 1982* (UK), 1982, c. 11.

22 Michael McCrossan and Kiera Ladner, "Eliminating Indigenous Jurisdictions: Federalism, the Supreme Court of Canada, and Territorial Rationalities of Power," *Canadian Journal of Political Science* 49, 3 (2016): 411–31; *Canadian Charter of Rights and Freedoms,* Part 1 of the *Constitution Act, 1982,* being Schedule B to the *Canada Act 1982* (UK), 1982, c. 11.

23 John Borrows, "Challenging Historical Frameworks: Aboriginal Rights, The Trickster, and Originalism," *Canadian Historical Review* 98, 1 (2017): 114–35.

24 *R v Van der Peet,* [1996] 2 SCR 507 [*Van der Peet*].

25 *Haida Nation v British Columbia (Ministry of Forests),* 2004 SCC 73, [2004] 3 SCR 511, para. 1 [*Haida Nation*].

26 Dwight Newman, "Reconciliation: Legal Conception(s) and Faces of Justice," in *Moving Toward Justice: Legal Traditions and Aboriginal Justice,* ed. John Whyte (Saskatoon: Purich Publishing, 2008), 85.
27 *Haida Nation,* para. 41.
28 Peter Russell, *Canada's Constitutional Odyssey: Can Canadians Become a Sovereign People?* (Toronto: University of Toronto Press, 2004).
29 James Tully, *Strange Multiplicity: Constitutionalism in an Age of Diversity* (Cambridge, UK: Cambridge University Press, 2010).
30 *Haida Nation,* para. 14.
31 Minh Do, "Lessons from Public Policy Theories: Ask About Policy Change First, Courts Second," in *Policy Change, Courts, and the Canadian Constitution,* ed. Emmett Macfarlane (Toronto: University of Toronto Press, 2018), 21–39.
32 B. Guy Peters and Jon Pierre, *Comparative Governance: Rediscovering the Functional Dimension of Governing* (Cambridge, UK: Cambridge University Press, 2016), 60.
33 See, for example, Macfarlane, *Policy Change.*
34 James Kelly, *Governing with the Charter: Legislative and Judicial Activism* (Vancouver: UBC Press, 2005).
35 Matthew A. Hennigar, "Players and the Process: Charter Litigation and the Federal Government," *Windsor Yearbook of Access to Justice* 21 (2002): 91–110.
36 Janet Hiebert, "The Charter's Influence on Legislation: Political Strategizing About Risk" (Presidential address to the Canadian Political Science Association, Regina), Canadian Journal of Political Science 51, 4 (2018): 727–47; see also James Kelly and Matthew Hennigar, "The Canadian Charter of Rights and the Minister of Justice: Weak-form Review within a Constitutional Charter of Rights," *International Journal of Constitutional Law* 10, 1 (2012): 35–68; and Janet Hiebert, "The Notwithstanding Clause and Charter Compliance: Why Infrequent Use Should Not Be Equated with Charter Compliance," in *Oxford Handbook of the Canadian Constitution,* ed. Nathalie Des Rosiers, Patrick Macklem, and Peter Oliver (Oxford: Oxford University Press, 2017), 695–714.
37 Peters and Pierre, *Comparative Governance,* 29.
38 Martin Papillon, "Introduction," in Papillon and Juneau, *Canada: The State of the Federation,* 8.
39 Papillon, "Introduction," 8; Michael Howlett, "Managing the 'Hollow State': Procedural Policy Instruments and Modern Governance," *Canadian Public Administration* 43, 4 (2000): 419.
40 Fritz Scharpf, *Governing in Europe: Effective and Democratic?* (Oxford: Oxford University Press, 1999).

41 Grace Skogstad, "Who Governs? Who Should Govern?: Political Authority and Legitimacy in Canada in the Twenty-Frist Century," *Canadian Journal of Political Science* 36, 5 (2003): 956. The original concept was expressed by Scharpf, *Governing in Europe*.

42 Skogstad, "Who Governs?," 956.

43 See Neil Bradford, "Place Matters and Multi-level Governance: Perspectives on a New Urban Policy Paradigm," *Policy Options* 25, 2 (2004): 39–44; Arthur Benz, "Multilevel Parliaments in Canada and Europe," *International Journal* 66, 1 (2010): 109; Rachel Laforest, "Shifting Scales of Governance and Civil Society Participation in Canada and the European Union," *Canadian Public Administration* 56, 2 (2013): 235–51; Heather Millar, "Comparing Accountability Relationships between Governments and Non-state Actors in Canadian and European International Development Policy," *Canadian Public Administration* 56, 2 (2013): 252–69; Eric Monpetit, "Policy Design for Legitimacy: Expert Knowledge, Citizens, Time and Inclusion in the United Kingdom's Biotechnology Sector," *Public Administration* 86, 1 (2008): 259–77; and Amy Verdun and Donna Wood, "Governing the Social Dimension in Canadian Federalism and European Integration," *Canadian Public Administration* 56, 2 (2013): 173–84.

44 Barbara Finke, "Civil Society Participation in EU Governance," *Living Reviews in European Governance* 2, 2 (2007): 4–31; Justin Greenwood, "Organized Civil Society and Democratic Legitimacy in the European Union," *British Journal of Political Science* 37 (2007): 333–57; Beate Kohler-Koch, "How to Put Matters Right? Assessing the Role of Civil Society in EU Accountability," *West European Politics* 33, 5 (2010): 1117–41.

45 Vivien Schmidt, "Democracy and Legitimacy in the European Union Revisited: Input, Output and 'Throughput,'" *Political Studies* 61, 1 (2013): 5, 6.

46 Vivien Schmidt and Matthew Wood, "Conceptualizing Throughput Legitimacy: Procedural Mechanisms of Accountability, Transparency, Inclusiveness and Openness in EU Governance," *Public Administration* 97, 4 (2019): 730.

47 Schmidt, "Democracy and Legitimacy," 6.

48 Howlett, "Managing the 'Hollow State,'" 412–31; Justin Greenwood, "Organized Civil Society and Democratic Legitimacy in the European Union," *British Journal of Political Science* 37, 2 (2007): 333–57; Ingi Iusmen and John Boswell, "The Dilemmas of Pursuing 'Throughput Legitimacy' through Participatory Mechanisms," *West European Politics* 40, 2 (2017): 459–78; Mario Levesque, "Mapping a Way Forward: Interest Group Selection and Roles Performed in Engagement Processes," *Canadian Public Administration* 55, 4 (2012): 531–52; Ingmar van Meerkerk, Jurien Edelenbos, and Erik-Hans Klijn,

"Connective Management and Governance Network Performance: The Mediating Role of Throughput Legitimacy. Findings from Survey Research on Complex Water Projects in the Netherlands," *Environment and Planning C: Government and Policy* 33, 4 (2017): 746–64; Carey Doberstein and Heather Millar, "Balancing a House of Cards: Throughput Legitimacy in Canadian Governance Networks," *Canadian Journal of Political Science* 47, 2 (2014): 259–80.

49 See Peter G. Stillman, "The Concept of Legitimacy," *Polity* 7, 1 (1974): 32–56; Mark C. Suchman, "Managing Legitimacy: Strategic and Institutional Approaches," *Academy of Management Review* 20, 3 (1995): 571–610.

50 See Robert K. Leik, "New Directions for Network Exchange Theory: Strategic Manipulation of Network Linkages," *Social Networks* 14, 3 (1992): 309–23; Johan A. de Bruijn and Ernst F. ten Heuvelhof, "Policy Networks and Governance," in *Institutional Design*, ed. David L. Weimer (Boston: Kluwer Academic, 1995), 161–79; Erik-Hans Klijn, "Analyzing and Managing Policy Processes in Complex Networks: A Theoretical Examination of the Concept Policy Network and Its Problems," *Administration and Society* 28, 1 (1996): 90–119; Johan A. de Bruijn and Ernst F. ten Heuvelhof, "Instruments for Network Management," in *Managing Complex Networks: Strategies for the Public Sector*, ed. W.J.M. Kickert, Erik-Hans Klijn, and J.F.M. Koppenjan (London: Sage Publications, 1997), 119–36.

51 Howlett, "Managing the 'Hollow State,'" 412–31.

52 Howlett, "Managing the 'Hollow State,'" 422.

53 Howlett, "Managing the 'Hollow State,'" 419.

54 Van Meerkerk, Edelenbos, and Klijn, "Connective Management," 460. Some exceptions include Arwin van Buuren, Ingmar van Meerkerk, and Cecilia Tortajada, "Understanding Emergent Participation Practices in Water Governance," *International Journal of Water Resources Development* 35, 3 (2019): 367–82; and Andrew Song et al., "Measuring, Mapping and Quantifying the Effects of Trust and Informal Communication on Transboundary Collaboration in the Great Lakes Fisheries Policy Network," *Global Environmental Change* 54 (2019): 6–18.

55 See Helena Catt and Michael Murphy, "What Voice for the People? Categorizing Methods of Public Consultation," *Australian Journal of Political Science* 38, 3 (2003): 416–18; and Jon Pierre, "Public Consultation and Citizen Participation: Dilemmas of Policy Advice," in *Taking Stock: Assessing Public Sector Reforms*, ed. Guy Peters and Donald Savoie (Montreal and Kingston: McGill-Queen's University Press and Canadian Centre for Management Development, 1998), 146.

56 See Catt and Murphy, "What Voice for the People," 419; and Lawrence Pratchett, "New Fashions in Public Participation: Towards Greater Democracy?" *Parliamentary Affairs* 52, 4 (1999): 618, 630.

57 See Catt and Murphy, "What Voice for the People," 416–18; and Pierre, "Public Consultation," 146.

58 See Catt and Murphy, "What Voice for the People," 408–9; Pierre, "Public Consultation," 150; Pratchett, "New Fashions in Public Participation," 630–31; and Gene Rowe and Lyn Frewer, "Public Participation Methods: A Framework for Evaluation," *Science, Technology and Human Values* 25, 1 (2000): 12–13.

59 See Margot Hulbert, "Evaluating Public Consultation in Nuclear Energy: The Importance of Problem Structuring and Scale," *International Journal of Energy Sector Management* 8, 1 (2014): 60; Laurie Skuba Jackson, "Contemporary Public Involvement: Toward a Strategic Approach," *Local Environment* 6, 2 (2001): 145–46; Steve Patten, "Democratizing the Institutions of Policy-Making: Democratic Consultation and Participatory Administration," *Journal of Canadian Studies* 35, 4 (2001): 237; Pratchett, "New Fashions in Public Participation," 629; Rowe and Frewer, "Public Participation Methods," 15–17.

60 Patten, "Democratizing the Institutions," 237; Rowe and Frewer, "Public Participation Methods," 15–17.

61 Robert Ratner, "Communicative Rationality in the Citizens' Assembly and Referendum Processes," in *Designing Deliberative Democracy: The British Columbia Citizens' Assembly,* ed. Mark Warren and Hilary Pearse (Cambridge, UK: Cambridge University Press, 2008), 148; Pratchett, "New Fashions in Public Participation," 629.

62 Antonio Floridia, *From Participation to Deliberation: A Critical Genealogy of Deliberative Democracy* (Colchester, UK: ECPR Press, 2017); Amy Guttman and Dennis Thompson, *Why Deliberative Democracy?* (Princeton, NJ: Princeton University Press, 2009).

63 Doberstein and Millar, "Balancing a House of Cards," 266.

64 Eric Montpetit, "Public Consultations in Policy Network Environments: The Case of Assisted Reproductive Technology Policy in Canada," *Canadian Public Policy* 29, 1 (2003): 98.

65 Sarah Marie Wiebe and Leah Levac, "Introduction," in *Creating Spaces of Engagement: Policy Justice and the Practical Craft of Deliberative Democracy,* ed. Sarah Marie Wiebe and Leah Levac (Toronto: University of Toronto Press, 2020), 6.

66 Anna Drake, *Activism, Inclusion, and the Challenges of Deliberative Democracy* (Vancouver: UBC Press, 2021), 72.

67 Van Buuren, van Meerkerk, and Tortajada, "Understanding Emergent Participation Practices."

68 See Gerald Taiaiake Alfred, *Wasáse: Indigenous Pathways of Action and Freedom* (Toronto: University of Toronto Press, 2005); and Kiera Ladner, "Political Genocide: Killing Nations through Legislation and Slow Moving Poisons," in *Colonial Genocide and Indigenous North America,* ed. Andrew Woolford, Jeff Benvenuto, and Alexander Hinton (Durham, NC: Duke University Press, 2014), 226–45; these authors raise concerns that Indigenous forms of governance are incompatible with Westphalia-based systems of governance). In contrast, see Meaghan Williams and Robert Scherzter, "Is Indigeneity Like Ethnicity? Theorizing and Assessing Models of Indigenous Political Representation," *Canadian Journal of Political Science* 52, 4 (2019): 677–96, as they explain how these different forms of governance might find equal expression in state-based institutions.

69 Jens Steffek, "The Limits of Proceduralism: Critical Remarks on the Rise of Throughput Legitimacy," *Public Administration* 97, 4 (2019): 784–96.

70 See Coulthard, *Red Skin, White Masks*; Lorenzo Veracini, "Introducing Settler Colonial Studies," *Settler Colonial Studies* 1, 1 (2011): 8; and Andrée Boiselle et al., eds., *Recognition versus Self-Determination: Dilemmas of Emancipatory Politics* (Vancouver: UBC Press, 2014).

71 See Roderick Arthur William Rhodes, "The Hollowing Out of the State: The Changing Nature of the Public Service in Britain," *Political Quarterly* 65 (1994): 138–51; H. Brinton Milward, Keith G. Provan, and Barbara A. Else, "What Does the 'Hollow State' Look Like?" in *Public Management: The State of the Art,* ed. Barry Bozeman (San Francisco: Jossey-Bass, 1993), 309–23; and H. Brinton Milward and Keith G. Provan, "Governing the Hallow State," *Journal of Public Administration Research and Practice* 10 (2000): 359–80.

72 See Ian Holliday, "Is the British State Hollowing Out?" *Political Quarterly* 71 (2000): 167–76; and Adrienne Hértier and Dirk Lehmkuhl, "The Shadow of Hierarchy and New Modes of Governance," *Journal of Public Policy* 28, 1 (2008): 1–17.

73 *Mikisew Cree First Nation v Canada (Governor General in Council),* 2018 SCC 40, para. 156.

74 *Chippewas of the Thames First Nation v Enbridge Pipelines Inc,* 2017 SCC 41, para. 2.

75 Neil Craik, "Process and Reconciliation: Integrating the Duty to Consult with Environmental Assessment," *Osgoode Hall Law Journal* 53, 2 (2016): 672.

76 See Ria Tzimas, "To What End the Dialogue?" *Supreme Court Law Review* 54 (2011): 493–527.

77 See Jürgen Habermas, *The Structural Transformation of the Public Sphere* (Cambridge, MA: MIT Press, 1989); and Simone Chambers, "Deliberative Democratic Theory," *Annual Review of Political Science* 6, 1 (2003): 307–26.

78 *Mikisew Cree First Nation v Canada (Minister of Canadian Heritage),* 2005 SCC 69, para. 54.

79 Ryan Beaton, "*De Facto* and *de jure* Crown Sovereignty: Reconciliation and Legitimation at the Supreme Court of Canada," *Constitutional Forum* 25, 1 (2017–18): 31.

80 Avigail Eisenberg, "Decolonizing Authority: The Conflict on Wet'suwet'en Territory," *Canadian Journal of Political Science* 55, 1 (2022): 48.

81 *Van der Peet,* para. 50.

Chapter 2: The Supreme Court of Canada and the Duty to Consult

1 Dwight Newman, "Reconciliation: Legal Conception(s) and Faces of Justice," in *Moving Toward Justice: Legal Traditions and Aboriginal Justice,* ed. John Whyte (Saskatoon: Purich Publishing, 2008), 85; *Constitution Act, 1982,* being Schedule B to the *Canada Act 1982* (UK), 1982, c. 11.

2 Ryan Beaton, "*De Facto* and *de jure* Crown Sovereignty: Reconciliation and Legitimation at the Supreme Court of Canada," *Constitutional Forum* 26, 1 (2017–18): 28.

3 *Haida Nation v British Columbia (Ministry of Forests),* 2004 SCC 73; *Taku River Tlingit First Nation v British Columbia (Project Assessment Director),* 2004 SCC 74 [*Taku River*]; *Mikisew Cree v Canada (Minister of Canadian Heritage),* 2005 SCC 69 [*Mikisew Cree* 2005].

4 *Rio Tinto Alcan v Carrier Sekani,* 2010 SCC 43 [*Rio Tinto*]; *Beckman v Little Salmon/Carmacks First Nation,* 2010 SCC 53 [*Beckman*].

5 *Behn v Moulton Contracting Ltd,* 2013 SCC 26 [*Behn*].

6 *Tsilhqot'in Nation v British Columbia,* 2014 SCC 44 [*Tsilhqot'in Nation*].

7 *Chippewas of the Thames First Nation v Enbridge Pipelines Inc.,* 2017 SCC 41 [*Chippewas*]; *Clyde River (Hamlet) v Petroleum Geo-Services,* 2017 SCC 40 [*Clyde River*]; *Ktunaxa Nation v British Columbia (Forests, Lands and Natural Resource Operations),* 2017 SCC 54 [*Ktunaxa*].

8 *Mikisew Cree First Nation v Canada (Governor General in Council),* 2018 SCC 40 [*Mikisew Cree* 2018].

9 See Dwight Newman, *Revisiting the Duty to Consult Aboriginal Peoples* (Saskatoon: Purich Publishing, 2014); and Thomas Isaac and Anthony Knox, "The Crown's Duty to Consult Aboriginal People," *Alberta Law Review* 41, 1 (2003): 49–77.

10 See Anthony Wicks, "Beyond Audi Alterum Partem: The Duty to Consult Aboriginal Peoples in Canada and New Zealand," *Journal of South Pacific Law* 13, 1 (2009): 40–46; Lorne Sossin, "The Duty to Consult and Accommodate: Procedural Justice as Aboriginal Rights," *Canadian Journal of Administrative Law and Practice* 23, 1 (2010): 93–113; Zena Charowsky, "The Aboriginal Law

Duty to Consult: An Introduction for Administrative Tribunals," *Saskatchewan Law Review* 74, 2 (2011): 213–30; David Mullan, "The Supreme Court and the Duty to Consult Aboriginal Peoples: A Lifting of the Fog?" *Canadian Journal of Administrative Law and Practice* 24, 3 (2011): 233–60; and Janna Promislow, "Irreconcilable? The Duty to Consult and Administrative Decision Makers, *Constitutional Forum* 22, 1 (2013): 63–78.

11 See Courtney Fidler and Michael Hitch, "Impact and Benefit Agreements: A Contentious Issue for Environmental and Aboriginal Justice," *Environments Journal* 35, 2 (2007): 49–69; Brad Gilmour and Bruce Mellet, "The Role of Impact and Benefit Agreements in the Resolution of Project Issues with First Nations," *Alberta Law Review* 51, 2 (2013): 385–400; and Martin Papillon and Thierry Rodon, "Proponent-Indigenous Agreements and the Implementation of the Right to Free, Prior, and Informed Consent in Canada," *Environmental Assessment Review* 62, 1 (2016): 216–24.

12 David Newman, "The Section 35 Duty to Consult," in *The Oxford Handbook of the Canadian Constitution,* ed. Peter Oliver, Patrick Macklem, and Nathalie Des Rosiers (New York: Oxford University Press, 2017), 351.

13 Sonia Lawrence and Patrick Macklem, "From Consultation to Reconciliation: Aboriginal Rights and the Crown's Duty to Consult," *Canadian Bar Review* 79, 1 (2000): 274–75.

14 E. Ria Tzimas, "To What End the Dialogue?" *Supreme Court Law Review* 54 (2011): 493–527.

15 Kaitlin Ritchie, "Issues Associated with the Implementation of the Duty to Consult and Accommodate Aboriginal Peoples: Threatening the Goals of Reconciliation and Meaningful Consultation," *UBC Law Review* 46, 2 (2013): 397–438.

16 Dwight Newman, "Consultation and Economic Reconciliation," in *From Recognition to Reconciliation: Essays on the Constitutional Entrenchment of Aboriginal and Treaty Rights,* ed. Patrick Macklem and Douglas Sanderson (Toronto: University of Toronto Press, 2016), 207–22; Dwight Newman, ed., *Business Implications of Aboriginal Law* (Toronto: LexisNexis Canada, 2018).

17 Veronica Potes, "The Duty to Accommodate Aboriginal Peoples' Rights: Substantive Consultation?" *Journal of Environmental Law and Practice* 17, 1 (2006): 27–45; Arthur Pape, "The Duty to Consult and Accommodation: A Judicial Innovation Intended to Promote Reconciliation," in *Aboriginal Law Since Delgamuukw,* ed. Maria Morellato (Aurora, ON: Canada Law Book, 2009), 313–31; Rachael Ariss, Clara MacCallum, and Diba Nazneen Somani, "Crown Policies on the Duty to Consult and Accommodate: Towards Reconciliation?" *McGill Journal of Sustainable Development Law* 13, 1 (2017): 1–54.

18 *Haida Nation,* para. 27; *Taku River,* para. 21.

19 *Mikisew Cree* 2005, para. 3.
20 *Haida Nation*, paras. 26, 32, 53; *Taku River*, paras. 24, 42; *Mikisew Cree* 2005, para. 50.
21 *Haida Nation*, para. 25.
22 Mark Walters, "The Jurisprudence of Reconciliation," in *The Politics of Reconciliation in Multinational Societies*, ed. Will Kymlicka and Bashir Bashir (Oxford: Oxford University Press, 2008), 186.
23 *Haida Nation*, para. 33.
24 *Haida Nation*, para. 25.
25 *Haida Nation*, para. 16.
26 *Haida Nation*, para. 20. Indeed, this expectation for honourable dealing has been interpreted as replacing fiduciary obligations altogether, such that the full scope of remedies and obligations that flow from the honour of the Crown remain unknown. See Jamie Dickson, *The Honour and Dishonour of the Crown: Making Sense of Aboriginal Law in Canada* (Saskatoon: Purich Publishing, 2015).
27 *Haida Nation*, para. 42.
28 *Haida Nation*, para. 25.
29 *Haida Nation*, para. 45.
30 *Haida Nation*, para. 42.
31 *Haida Nation*, para. 48; *Mikisew Cree* 2005, para. 66.
32 *Haida Nation*, para. 49.
33 *Haida Nation*, para. 49.
34 *Haida Nation*, para 42; see also *Taku River*, paras. 2, 22; *Mikisew Cree* 2005, para. 66.
35 *Haida Nation*, para. 35; *Taku River*, para. 25.
36 *Haida Nation*, para. 43.
37 *Haida Nation*, para. 44.
38 *Haida Nation*, paras. 14, 45, 49, 50; *Taku River*, paras. 2, 42; *Mikisew Cree*, para. 50.
39 *Haida Nation*, para. 45.
40 *Haida Nation*, para. 27.
41 *Haida Nation*, para. 42.
42 James (Sa'ke'j) Youngblood Henderson, "Dialogical Governance: A Mechanism of Constitutional Governance," *Saskatchewan Law Review* 72 (2009): 59.
43 *Haida Nation*, para. 51.
44 Gordon Christie, "Developing Case Law: The Future of Consultation and Accommodation," *UBC Law Review* 39, 1 (2006): 160.
45 *Rio Tinto*, para. 2.
46 *Rio Tinto*, paras. 31, 39–50.

47 *Rio Tinto,* para. 51.

48 *Rio Tinto,* para. 53.

49 *Rio Tinto,* para. 60. The Supreme Court of Canada (SCC) recognized that the Crown could avoid the duty to consult by purposefully withholding from tribunals the power to fulfill or evaluate consultation with Indigenous peoples; the Court only suggested that, in these instances, the Indigenous party should seek remedies in the courts (para. 63). If the Crown does try to shirk its responsibilities by using disempowered tribunals to avoid the duty, Indigenous parties would have a strong case when seeking remedies through judicial review.

50 The SCC clarified that, regardless of the express terms of a modern treaty, "the Crown cannot contract out of its duty of honourable dealing with Aboriginal people" (*Beckman,* para. 61). The scope of the duty may be determined by the terms of the treaty, but the duty exists independently (para. 67).

51 *Haida Nation,* para. 62.

52 *Haida Nation,* para. 63.

53 Sossin, "The Duty to Consult and Accommodate," 101.

54 See Lorne Sossin, "Public Fiduciary Obligations, Political Trusts, and the Equitable Duty of Reasonableness in Administrative Law," *Saskatchewan Law Review* 66, 1 (2003): 180; and David Mullan, "The Supreme Court and the Duty to Consult Aboriginal Peoples: A Lifting of the Fog?" *Canadian Journal of Administrative Law and Practice* 24, 3 (2011): 250.

55 In *Canada (Minister of Citizenship and Immigration) v Vavilov,* the SCC may reveal some insights about how the court may be changing the appropriate standard of review for tribunals in administrative law; *Canada (Minister of Citizenship and Immigration) v Vavilov,* 2019 SCC 65. The SCC made a distinction between statutory appeals and judicial review to determine the appropriate standard of review. Within a statutory appeal process, questions of mixed fact and law, like matters concerning the duty to consult, are reviewed under the more deferential "palpable and overriding error" standard rather than reasonableness. It remains to be seen whether the duty to consult is exempt from this standard as it is related to constitutional rights under section 35 of the *Constitution Act, 1982,* being Schedule B to the *Canada Act 1982* (UK), 1982, c 11.

56 *R v Van der Peet,* [1996] 2 SCR 507, para. 50.

57 *Beckman,* para. 47.

58 *Beckman,* para. 47.

59 *Behn,* para. 1. The question of whether a subset of an Indigenous nation can claim consultation apart from the rest of the community was set aside (paras. 35–36).

60 *Behn,* para. 37.

61 *Behn,* para. 42.

62 *Behn,* para. 42.

63 See Sossin, "Public Fiduciary Obligations"; and Sari Graben, "Resourceful Impacts: Harm and Valuation of the Sacred," *University of Toronto Law Journal* 64, 1 (2014): 61–105.

64 Potes, "Duty to Accommodate," 27–45.

65 Potes, "Duty to Accommodate," 41–42.

66 D'Arcy Vermette, "Dizzying Dialogue: Canadian Courts and the Continuing Justification of the Dispossession of Aboriginal Peoples," *Windsor Yearbook of Access to Justice* 29, 1 (2011): 69–71.

67 *Tsilhqot'in Nation.* See Ravina Bains, "A Real Game Changer: An Analysis of the Supreme Court of Canada Tsilhqot'in *Nation v. British Columbia* Decision," *Fraser Institute Research Bulletin,* July 10, 2014, https://www.fraserinstitute.org/sites/default/files/real-game-changer-supreme-court-of-canada-tsilhqotin-decision.pdf; and Duncan McCue, "Tsilhqot'in Land Ruling Was a Game Changer for BC," *CBC News,* December 23, 2014, http://www.cbc.ca/news/aboriginal/tsilhqot-in-land-ruling-was-a-game-changer-for-b-c-1.2875262.

68 *Tsilhqot'in Nation,* para. 9.

69 *Tsilhqot'in Nation,* para. 77; *Delgamuukw v British Columbia,* [1997] 3 SCR 1010.

70 *Tsilhqot'in Nation,* para. 90.

71 *Tsilhqot'in Nation,* para. 90.

72 *Tsilhqot'in Nation,* para. 97.

73 Although the SCC recognized Aboriginal title in this case, the court's logic underpinning this recognition arguably continued Eurocentric understandings of occupancy and maintained the supremacy of federal and provincial jurisdictions. See John Borrows, "The Durability of *Terra Nullius: Tsilhqot'in Nation v British Columbia,*" *UBC Law Review* 48, 3 (2015): 701–42; and Michael McCrossan and Kiera Ladner, "Eliminating Indigenous Jurisdictions: Federalism, the Supreme Court of Canada, and Territorial Rationalities of Power," *Canadian Journal of Political Science* 49, 3 (2016): 411–31.

74 *United Nations Declaration on the Rights of Indigenous Peoples,* GA Resolution 61/295, UNGAOR, 61st Sess., Supp. no. 49, UN Doc. A/61/49, September 13, 2007 [*UNDRIP*]. See Tim Fontaine, "Canada Officially Adopts UN Declaration

on Rights of Indigenous Peoples," *CBC News,* May 10, 2016, https://www.cbc.ca/news/aboriginal/canada-adopting-implementing-un-rights-declaration-1.3575272.

75 Truth and Reconciliation Commission of Canada, *Truth and Reconciliation Commission of Canada: Calls to Action* (Ottawa: Truth and Reconciliation Commission of Canada, 2015), 4, ss. 43–44.

76 *Clyde River,* para. 34.

77 *Clyde River,* para. 27.

78 *Clyde River,* para. 29.

79 *Clyde River,* para. 40.

80 *Clyde River,* para. 42.

81 *Clyde River,* para. 10.

82 *Clyde River,* para. 11.

83 *Clyde River,* para. 45.

84 *Clyde River,* paras. 46–47.

85 *Chippewas,* para. 62.

86 *Chippewas,* para. 63.

87 Sari Graben and Abbey Sinclair, "Tribunal Administration and the Duty to Consult: A Study of the National Energy Board," *University of Toronto Law Journal* 65, 4 (2015): 384. Not all scholars share the concern that tribunals inadequately approach and apply the duty to consult. See Dwight Newman, "The Section 35 Duty to Consult," in *The Oxford Handbook of the Canadian Constitution,* ed. Peter Oliver, Patrick Macklem, and Nathalie Des Rosiers (New York: Oxford University Press, 2017), 362.

88 *Clyde River,* para. 24 (emphasis in original).

89 *Ktunaxa,* para. 115.

90 *Canadian Charter of Rights and Freedoms,* Part 1 of the *Constitution Act, 1982,* being Schedule B to the *Canada Act 1982* (UK), 1982, c. 11.

91 *Ktunaxa,* para. 5.

92 *Ktunaxa,* para. 9.

93 *Ktunaxa,* para. 94.

94 *Ktunaxa,* para. 100.

95 *Ktunaxa,* para. 112.

96 *Ktunaxa,* para. 114.

97 *Ktunaxa,* para. 133.

98 For a commentary on issues with a tribunal's assessment of risk due to differences in cost-benefit analyses, see Sari Graben, "Rationalizing Risks to Cultural Loss in Resource Development," *Canadian Journal of Law and Jurisprudence* 26, 1 (2013): 83–114.

99 *Haida Nation*, para. 27.

100 *Ktunaxa*, para. 145. For a commentary on issues with tribunals evaluating the substance of Aboriginal rights, see Sari Graben, "Resourceful Impacts: Harm and Valuation of the Sacred," *University of Toronto Law Journal* 64, 1 (2014): 61–105.

101 *Ktunaxa*, para. 86.

102 *Mikisew Cree* 2018, paras. 33, 102, 128.

103 *Mikisew Cree* 2018, paras. 34, 117.

104 *Mikisew Cree* 2018, para. 32.

105 *Mikisew Cree* 2018, paras. 35–38, 122.

106 *Mikisew Cree* 2018, para. 86 (emphasis in original); *R v Sparrow*, [1990] 1 SCR 1075.

107 *Mikisew Cree* 2018, para. 84.

108 *Mikisew Cree* 2018, para. 52.

109 *Mikisew Cree* 2018, para. 49.

110 *Mikisew Cree* 2018, para. 139.

111 *Mikisew Cree* 2018, paras. 145, 155.

112 *Mikisew Cree* 2018, para. 142.

113 *Kebaowek First Nation v Canadian Nuclear Laboratories*, 2025 FC 319, para. 26 [*Kebaowek*].

114 *Kebaowek*, para. 55.

115 *Kebaowek*, para. 75.

116 *Kebaowek*, para. 76.

117 *Kebaowek*, para. 85.

118 *Kebaowek*, para. 119.

119 *Kebaowek*, paras. 128, 130.

120 *Kebaowek*, para. 135.

121 *Kebaowek*, para. 139.

122 *Kebaowek*, paras. 229, 228.

123 *Yahey v British Columbia*, 2021 BCSC 1287 [*Yahey*].

124 *Yahey*, para. 2.

125 *Yahey*, para. 511.

126 *Yahey*, para. 510.

127 The province of British Columbia argued that there was no treaty infringement because the projects fell within the Crown's right to take up land from time to time under Treaty 8 (*Yahey*, para. 471). According to the province, infringement is only considered to have occurred when "the Crown has taken up so much land that 'no meaningful right' to hunt, fish, or trap remains" (para. 494). The Blueberry River First Nations (BRFN) completely opposed the province's

interpretation of infringement. The BRFN claimed that the province "is essentially starting at nothing [that is, no rights] and is 'counting up from nothing' to find specific instances of Blueberry members exercising their treaty rights, thereby confirming the Province's position that rights remain" (para. 496). The BC Supreme Court agreed with the BRFN's argument, asserting that "the Province puts forward an approach to infringement that essentially relies on an unfettered taking up clause and disregards the essential element of Treaty 8" (para. 511).

128 *Yahey,* para. 534.

129 *Yahey,* para. 535.

130 *Yahey,* para. 501.

131 *Yahey,* para. 1802.

132 *Yahey,* para. 1802.

133 *Yahey,* para. 1783.

134 *Yahey,* para. 1780.

135 *Yahey,* para. 1807.

136 *Yahey,* para. 1780.

137 "Province, Blueberry River First Nations Reach Agreement," *BC Government News,* January 18, 2023, https://news.gov.bc.ca/28086.

138 "Province, Blueberry River First Nations."

139 "Province, Blueberry River First Nations."

140 Sarah Cox, "'We're Going to Court': BC First Nation to Proceed with Site C Dam 'Megatrial,'" *The Narwhal,* August 27, 2019, https://thenarwhal.ca/were-going-court-b-c-first-nation-to-proceed-site-c-dam-megatrial.

141 "West Moberly First Nations, BC Hydro and Canada Reach Settlement Related to the Site C Project," *BC Government News,* June 27, 2022, https://news.gov.bc.ca/27066.

142 "West Moberly First Nations."

143 "West Moberly First Nations."

144 *Environmental Assessment Act,* SBC 2018, c. 51.

145 Jackson Smith and Terry Mitchell, "Development of an UNDRIP Compliance Assessment Tool: How a Performance Framework Could Improve State Compliance," *International Indigenous Policy Journal* 11, 2 (2020): 1–23.

146 Gordon Christie, "Implementation of UNDRIP within Canadian and Indigenous Law: Assessing Challenges," in *UNDRIP Implementation: More Reflections on the Braiding of International, Domestic, and Indigenous Laws* (Waterloo, ON, and Saskatoon: Centre for International Governance Innovation and Wiyasiwewin Mikiwahp Native Law Centre, 2018), 25–32.

Chapter 3: The BC Court of Appeal and the Duty to Consult

1 *Musqueam Indian Band v British Columbia (Minister of Sustainable Resource Management),* 2005 BCCA 128, para. 62 [*Musqueam Indian Band*]; *Haida Nation v British Columbia (Ministry of Forests),* 2004 SCC 73 [*Haida Nation*].
2 *Musqueam Indian Band,* para. 97; *Lax Kw'Alaams Indian Band v British Columbia (Minister of Forests),* 2002 BCCA 403, para. 24.
3 *Rio Tinto Alcan v Carrier Sekani,* 2010 SCC 43, [2010] 2 SCR 650, para. 56 [*Rio Tinto*].
4 *Nlaka'pamux Nation Tribal Council v British Columbia (Environmental Assessment Office),* 2011 BCCA 78 [*Nlaka'pamux Nation*].
5 *Nlaka'pamux Nation,* para. 88.
6 *Nlaka'pamux Nation,* para. 99.
7 *Paul v British Columbia (Forest Appeals Commission),* 2001 BCCA 411 [*Paul*].
8 *Paul,* para. 2.
9 *Paul,* para. 95.
10 *Paul,* para. 95.
11 *Rio Tinto,* para. 70.
12 *Lax Kw'Alaams Indian Band v British Columbia (Minister of Forests),* 2002 BCCA 403, para. 27.
13 *Beckman v Little Salmon/Carmacks First Nation,* 2010 SCC 53 [*Beckman*].
14 *Halalt First Nation v British Columbia,* 2012 BCCA 472, para. 118 [*Halalt First Nation*].
15 *Halalt First Nation,* para. 127.
16 *Clyde River (Hamlet) v Petroleum Geo-Services,* 2017 SCC 40, para. 42.
17 *Halalt First Nation,* para. 123.
18 *Halalt First Nation,* para. 126.
19 *West Moberly First Nations v British Columbia (Chief Inspector of Mines),* 2011 BCCA 247 [*West Moberly First Nations*].
20 *West Moberly First Nations,* para. 117.
21 *West Moberly First Nations,* para. 181. This opinion was expressed because the majority's decision ruled that the outcome of consultation was unreasonable in part because the final decision did not adequately explain why the West Moberly First Nations' demands for the restoration of the Burnt Pine caribou herd was rejected (para. 148, see also para. 59). The concurrent decision asserted that such an accommodation measure was not necessary to address because the caribou herd was diminished prior to the events of the proposed project.
22 *Chippewas of the Thames First Nation v Enbridge Pipelines Inc.,* 2017 SCC 41 [*Chippewas*].
23 *Chippewas,* para. 42.

24 *Yahey v British Columbia,* 2021 BCSC 1287 [*Yahey*].
25 *West Moberly First Nations.*
26 *West Moberly First Nations,* para. 123.
27 *West Moberly First Nations,* para. 240.
28 *R. v Douglas et al.,* 2007 BCCA 265, para. 40.
29 *Chartrand v British Columbia (Forests, Lands and Natural Resources Operations),* 2015 BCCA 345, para. 20.
30 *Louis v British Columbia (Minister of Energy, Mines, and Petroleum Resources),* 2013 BCCA 412, paras. 37, 48.
31 *Nlaka'pamux Nation Tribal Council v British Columbia (Environmental Assessment Office),* 2011 BCCA 236 [*Nlaka'pamux Nation Tribal Council*].
32 *Nlaka'pamux Nation Tribal Council,* para. 58.
33 *Nlaka'pamux Nation Tribal Council,* para. 58.
34 *Spookw v Gitxsan Treaty Society,* 2017 BCCA 16 [*Spookw*].
35 *Spookw,* para. 3.
36 *Spookw,* paras. 27, 71.
37 *Nlaka'pamux Nation Tribal Council,* para. 68.
38 *Nlaka'pamux Nation Tribal Council,* paras. 81–82.
39 *Haida Nation,* para. 62. Although the Supreme Court of Canada (SCC) deviated from this assertion in 2010 in *Beckman* by stating that a standard of correctness determines the adequacy of the consultation process, it has now been firmly established that a standard of reasonableness is applied. See *Beckman,* para. 48; and *Neskonlith Indian Band v Salmon Arm (City),* 2012 BCCA 379, paras 60, 84.
40 *Paul,* para. 148.
41 *Paul,* para. 148; *Canadian Charter of Rights and Freedoms,* Part 1 of the *Constitution Act, 1982,* being Schedule B to the *Canada Act 1982* (UK), 1982, c. 11.
42 *Fort Nelson First Nation v British Columbia (Environmental Assessment Office),* 2016 BCCA 500, para. 82.
43 *William v British Columbia (Attorney General),* 2019 BCCA 74, para. 46.
44 *West Moberly First Nations,* para. 144.
45 Indeed, the BC Court of Appeal (BCCA) has asserted that the public interest may change over time, making a veto for Indigenous parties inappropriate in the pursuit of compromise between competing interests. *Prophet River First Nation v British Columbia (Environment),* 2017 BCCA 58, para. 58 [*Prophet River First Nation*].
46 *Musqueam Indian Band v British Columbia (Minister of Sustainable Resource Management),* 2005 BCCA 128, para. 99 [*Musqueam Indian Band*].
47 *Musqueam Indian Band,* para. 99.

48 *West Moberly First Nations*, para. 287.
49 *Prophet River First Nation*, para. 33; *R v Sparrow*, [1990] 1 SCR 1075.
50 *Prophet River First Nation*, para. 33.
51 *Prophet River First Nation*, para. 36.
52 *Prophet River First Nation*, para. 36.
53 *Prophet River First Nation*, para. 58.
54 *Prophet River First Nation*, para. 58.
55 The BCCA asserted that the Prophet River First Nation did not advance "any specific alternatives [that] should have been but were not considered in the course of the consultation process" (*Prophet River First Nation*, para. 59). Since the proposed action involved the construction of a hydroelectric dam, the court stated that the First Nation did not "specify sources of electricity that might be sufficiently viable in terms of comparable cost, power production, and availability that ought to have been, but were not, considered as alternatives" (para. 59).

Chapter 4: Participation in the Environmental Assessment Process in British Columbia

1 Government of Canada, *Aboriginal Consultation and Accommodation: Updated Guidelines for Federal Officials to Fulfill the Duty to Consult*, 2011, 14.
2 See Kirk Lambrecht, *Aboriginal Consultation, Environmental Assessment, and Regulatory Review in Canada* (Regina: University of Regina Press, 2013).
3 *Reviewable Projects Regulation*, BC Reg. 370/2002; *Environmental Assessment Act*, SBC 2002, c. 43.
4 *Environmental Assessment Act*, s. 11(1).
5 *Environmental Assessment Act*, s. 11(2).
6 Mark Haddock, *Environmental Assessment in British Columbia* (Victoria: Environmental Law Centre, 2010), 28.
7 Environmental Assessment Office, *Guideline for the Selection of Valued Components and Assessment of Potential Effects*, September 9, 2013, 4 (approved by Doug Caul, associate deputy minister).
8 *Environmental Assessment Act*, SBC 2018, c. 51.
9 *Declaration on the Rights of Indigenous Peoples Act*, SBC 2019, c. 44; *United Nations Declaration on the Rights of Indigenous Peoples*, GA Resolution 61/295, UNGAOR, 61st Sess., Supp. no. 49, UN Doc. A/61/49, September 13, 2007.
10 *Rio Tinto Alcan v Carrier Sekani*, 2010 SCC 43, para. 56 [*Rio Tinto*].
11 Interview with anonymous legal representative for Indigenous nations, September 19, 2018; interview with anonymous consultant for Indigenous nations, October 2, 2018; interview with anonymous consultant for Indigenous nations, December 21, 2018.

12 Minh Do, "Salient Indigenous Acts of Resistance in Canada, 2010–2020: Current Trends," *Canadian Journal of Political Science* 56, 4 (2023): 936–49.

13 See Annie Booth and Norm Skelton, "Improving First Nations' Participation in Environmental Assessment Process: Recommendations from the Field – Impact Assess," *Project Appraisal* 29, 1 (2011): 49–58; Denis Kirchoff, Holly Gardner, and Leonard Tsuji, "The Canadian Environmental Assessment Act 2012 and Associated Policy: Implications for Aboriginal Peoples," *International Indigenous Policy Journal* 4, 3 (2013): 1–16; Joel Krupta, Lindsay Galbraith, and Sarah Burch, "Participatory and Multi-level Governance: Applications to Aboriginal Renewable Energy Projects," *Local Environment* 20, 1 (2015): 81–101; Kirk Lambrech, *Aboriginal Consultation, Environmental Assessment and Regulatory Review in Canada* (Regina: University of Regina Press, 2013); Bram Noble and Aniekan Udofia, *Protectors of the Land: Toward an EA Process That Works for Aboriginal Communities and Developers* (Ottawa: MacDonald-Laurier Institute, 2015); and Ciarian O'Faircheallaigh, "Environmental Agreements, EIA Followup and Aboriginal Participation in Environmental Management: The Canadian Experience," *Environmental Impact Assessment Review* 27, 4 (2007): 319–42.

14 See Derek Armitage, "Collaborative Environmental Assessment in the Northwest Territories, Canada," *Environmental Impact Assessment Review* 25, 3 (2005): 239–58; Lindsay Galbraith, Ben Bradshaw, and Murray Rutherford, "Towards a New Supraregulatory Approach to Environmental Assessment in Northern Canada," *Impact Assessment Project Appraisal* 25, 1 (2007): 27–41; Bram Noble et al., "Strategic Environmental Assessment Opportunities and Risks for Arctic Offshore Energy Planning and Development," *Marine Policy* 39 (2013): 296–302; Bram Noble and Kevin Hanna, "Environmental Assessment in the Arctic: A Gap Analysis and Research Agenda," *Arctic* 68, 3 (2015): 341–55; and Kevin O'Rielly, "Diamond Mining and the Demise of Environmental Assessment in the North," *Northern Perspectives* 24 (1996): 1–4.

15 See Douglas Baker and James McLelland, "Evaluating the Effectiveness of British Columbia's Environmental Assessment Process for First Nations' Participation in Mining Development," *Environmental Impact Assessment Review* 23, 5 (2003): 581–603; and Annie Booth and Norm Skelton, "Industry and Government Perspectives on First Nations' Participation in the British Columbia Environmental Assessment Process," *Environmental Impact Assessment Review* 31 (2011): 216–25.

16 See Stephen Ellis, "Meaning Consideration? A Review of Traditional Knowledge in Environmental Decision Making," *Arctic* 58, 1 (2005): 66–77; Einar Eyporsson and Alma Elizabeth Thuestad, "Incorporating Traditional Knowledge in Environmental Impact Assessment: How Can It Be Done?" *Arctic Review on Law and Politics* 6, 2 (2015): 132–50; Chris Paci, Ann Tobin, and Peter Robb,

"Reconsidering the Canadian Environmental Impact Assessment Act: A Place for Traditional Environmental Knowledge," *Environmental Impact Assessment Review* 22 (2002): 111–27; Peter Usher, "Traditional Knowledge in Environmental Assessment and Management," *Arctic* 53, 2 (2000): 183–93; and Chris Tollefson and Karen Wipond, "Cumulative Environmental Impacts and Aboriginal Rights," *Environmental Impact Assessment Review* 18, 4 (1998): 371–90.

17 See Bram Noble and Courtney Fidler, "Advancing Indigenous-community Corporate Agreements: Lessons from Practice in the Canadian Mining Sector," *Oil Gas and Energy Law* 9, 4 (2011): 1–30; and Cirian O'Faircheallaigh and Tony Corbett, "Indigenous Participation in Environmental Management of Mining Projects: The Role of Negotiated Agreements," *Environmental Politics* 14, 5 (2005): 629–47.

18 It is noted whether multiple Indigenous nations involved in a single environmental assessment (EA) mentioned the same issue. This duplication may reflect each Indigenous nation's due diligence to keep a record of the proceedings in the EA in the event that legal challenges need to be made. As such, there are no assurances that multiple instances of the same issue within an EA mean that the issue is more severe, but it is still noted in the database.

19 Indeed, the absence of issues expressed by Indigenous parties is also interpreted by the Crown's actors to mean satisfaction over how the Crown discharged the duty to consult.

20 Vivien Schmidt, "Democracy and Legitimacy in the European Union Revisited: Input, Output and 'Throughput,'" *Political Studies* 61, 1 (2013): 4.

21 See Helena Catt and Michael Murphy, "What Voice for the People? Categorizing Methods of Public Consultation," *Australian Journal of Political Science* 38, 3 (2003): 407–21; Jon Pierre, "Public Consultation and Citizen Participation: Dilemmas of Policy Advice," in *Taking Stock: Assessing Public Sector Reforms*, ed. Guy Peters and Donald Savoie (Montreal and Kingston: McGill-Queen's University Press and Canadian Centre for Management Development, 1998), 137–63; Lawrence Pratchett, "New Fashions in Public Participation: Towards Greater Democracy?" *Parliamentary Affairs* 52, 4 (1999): 616–33; Gene Rowe and Lyn Frewer, "Public Participation Methods: A Framework for Evaluation," *Science, Technology and Human Values* 25, 1 (2000): 3–29; Margot Hulbert, "Evaluating Public Consultation in Nuclear Energy: The Importance of Problem Structuring and Scale," *International Journal of Energy Sector Management* 8, 1 (2014): 56–75; Laurie Skuba Jackson, "Contemporary Public Involvement: Toward a Strategic Approach," *Local Environment* 6, 2 (2001): 135–47; and Steve Patten, "Democratizing the Institutions of Policy-Making: Democratic Consultation and Participatory Administration," *Journal of Canadian Studies* 35, 4 (2001): 221–39.

22 For a discussion on the difficulties of gaining the approval of all members of an Indigenous nation, see Martin Papillon and Thierry Rodon, "Proponent-Indigenous Agreements and the Implementation of the Right to Free, Prior and Informed Consent in Canada," *Environmental Impact Assessment Review* 62 (2017): 216–24.

23 Schmidt, "Democracy and Legitimacy."

24 Vivien Schmidt and Matthew Wood, "Conceptualizing Throughput Legitimacy: Procedural Mechanisms of Accountability, Transparency, Inclusiveness and Openness in EU Governance," *Public Administration* 97, 4 (2019): 731.

25 For the purposes of this book, the principles of openness will be subsumed into the principle of inclusiveness. Although Vivien Schmidt differentiates these two principles, operationalizing openness is not distinct from the other principles outlined.

26 *Beckman v Little Salmon/Carmacks First Nation,* 2010 SCC 53, para. 41.

27 *Mikisew Cree First Nation v Canada (Minister of Canadian Heritage),* 2005 SCC 69, para. 54 [*Mikisew Cree*].

28 Richard Bellamy, "Democracy without Democracy? Can the EU's Democratic 'Outputs' Be Separated from the Democratic 'Inputs' Provided by Competitive Parties and Majority Rule?" *Journal of European Public Policy* 17, 1 (2010): 3.

29 *Haida Nation v British Columbia (Ministry of Forests),* 2004 SCC 73, para. 42 [*Haida Nation*]. See also *Taku River Tlingit First Nation v British Columbia (Project Assessment Director),* 2004 SCC 74, paras. 2, 22 [*Taku River*]; and *Mikisew Cree,* para. 66.

30 Ian Peach, "Who Speaks for Whom? Implementing the Crown's Duty to Consult in the Case of Divided Aboriginal Political Structures," *Canadian Public Administration* 59, 1 (2016): 95–112.

31 *Cache Creek Landfill Project Assessment Report,* 2010, 66 (on file with author).

32 *Cache Creek Report,* 67.

33 *Red Chris Porphyry Copper-Gold Mine Project Assessment Report,* 2005, 51 (on file with author).

34 *Red Chris Porphyry Report,* 51.

35 Interview with anonymous BC Environmental Assessment Office (EAO) official, January 9, 2019.

36 *Nlaka'pamux Nation Tribal Council v British Columbia (Environmental Assessment Office),* 2011 BCCA 236, paras. 81–82 [*Nlaka'pamux Nation Tribal Council*].

37 Interview with anonymous EAO official, January 9, 2019.

38 *Rio Tinto Alcan v Carrier Sekani,* 2010 SCC 43, para. 56 [*Rio Tinto*].

39 Interview with anonymous Indigenous official, October 23, 2018.

40 See Peach, "Who Speaks for Whom," 95–112.

41 *Spookw v Gitxsan Treaty Society,* 2017 BCCA 16, paras. 27, 71.

42 *Nlaka'pamux Nation Tribal Council*, paras. 81–82.

43 "Timeline of Wet'suwet'en Solidarity Protests and the Dispute That Sparked Them," *CBC News*, February 19, 2020, https://www.cbc.ca/news/indigenous/blockade-railway-mowhak-wet-suwet-en-1.5467234.

44 "Why Two Different Kinds of Wet'suwet'en Leaders Support and Oppose the Gas Pipeline," *CBC News*, February 17, 2020, https://globalnews.ca/news/6560125/timeline-wetsuweten-pipeline-protests/

45 "Why Two Different Kinds."

46 Kaitlin Ritchie, "Issues Associated with the Implementation of the Duty to Consult and Accommodate Aboriginal Peoples: Threatening the Goals of Reconciliation and Meaningful Consultation," *UBC Law Review* 46, 2 (2013): 423.

47 Interview with anonymous Indigenous political representative, April 6, 2018.

48 Interview with anonymous legal representative for the Crown and Indigenous nations, January 24, 2018; interview with anonymous consultant for Indigenous nations, December 12, 2018.

49 Interview with anonymous consultant for the Crown and Indigenous nations, October 2, 2018.

50 Interview with anonymous Indigenous political representative, April 24, 2018.

51 Interview with anonymous legal representative for Indigenous nations, December 10, 2018; interview with anonymous consultant for Indigenous nations, April 17, 2019.

52 Interview with anonymous Indigenous official, April 17, 2018; interview with anonymous consultant for Indigenous nations, October 23, 2018.

53 Interview with anonymous Indigenous political representative, April 24, 2018; interview with anonymous Indigenous official, October 18, 2018.

54 Interview with anonymous legal representative for Indigenous nations, December 21, 2017; *Behn v Moulton Contracting Ltd*, 2013 SCC 26.

55 Interview with anonymous legal representative for Indigenous nations, February 27, 2018.

56 See also Armitage, "Collaborative Environmental Assessment"; Baker and McLelland, "Evaluating the Effectiveness"; Lindsay Galbraith, Ben Bradshaw, and Murray Rutherford, "Towards a New Supraregulatory Approach to Environmental Assessment in Northern Canada," *Impact Assessment and Project Appraisal* 25, 1 (2007): 27–41; O'Faircheallaigh, "Environmental Agreements"; and Elmar Plate, Malcolm Foy, and Rick Krehbiel, *Best Practices for First Nation Involvement in Environmental Assessment Reviews of Development Projects in British Columbia* (West Vancouver, BC: New Relationship Trust, 2009).

57 Interview with anonymous Indigenous official, April 27, 2018; interview with anonymous consultant for Indigenous nations, October 23, 2018; interview with anonymous consultant for Indigenous nations, December 21, 2018.

58 Interview with anonymous Indigenous political representative, April 6, 2018.
59 Interview with anonymous Indigenous official, October 23, 2018; interview with anonymous consultant for Indigenous nations, December 21, 2018.
60 Interview with anonymous consultant for Indigenous nations, December 21, 2018.
61 Interview with anonymous Indigenous official, October 23, 2018.
62 Interview with anonymous Indigenous representative, April 26, 2018.

Chapter 5: Assessment of Impacts in the Application Review Phase

1 *Haida Nation v British Columbia (Ministry of Forests),* 2004 SCC 73, para. 37 [*Haida Nation*].
2 *Environmental Assessment Act,* SBC 2002, c. 43, s. 11.
3 *Environmental Assessment Act,* ss. 11.1.
4 This analysis on throughput legitimacy is reprinted with permission from the original article by Minh Do, "Throughput Legitimacy and the Duty to Consult: The Limits of the Law to Produce Quality Interactions in British Columbia's EA Process," *Canadian Journal of Political Science* 53, 3 (2020): 577–95, © Canadian Political Science Association and the Société québécoise de science politique, reproduced with permission.
5 Letter from the Namgis First Nation to the BC Environmental Assessment Office, December 6, 2010.
6 Letter from Fort Nelson First Nation Lands and Resources Department to CCS Midstream Services, February 12, 2009.
7 Interview with anonymous Indigenous political representative, April 6, 2018; interview with anonymous consultant for Indigenous nations, December 12, 2018.
8 Interview with anonymous legal representative for Indigenous nations, December 10, 2018.
9 This observation is corroborated by interview data. Interview with anonymous legal representative for Indigenous nations, December 21, 2017; interview with anonymous Indigenous political representative, April 24, 2018; interview with anonymous legal representative for Indigenous nations, December 10, 2018.
10 Ministry of Transport Responses to Kwantlen First Nation Comments on PMH1 EAC Application, Comment 3.3, March 20, 2008, 4 (on file with author).
11 Letter from Tahltan Central Council to BC Environmental Assessment Office, September 23, 2010, 5.
12 *Tsleil-Waututh v Canada (Attorney General),* 2018 FCA 153, para. 603.
13 Interview with anonymous Indigenous political representative, April 6, 2018.
14 *Chippewas of the Thames v Enbridge Pipelines Inc.*, 2017 SCC 41, para. 63 [*Chippewas*]; see also Sari Graben and Abbey Sinclair, "Tribunal Administration

and the Duty to Consult: A Study of the National Energy Board," *University of Toronto Law Journal* 65, 4 (2015): 382–433.

15 Submission from the Syilx Okanagan Nation to the BC Environmental Assessment Office's Assistant Deputy Minister, August 13, 2018.

16 Submission from the Tsleil-Waututh First Nation to the Minister of Environment and Minster of Natural Gas Development, August 18, 2015, 8.

17 *Haida Nation,* para. 44.

18 *Chippewas,* para. 64.

19 This position is also corroborated by the interviews. Interview with anonymous Indigenous political representative, April 6, 2018.

20 This position is also corroborated by the interviews. Interview with anonymous Indigenous political representative, April 24, 2018.

21 BC Environmental Assessment Office (EAO), *Deltaport Third Berth Project: Recommendations of the Executive Director and Reasons for Recommendation,* June 30, 2006, 3.

22 Letter from the Tsleil-Waututh First Nation to the Minister of Environment and Minister of Natural Gas Development, August 18, 2015, 2.

23 *Final Report Third Party Review,* July 7, 2006, 4 (on file with author).

24 This position is also corroborated by the interviews. Interview with anonymous Indigenous legal representative, December 21, 2017.

25 EAO, *Summary Assessment Report for Red Mountain Underground Gold Project (Red Mountain),* August 28, 2018, 16–17 (on file with author).

26 This issue is corroborated by the interviews. Interview with anonymous legal representative for Indigenous nations, April 19, 2019.

27 Anonymous personal communication, October 2, 2018; anonymous personal communication, October 17, 2018.

28 Anonymous personal communication, April 17, 2018; anonymous personal communication, October 17, 2018; anonymous personal communication, December 12, 2018.

29 Interview with anonymous Indigenous political representative, April 6, 2018; anonymous personal communication, April 25, 2018; interview with anonymous consultant for Indigenous nations, October 18, 2018.

30 Interview with anonymous Indigenous political representative, April 6, 2018.

31 Interview with anonymous consultant for Indigenous nations, October 18, 2018.

32 Interview with anonymous consultant for Indigenous nations, October 18, 2018.

33 Semiahmoo First Nation, *Vancouver Airport Fuel Facilities Corporation Environmental Assessment Review,* April 2011, 13 (on file with author).

34 *R v Van der Peet,* [1996] 2 SCR 507 [*Van der Peet*]; *Delgamuukw v British Columbia,* [1997] 3 SCR 1010 [*Delgamuukw*].

35 Anonymous personal communication, January 24, 2018; see also John Borrows, "Frozen Rights in Canada: Constitutional Interpretation and the Trickster," *American Indian Law Review* 22, 1 (1997–98): 37–64; Avigail Eisenberg, *Reasons of Identity: A Normative Guide to the Political and Legal Assessment of Identity Claims* (Oxford: Oxford University Press, 2009), 123–28; and Jonathan Rudin, "One Step Forward, Two Steps Back: The Political and Institutional Dynamics behind the Supreme Court of Canada's Decisions in *R. v. Sparrow*, *R. v. Van der Peet* and *Delgamuukw v. British Columbia*," *Journal of Law and Social Policy* 13 (1998): 67–94.

36 *Van der Peet*, para. 191.

37 *Delgamuukw*, para 155.

38 *Tsilhqot'in Nation v British Columbia*, 2014 SCC 44, para. 66.

39 Interview with anonymous Indigenous political representative, April 6, 2018.

40 *Rio Tinto Alcan v Carrier Sekani*, 2010 SCC 43, para. 36.

41 *Haida Nation*, para. 53.

42 Interview with anonymous legal representative for Indigenous nations, December 11, 2017; interview with anonymous legal representative for Indigenous nations, February 27, 2018; interview with anonymous consultant for Indigenous nations, December 21, 2018.

43 Interview with anonymous consultant for Indigenous nations, December 21, 2018.

44 Interview with anonymous consultant for Indigenous nations, December 21, 2018.

45 Interview with anonymous legal representative for Indigenous nations, January 24, 2018; interview with anonymous consultant for Indigenous nations, October 23, 2018.

46 Interview with anonymous consultant for Indigenous nations, October 23, 2018.

47 Interviews with anonymous EAO officials, January 9, 2019, and March 1, 2019.

48 See *Nisga'a Final Agreement Act*, RSBC 1999, c. 2, s. 3 (on environmental assessment and protection).

49 *Mikisew Cree First Nation v Canada (Minister of Canadian Heritage)*, 2005 SCC 69, para. 54.

50 This word was chosen because it is the language adopted by the Supreme Court of Canada in *Haida Nation* to explain the Crown's honourable consultation (para. 10).

51 It is highly likely that these issues together create a lack of meaningfulness and effectiveness for the overall environmental assessment process.

52 Letter from West Moberly First Nations to the EAO's Project Assessment Manager, February 26, 2007, 2.

53 Letter from Carrier Sekani Tribal Council to EAO's Executive Project Director and Premier of British Columbia, January 27, 2014, 6.
54 Interview with anonymous Indigenous official, October 18, 2018.
55 Interview with anonymous Indigenous official, October 18, 2018.

Chapter 6: Accommodations in the Decision Phase

1 *Ktunaxa Nation v British Columbia (Forests, Lands and Natural Resource Operations),* 2017 SCC 54, para. 119 [*Ktunaxa Nation*]. As stated in Chapter 4, the court evaluated whether the minister balanced their statutory objective with the Ktunaxa Nation's section 2(a) right under the *Canadian Charter of Rights and Freedoms* but did not evaluate the stakes involved for the Ktunaxa Nation if their right was not protected. *Canadian Charter of Rights and Freedoms,* Part 1 of the *Constitution Act, 1982*, being Schedule B to the *Canada Act 1982* (UK), 1982, c. 11.
2 *Musqueam Indian Band v British Columbia (Minister of Sustainable Resource Management),* 2005 BCCA 128, para. 99.
3 *West Moberly First Nations v British Columbia (Chief Inspector of Mines),* 2011 BCCA 247, para. 144 [*West Moberly First Nations*].
4 *Prophet River First Nation v British Columbia (Environment),* 2017 BCCA 58, para. 59.
5 Letter from Kitsumkalum Indian Band to BC Environmental Assessment Office (EAO) Project Assessment Manager, October 24, 2014, 3.
6 Letter from Kitsumkalum Indian Band to EAO Project Assessment Manager, October 24, 2014, 3.
7 Letter from Musqueam Indian Band to BC Minister of Environment and Minister of Community, Sport and Cultural Development, January 17, 2016, 4.
8 EAO, *Line Creek Operations Phase II Assessment Report*, August 30, 2013, 164 (on file with author).
9 EAO, *Line Creek Operations Report,* 164.
10 EAO, *Line Creek Operations Report,* 164, 179–80.
11 Projects were counted if more than 50 percent of participating Indigenous nations in an assessment explicitly opposed a project receiving an environmental assessment (EA) certificate. This count does not consider how certain nations have higher stakes across projects over others.
12 "Frequently Asked Questions," *Government of British Columbia,* May 23, 2018, https://www2.gov.bc.ca/gov/content/environment/natural-resource-stewardship /environmental-assessments/frequently-asked-questions#whyaresofewpro -jectsrefusedanenvironmentalassessmentcertificate.
13 *Tsilhqot'in Nation v British Columbia,* 2014 SCC 44.

14 *United Nations Declaration on the Rights of Indigenous Peoples,* GA Resolution 61/295, UNGAOR, 61st Sess., Supp. no. 49, UN Doc. A/61/49, September 13, 2007 [*UNDRIP*].

15 Interview with anonymous EAO official, January 9, 2019.

16 *Ktunaxa Nation.*

17 Interview with anonymous legal representative for Indigenous nations, December 21, 2017.

18 Interview with anonymous legal representative for Indigenous nations, December 19, 2018; interview with anonymous consultant for Indigenous nations, April 17, 2019.

19 Interview with anonymous consultant for Indigenous nations, April 17, 2019.

20 Interview with anonymous legal representative for Indigenous nations, December 19, 2018.

21 *Rio Tinto Alcan v Carrier Sekani,* 2010 SCC 43, para. 44 [*Rio Tinto*].

22 Interview with anonymous legal representative for Indigenous nations, February 27, 2018; interview with anonymous consultant for Indigenous nations, October 23, 2018; interview with anonymous consultant for Indigenous nations, December 21, 2018; interview with anonymous consultant for Indigenous nations, April 17, 2019.

23 Interview with anonymous EAO official, March 1, 2019.

24 Interview with anonymous consultant for Indigenous nations, December 21, 2018.

25 Interview with anonymous legal representative for Indigenous nations, December 10, 2018.

26 Interview with anonymous consultant for Indigenous nations, December 12, 2018.

27 Interview with anonymous legal representative for Indigenous nations, December 10, 2018.

28 Interview with anonymous Indigenous official, October 23, 2018.

29 Interview with anonymous legal representative for Indigenous nations, December 10, 2018.

30 Interview with anonymous legal representative for Indigenous nations, December 10, 2018.

31 Interview with anonymous Indigenous representative, April 6, 2018.

32 See Brenden Boyd and Sophie Lorefice, "Understanding Consultation and Engagement of Indigenous Peoples in Resource Development: A Policy Framing Approach," *Canadian Public Administration* 61, 4 (2018): 572–95.

33 Interview with anonymous EAO official, March 1, 2019.

34 Interview with anonymous legal representative for Indigenous groups, December 11, 2017.

35 Interview with anonymous legal representative for Indigenous nations, February 27, 2018.
36 Interview with anonymous consultant for Indigenous nations, December 21, 2018.
37 Interview with anonymous Indigenous political representative, April 24, 2018.
38 Mark Haddock, "Current Issues in Environmental Assessment in British Columbia," *Journal of Environmental Law and Practice* 21 (2010): 223.
39 Interview with anonymous legal representative for Indigenous nations, April 19, 2019.
40 Interview with anonymous consultant for Indigenous nations, December 21, 2017; anonymous personal communication, October 17, 2018; interview with anonymous consultant for Indigenous nations, October 18, 2018; anonymous personal communication, December 21, 2018.
41 Interview with anonymous consultant for Indigenous peoples, October 17, 2018.
42 See Malcolm Lavoie, *Assessing the Duty to Consult* (Vancouver: Fraser Institute, 2019), 30.
43 Anonymous personal communication, February 27, 2018.
44 *Rio Tinto,* para. 83.
45 *West Moberly First Nations.*
46 *Chippewas of the Thames First Nation v Enbridge Pipelines Inc.*, 2017 SCC 41, para. 42.
47 Fair Mining Collaborative, *Preliminary Technical Review of KSM EA Application,* October 10, 2013, 10 (on file with author).
48 EAO, *KSM Project Assessment Report,* June 2014, 326 (on file with author).
49 Interviews with anonymous legal representative for Indigenous nations, September 19, 2018, and April 19, 2019.
50 Bram Noble, *Introduction to Environmental Impact Assessment: A Guide to Principles and Practice,* 4th ed. (Don Mills, ON: Oxford University Press, 2020).
51 EAO, *KSM Project Assessment Report,* 312.
52 EAO, *KSM Project Assessment Report,* 312.
53 Interview with anonymous EAO official, March 1, 2019.
54 Interview with anonymous EAO official, March 1, 2019.
55 Interview with anonymous Indigenous official, April 17, 2018; see also interview with anonymous lawyer representing Indigenous nations, December 19, 2018.
56 *Haida Nation,* para. 14.
57 For a discussion on the relationship between tribunals and impartiality, see Rowland Harrison, "The Elusive Goal of Regulatory Independence and the National Energy Board: Is Regulatory Independence Achievable? What Does Regulatory 'Independence' Mean? Should We Pursue It?" *Alberta Law Review*

50, 4 (2013): 757–82; and Laverne Jacobs, "Caught between Judicial Paradigms and the Administrative Stat's Pastiche: 'Tribunal' Independence, Impartiality, and Bias," in *Administrative Law in Context,* ed. Colleen Flood and Lorne Sossin (Toronto: Emond Montgomery, 2013), 233–78.

58 Interview with anonymous Indigenous and Crown consultant, October 2, 2018.

Chapter 7: *UNDRIP* and the Duty to Consult

1 *United Nations Declaration on the Rights of Indigenous Peoples,* GA Resolution 61/295, UNGAOR, 61st Sess., Supp. no. 49, UN Doc. A/61/49, September 13, 2007 [*UNDRIP*]. See Sheryl Lightfoot, "Indigenous-Crown Relations at the Sesquicentennial: An Opportunity for Real and Lasting Transformation," in *Policy Transformation in Canada: Is the Past Prologue?,* ed. Carolyn Tuohy et al. (Toronto: University of Toronto Press, 2019), 124–31; and Martin Papillon and Thierry Rodon, "Indigenous Consent and Natural Resource Extraction: Foundations for a Made-in-Canada Approach," *Institute for Research on Public Policy Insight* 16 (2017): 1–25.

2 *Declaration on the Rights of Indigenous Peoples Act,* SBC 2019, c. 44 [BC *UNDRIP Act*]; Karin Larsen, "'We Are Moving Forward Together': Premier Urges Feds to Follow BC's Lead in Enshrining UNDRIP," *CBC News,* December 3, 2019, https://www.cbc.ca/news/canada/british-columbia/assembly-of-first-nations-recognizes-b-c-s-historic-undrip-legislation-1.5382649.

3 *United Nations Declaration on the Rights of Indigenous Peoples Act,* SC 2021, c. 14.

4 "*United Nations Declaration on the Rights of Indigenous Peoples Act* Action Plan 2023–2028," *Department of Justice Canada,* November 23, 2023, https://www.justice.gc.ca/eng/declaration/ap-pa/index.html ["Action Plan 2023–2028"].

5 "United Nations Declaration on the Rights of Indigenous Peoples Act Action Plan," *Department of Justice Canada,* 2023, 18, https://www.justice.gc.ca/eng/declaration/ap-pa/ah/pdf/2023-06-20_UNDA_Action_Plan_EN.pdf ["UNDRIP Action Plan"].

6 "UNDRIP Action Plan," 35; *Impact Assessment Act,* SC 2019, c. 28, s. 1.

7 BC *UNDRIP Act.*

8 Government of British Columbia, *Environmental Assessment Revitalization Intentions Paper,* 2018, 8.

9 Interviews with anonymous BC Environmental Assessment Office (EAO) officials, January 9, 2019, and March 1, 2019.

10 *Environmental Assessment Act,* SBC 2018, c. 51, s. 14(1) [*Environmental Assessment Act* 2018].

11 EAO, *Early Engagement Policy,* version 1.0, December 16, 2019, s. 4.2.

12 *Environmental Assessment Act* 2018, s. 14(2).

13 *Environmental Assessment Act* 2018, s. 14(3).

14 EAO, *Early Engagement Policy,* s. 4.1; *Constitution Act, 1982,* being Schedule B to the *Canada Act 1982* (UK), 1982, c. 11.

15 Sam Adkins et al., "*UNDRIP* as a Framework for Reconciliation in Canada: Challenges and Opportunities for Major Energy and Natural Resources Projects," *Alberta Law Review* 58, 2 (2020): 357.

16 EAO, *Early Engagement Policy,* s. 4.2.

17 *Environmental Assessment Act* 2018, s. 38(1)(a).

18 *Environmental Assessment Act* 2018, s. 5(2).

19 *Environmental Assessment Act* 2018, s. 5(7).

20 *Environmental Assessment Act,* SBC 2002, c. 43.

21 "Indigenous Nation Guidance," *Government of British Columbia,* January 25, 2024, https://www2.gov.bc.ca/gov/content/environment/natural-resource-stewardship/environmental-assessments/environmental-assessment-process/guidance-materials/indigenous-nation-guidance.

22 *Environmental Assessment Act* 2018, s. 48(1).

23 EAO, *Free, Prior and Informed Consent within the Context of UNDRIP and Environmental Assessments,* https://www2.gov.bc.ca/assets/gov/environment/natural-resource-stewardship/environmental-assessments/environmental-assessment-revitalization/documents/free_prior_informed_consent_in_an_ea_context.pdf.

24 EAO, *Process Planning Policy,* version 1.0, April 2020, s. 1.1.

25 *Environmental Assessment Act* 2018, s. 19(4).

26 EAO, *Process Planning Policy,* 9, Table 1.

27 EAO, *Process Planning Policy,* 8, s. 2.1.

28 EAO, *Guide to Indigenous Knowledge in Environmental Assessments,* version 2.0, September 2022, 7, s. 2.1.

29 EAO, *Guide to Indigenous Knowledge,* 8, s. 2.3.

30 EAO, *Guide to Indigenous Knowledge,* 9–10, s. 2.6; 8–9, s. 2.4.

31 EAO, *Guide to Indigenous Knowledge,* 16, s. 5.7.

32 EAO, *Guide to Indigenous Knowledge,* 16, s. 5.7.

33 Robert Argent, "Components of Adaptive Management," in *Adaptive Environmental Management: A Practitioner's Guide,* ed. Catherine Allan and George Stankey (Collingwood, Australia: Springer and SCIRO Publishing, 2009), 12–13.

34 Lawrence Susskind, Alejandro E. Camacho, and Todd Schenk, "A Critical Assessment of Collaborative Adaptive Management in Practice," *Journal of Applied Ecology* 49, 1 (2012): 48.

35 *Environmental Assessment Act* 2018, s. 35(1).

36 *Environmental Assessment Act* 2018, s. 35(2).

37 *Yahey v British Columbia*, 2021 BCSC 1287.
38 EAO, *Process Planning Policy*, 14, s. 2.5.
39 EAO, *Process Planning Policy*, 14, s. 2.5.
40 EAO, *Free, Prior and Informed Consent*.
41 EAO, *Guide to Consensus-Seeking under the Environmental Assessment Act, 2018*, version 1.0, April 2020, 4, s. 1.1.
42 EAO, *Guide to Consensus-Seeking*, 7, s. 3.1.
43 EAO, *Guide to Consensus-Seeking*, 9, s. 3.1.
44 EAO, *User Guide*, version 1.02, April 23, 2021, 14.
45 *Environmental Assessment Act* 2018, s. 5(1).
46 EAO, *User Guide*, 14.
47 *Environmental Assessment Act* 2018, s. 5(4).
48 *Environmental Assessment Act* 2018, s. 5(7).
49 EAO, *Guide to Consensus-Seeking*, 10, s. 3.1.
50 Lake Babine Nation Foundation Agreement Team, "Lake Babine Nation's Recommendations for Dispute Resolution under BC's *Environmental Assessment Act*," July 2023, 1; Tsleil-Waututh Nation, "TWN's Written Submission for the Dispute Resolution Regulation Paper," August 2023, 2–3; First Nations Leadership Council, "FNLC Technical Comments on Draft Environmental Assessment Act Dispute Resolution Regulation," August 2023, 1–3.
51 EAO, *Guide to Consensus-Seeking*, 10, s. 3.1.
52 *Kebaowek First Nation v Canadian Nuclear Laboratories*, 2025 FC 319, para. 131 [*Kebaowek*].
53 EAO, *Readiness Decision Policy*, version 1.0, December 2019, 5.
54 EAO, *Readiness Decision Policy*, 9.
55 EAO, *Readiness Decision Policy*, 9.
56 EAO, *Free, Prior and Informed Consent*.
57 The Supreme Court of Canada (SCC) has responded to a reference question that addresses *UNDRIP* insofar as the federal government has expressed in domestic law its commitments to aligning existing legislation with *UNDRIP*. In *Reference re An Act Respecting First Nations, Inuit, and Métis Children, Youth and Families*, 2024 SCC 5, the court affirmed that the federal government has the jurisdiction to establish national standards and provide Indigenous peoples with control over culturally appropriate child and family services. Interestingly, the SCC clarified that Parliament can present its own position on the content of section 35 through statutory law, such as the interpretation that section 35 includes a right to self-government, which has never been affirmed by the courts (para. 110). The court then suggested that this recognition could have other legal effects, such as requiring the Crown to act consistently with the honour

of the Crown to fulfill those statutory obligations while awaiting a formal court ruling (paras. 63–66). Given this interpretation, the BC's government's legislative commitments to *UNDRIP* and the changes to the environmental assessment process in light of these commitments may similarly engage the honour of the Crown.

58 *Kebaowek*, para. 139.

Conclusion

1 Interview with anonymous legal representative for Indigenous nations, September 19, 2018; interview with anonymous consultant for Indigenous nations, October 2, 2018; interview with anonymous consultant for Indigenous nations, December 21, 2018.

2 Minh Do, "Salient Indigenous Acts of Resistance in Canada, 2010–2020: Current Trends," *Canadian Journal of Political Science* 56, 4 (2023): 936–49.

3 *United Nations Declaration on the Rights of Indigenous Peoples*, GA Resolution 61/295, UNGAOR, 61st Sess., Supp. no. 49, UN Doc. A/61/49, September 13, 2007 [*UNDRIP*].

4 *Haida Nation v British Columbia (Ministry of Forests)*, 2004 SCC 73, para. 27 [*Haida Nation*].

5 *Haida Nation*, para. 49.

6 *Constitution Act, 1982*, being Schedule B to the *Canada Act 1982* (UK), 1982, c. 11.

7 Interview with anonymous legal representative for Indigenous nations, December 17, 2017; interview with anonymous legal representative for Indigenous nations, December 21, 2017; interview with anonymous Indigenous political representative, April 6, 2018; interview with anonymous Indigenous official, April 17, 2018.

8 For example, Minh Do and Robert Schertzer, "How Should Courts Respond to Political Questions? Exploring the Dialogical Turn in the Supreme Court of Canada's Federalism and Indigenous Case Law," *Law and Social Inquiry* 49, 1 (2023): 478–508.

9 *Canadian Charter of Rights and Freedoms*, Part 1 of the *Constitution Act, 1982*, being Schedule B to the *Canada Act 1982* (UK), 1982, c. 11.

10 Interview with anonymous legal representative for Indigenous nations, February 27, 2018.

11 Kathleen Thelen, "How Institutions Evolve: Insights from Comparative-Historical Analysis," in *Comparative Historical Analysis in the Social Sciences*, ed. James Mahoney and Dietrich Rueschemeyer (New York: Cambridge University Press, 2003), 226–27.

12 James Mahoney and Kathleen Thelen, "A Theory of Gradual Institutional Change," in *Explaining Institutional Change: Ambiguity, Agency, and Power,* ed. James Mahoney and Kathleen Thelen (New York: Cambridge University Press, 2010), 28.
13 Mahoney and Thelen, "Theory of Gradual Institutional Change," 29.
14 Jeroen van der Heijden, "Institutional Layering: A Review of the Use of the Concept," *Politics* 31, 1 (2011): 15.
15 *Haida Nation.*
16 Giliberto Capano, "Reconceptualizing Layering: From Mode of Institutional Change to Mode of Institutional Design: Types and Outputs," *Public Administration (London)* 97, 3 (2019): 594.
17 See, for example, Thomas Burke and Jeb Barnes, "Layering, Kludgeocracy and Disability Rights: The Limited Influence of the Social Model in American Disability Policy," *Social Policy and Society* 17, 1 (2018): 101–16.
18 Interview with anonymous BC Environmental Assessment Office (EAO) official, January 9, 2018.
19 Interview with anonymous EAO official, January 9, 2018.
20 van der Heijden, "Institutional Layering," 15.
21 For studies on the incoherency between policy goals and instruments as a result of institutional layering, see Adam Wellstead, Jeremy Rayner, and Michael Howlett, "Alberta's Oil Sands Reclamation Policy Trajectory: The Role of Tense Layering, Policy Stretching, and Policy Patching in Long-Term Policy Dynamics," *Journal of Environmental Planning and Management* 59, 10 (2016): 1873–90; and Adrian Kay, "Tense Layering and Synthetic Policy Paradigms: The Politics of Health Insurance in Australia," *Australian Journal of Political Science* 42, 4 (2007): 579–91.
22 Gavin Smith, "BC's Proposed New Environmental Assessment Act: Some Things Have Really Changed ... Others, Not So Much," *West Coast Environmental Law Blog,* November 21, 2018, https://www.wcel.org/blog/bcs-proposed-new-environmental-assessment-act-some-things-have-really-changedothers-not-so-much.
23 "Backgrounder: United Nations Declaration on the Rights of Indigenous Peoples Act," *Department of Justice Canada,* December 20, 2021, https://www.justice.gc.ca/eng/declaration/about-apropos.html.
24 "Backgrounder: United Nations Declaration."
25 *Kebaowek First Nation v Canadian Nuclear Laboratories*, 2025 FC 319.

Bibliography

Adkins, Sam, Lisa Jamieson, Terri-Lee Oleniuk, and Sabrina Spencer. "*UNDRIP* as a Framework for Reconciliation in Canada: Challenges and Opportunities for Major Energy and Natural Resources Projects." *Alberta Law Review* 58, 2 (2020): 339–69.

Alcantara, Christopher. *Negotiating the Deal: Comprehensive Land Claims Agreements in Canada*. Toronto: University of Toronto Press, 2013.

Alcantara, Christopher, and Jen Nelles. "Indigenous Peoples and the State in Settler Societies: Toward a More Robust Definition of Multilevel Governance." *Publius: The Journal of Federalism* 44, 1 (2014): 183–204.

Alfred, Gerald Taiaiake. *Wasáse: Indigenous Pathways of Action and Freedom*. Toronto: University of Toronto Press, 2005.

Argent, Robert. "Components of Adaptive Management." In *Adaptive Environmental Management: A Practitioner's Guide,* ed. Catherine Allan and George Stankey, 11–32. Collingwood, Australia: Springer and SCIRO Publishing, 2009.

Ariss, Rachael, Clara MacCallum, and Diba Nazneen Somani. "Crown Policies on the Duty to Consult and Accommodate: Towards Reconciliation?" *McGill Journal of Sustainable Development Law* 13, 1 (2017): 1–54.

Armitage, Derek. "Collaborative Environmental Assessment in the Northwest Territories, Canada." *Environmental Impact Assessment Review* 25, 3 (2005): 239–58.

Asch, Michael. "Confederation Treaties and Reconciliation: Stepping Back into the Future." In *Resurgence and Reconciliation: Indigenous-Settler Relations and Earth Teachings,* ed. Michael Asch, John Borrows, and James Tully, 29–48. Toronto: University of Toronto Press, 2018.

Bains, Ravina. "A Real Game Changer: An Analysis of the Supreme Court of Canada *Tsilhqot'in Nation v. British Columbia* Decision." *Fraser Institute Research Bulletin,*

2014. https://www.fraserinstitute.org/sites/default/files/real-game-changer-supreme-court-of-canada-tsilhqotin-decision.pdf.

Bakan, Joel. "Constitutional Interpretation and Social Change: You Can't Always Get What You Want (Nor What You Need)." *Canadian Bar Review* 70, 2 (1991): 307–29.

Baker, Douglas, and James McLelland. "Evaluating the Effectiveness of British Columbia's Environmental Assessment Process for First Nations' Participation in Mining Development." *Environmental Impact Assessment Review* 23, 5 (2003): 581–603.

Bakvis, Herman. "In the Shadows of Hierarchy: Intergovernmental Governance in Canada and the European Union." *Canadian Public Administration* 56, 2 (2013): 203–18.

BC Government News. "Province, Blueberry River First Nations Reach Agreement." January 18, 2023. https://news.gov.bc.ca/28086.

–. "West Moberly First Nations, BC Hydro and Canada Reach Settlement Related to the Site C Project." June 27, 2022. https://news.gov.bc.ca/27066.

Beaton, Ryan. "*De Facto* and *de jure* Crown Sovereignty: Reconciliation and Legitimation at the Supreme Court of Canada." *Constitutional Forum* 25, 1 (2017–18): 25–33.

Bellamy, Richard. "Democracy without Democracy? Can the EU's Democratic 'Outputs' Be Separated from the Democratic 'Inputs' Provided by Competitive Parties and Majority Rule?" *Journal of European Public Policy* 17, 1 (2010): 2–19.

Benz, Arthur. "Multilevel Parliaments in Canada and Europe." *International Journal* 66 (2010): 109–25.

Boiselle, Andrée, Glen Coulthard, Avigail Eisenberg, and Jeremy Webber, eds. *Recognition versus Self-Determination: Dilemmas of Emancipatory Politics*. Vancouver: UBC Press, 2014.

Booth, Annie, and Norm Skelton. "Improving First Nations' Participation in Environmental Assessment Process: Recommendations from the Field." *Impact Assessment and Project Appraisal* 29, 1 (2011): 49–58.

–. "Industry and Government Perspectives on First Nations' Participation in the British Columbia Environmental Assessment Process." *Environmental Impact Assessment Review* 31 (2011): 216–25.

Borrows, John. "Challenging Historical Frameworks: Aboriginal Rights, The Trickster, and Originalism." *Canadian Historical Review* 98, 1 (2017): 114–35.

–. "The Durability of *Terra Nullius: Tsilhqot'in Nation v British Columbia*." *UBC Law Review* 48, 3 (2015): 701–42.

–. "Frozen Rights in Canada: Constitutional Interpretation and the Trickster." *American Indian Law Review* 22, 1 (1997–98): 37–64.

–. "Sovereignty's Alchemy: An Analysis of *Delgamuukw v. British Columbia*." *Osgoode Hall Law Review* 37, 3 (1999): 537–96.

Boyd, Brenden, and Sophie Lorefice. "Understanding Consultation and Engagement of Indigenous Peoples in Resource Development: A Policy Framing Approach." *Canadian Public Administration* 61, 4 (2018): 572–95.

Bradford, Neil. "Place Matters and Multi-level Governance: Perspectives on a New Urban Policy Paradigm." *Policy Options* 25, 2 (2004): 39–44.

Burke, Thomas, and Jeb Barnes. "Layering, Kludgeocracy and Disability Rights: The Limited Influence of the Social Model in American Disability Policy." *Social Policy and Society* 17, 1 (2018): 101–16.

Capano, Giliberto. "Reconceptualizing Layering: From Mode of Institutional Change to Mode of Institutional Design: Types and Outputs." *Public Administration* 97, 3 (2019): 590–604.

Catt, Helena, and Michael Murphy. "What Voice for the People? Categorizing Methods of Public Consultation." *Australian Journal of Political Science* 38, 3 (2003): 407–21.

CBC News. "Timeline of Wet'suwet'en Solidarity Protests and the Dispute that Sparked Them." February 17, 2020. https://globalnews.ca/news/6560125/timeline-wetsuweten-pipeline-protests.

–. "Why Two Different Kinds of Wet'suwet'en Leaders Support and Oppose the Gas Pipeline." February 19, 2020. https://www.cbc.ca/news/indigenous/blockade-railway-mowhak-wet-suwet-en-1.5467234.

Chambers, Simone. "Deliberative Democratic Theory." *Annual Review of Political Science* 6, 1 (2003): 307–26.

Charowsky, Zena. "The Aboriginal Law Duty to Consult: An Introduction for Administrative Tribunals." *Saskatchewan Law Review* 74, 2 (2011): 213–30.

Christie, Gordon. *Canadian Law and Indigenous Self-Determination: A Naturalist Analysis*. Toronto: University of Toronto Press, 2019.

–. "Developing Case Law: The Future of Consultation and Accommodation." *UBC Law Review* 39, 1 (2006): 139–84.

–. "Implementation of UNDRIP within Canadian and Indigenous Law: Assessing Challenges." In *UNDRIP Implementation: More Reflections on the Braiding of International, Domestic, and Indigenous Laws*, 25–32. Waterloo, ON, and Saskatoon: Centre for International Governance Innovation and Wiyasiwewin Mikiwahp Native Law Centre, 2018. https://www.cigionline.org/static/documents/documents/UNDRIP%20Fall%202018%20lowres.pdf.

Coulthard, Glen. *Red Skin, White Masks: Rejecting the Colonial Politics of Recognition*. Minneapolis: University of Minnesota Press, 2014.

Cox, Sarah. "'We're Going to Court': BC First Nation to Proceed with Site C Dam 'Megatrial.'" *The Narwhal*, August 27, 2019. https://thenarwhal.ca/were-going-court-b-c-first-nation-to-proceed-site-c-dam-megatrial.

Craik, Neil. "Process and Reconciliation: Integrating the Duty to Consult with Environmental Assessment." *Osgoode Hall Law Journal* 53, 2 (2016): 632–80.

Crown-Indigenous Relations and Northern Affairs Canada. "Government of Canada and the Duty to Consult." *Government of Canada.* Last modified November 29, 2024. https://www.rcaanc-cirnac.gc.ca/eng/1331832510888/1609421255810.

De Bruijn, Johan A., and Ernst F. ten Heuvelhof. "Instruments for Network Management." In *Managing Complex Networks: Strategies for the Public Sector,* ed. W.J.M. Kickert, Erik-Hans Klijn, and J.F.M. Koppenjan, 119–36. London: Sage Publications, 1997.

–. "Policy Networks and Governance." In *Institutional Design,* ed. David L. Weimer, 161–79. Boston: Kluwer Academic, 1995.

Department of Justice Canada. "Backgrounder: United Nations Declaration on the Rights of Indigenous Peoples Act." December 20, 2021. https://www.justice.gc.ca/eng/declaration/about-apropos.html.

–. "United Nations Declaration on the Rights of Indigenous Peoples Act *Action Plan.*" 2023. https://www.justice.gc.ca/eng/declaration/ap-pa/ah/pdf/2023-06-20_UNDA_Action_Plan_EN.pdf.

–. "*United Nations Declaration on the Rights of Indigenous Peoples Act* Action Plan 2023–2028." November 23, 2023. https://www.justice.gc.ca/eng/declaration/ap-pa/index.html.

Dickson, Jamie. *The Honour and Dishonour of the Crown: Making Sense of Aboriginal Law in Canada.* Saskatoon: Purich Publishing, 2015.

Do, Minh. "Ask About Policy Change First, Courts Second." In *Policy Change, Courts, and the Canadian Constitution,* ed. Emmett Macfarlane, 21–39. Toronto: University of Toronto Press, 2018.

–. "Salient Indigenous Acts of Resistance in Canada, 2010–2020: Current Trends." *Canadian Journal of Political Science* 56, 4 (2023): 936–49.

–. "Throughput Legitimacy and the Duty to Consult: The Limits of the Law to Produce Quality Interactions in British Columbia's EA Process." *Canadian Journal of Political Science* 53, 3 (2020): 577–95.

Do, Minh, and Robert Schertzer. "How Should Courts Respond to Political Questions? Exploring the Dialogical Turn in the Supreme Court of Canada's Federalism and Indigenous Case Law." *Law and Social Inquiry* 49, 1 (2023): 478–508.

Doberstein, Carey, and Heather Millar. "Balancing a House of Cards: Throughput Legitimacy in Canadian Governance Networks." *Canadian Journal of Political Science* 47, 2 (2014): 259–80.

Drake, Anna. *Activism, Inclusion, and the Challenges of Deliberative Democracy.* Vancouver: UBC Press, 2021.

EAO (BC Environmental Assessment Office). *Early Engagement Policy.* Version 1.0. December 16, 2019.

–. *Free, Prior and Informed Consent within the Context of UNDRIP and Environmental Assessments.* https://www2.gov.bc.ca/assets/gov/environment/natural-resource-stewardship/environmental-assessments/environmental-assessment-revitalization/documents/free_prior_informed_consent_in_an_ea_context.pdf.

–. *Guide to Indigenous Knowledge in Environmental Assessments.* Version 2.0. September 2022.

–. *Guideline for the Selection of Valued Components and Assessment of Potential Effects.* September 9, 2013.

–. *Process Planning Policy.* Version 1.0. April 2020.

–. *Readiness Decision Policy.* Version 1.0. December 2019.

–. *User Guide.* Version 1.02. April 23, 2021.

Eisenberg, Avigail. "Decolonizing Authority: The Conflict on Wet'suwet'en Territory." *Canadian Journal of Political Science* 55, 1 (2022): 40–58.

–. *Reasons of Identity: A Normative Guide to the Political and Legal Assessment of Identity Claims.* Oxford: Oxford University Press, 2009.

Eliadis, Pearl, Margaret M. Hill, and Michael Howlett, ed. *Designing Government: From Instruments to Governance.* Montreal and Kingston: McGill-Queen's University Press, 2005.

Ellis, Stephen. "Meaning Consideration? A Review of Traditional Knowledge in Environmental Decision Making." *Arctic* 58, 1 (2005): 66–77.

Epp, Charles. *The Rights Revolution: Lawyers, Activists, and Supreme Courts in Comparative Perspective.* Chicago: University of Chicago Press, 1998.

Eyporsson, Einar, and Alma Elizabeth Thuestad. "Incorporating Traditional Knowledge in Environmental Impact Assessment: How Can It Be Done?" *Arctic Review on Law and Politics* 6, 2 (2015): 132–50.

Fidler, Courtney. "Increasing the Sustainability of a Resource Development: Aboriginal Engagement and Negotiated Agreements." *Environment Development Sustainability* 12, 2 (2010): 233–44.

Fidler, Courtney, and Michael Hitch. "Impact and Benefit Agreements: A Contentious Issue for Environmental and Aboriginal Justice." *Environments Journal* 35, 2 (2007): 49–69.

Finke, Barbara. "Civil Society Participation in EU Governance." *Living Reviews in European Governance* 2 (2007): 4–31.

Floridia, Antonio. *From Participation to Deliberation: A Critical Genealogy of Deliberative Democracy.* Colchester, UK: ECPR Press, 2017.

Fontaine, Tim. "Canada Officially Adopts UN Declaration on Rights of Indigenous Peoples." *CBC News,* May 10, 2016. https://www.cbc.ca/news/aboriginal/canada-adopting-implementing-un-rights-declaration-1.3575272.

Gagnon, Alain-G. *The Legitimacy Clash: Challenges to Democracy in Multinational States.* Toronto: University of Toronto Press, 2022.

Galbraith, Lindsay, Ben Bradshaw, and Murray Rutherford. "Towards a New Supraregulatory Approach to Environmental Assessment in Northern Canada." *Impact Assessment Project Appraisal* 25, 1 (2007): 27–41.

Gall, Christopher, and Brodie Douglas. "Shifting the Status Quo: The Duty to Consult and the Métis of British Columbia." In *Bead by Bead: Constitutional Rights and Métis Community*, ed. Yvonne Boyer and Larry Chartrand, 52–70. Vancouver: UBC Press, 2021.

Gilmour, Brad, and Bruce Mellet. "The Role of Impact and Benefit Agreements in the Resolution of Project Issues with First Nations." *Alberta Law Review* 51, 2 (2013): 385–400.

Government of British Columbia. *Environmental Assessment Revitalization Intentions Paper*. 2018.

–. "Frequently Asked Questions." May 23, 2018. https://www2.gov.bc.ca/gov/content/environment/natural-resource-stewardship/environmental-assessments/frequently-asked-questions#whyaresofewprojectsrefusedanenvironmentalassessmentcertificate.

–. "Indigenous Nation Guidance." January 25, 2024. https://www2.gov.bc.ca/gov/content/environment/natural-resource-stewardship/environmental-assessments/environmental-assessment-process/guidance-materials/indigenous-nation-guidance.

Government of Canada. *Aboriginal Consultation and Accommodation: Updated Guidelines for Federal Officials to Fulfill the Duty to Consult*. 2011.

Graben, Sari. "The Nisga'a Final Agreement: Negotiating Federalism." *Indigenous Law Journal* 6, 2 (2007): 63–94.

–. "Rationalizing Risks to Cultural Loss in Resource Development." *Canadian Journal of Law and Jurisprudence* 26, 1 (2013): 83–114.

–. "Resourceful Impacts: Harm and Valuation of the Sacred." *University of Toronto Law Journal* 64, 1 (2014): 61–105.

Graben, Sari, and Abbey Sinclair. "Tribunal Administration and the Duty to Consult: A Study of the National Energy Board." *University of Toronto Law Journal* 65, 4 (2015): 382–433.

Graham, Steve, and Simon Marvin. *Splintering Urbanism: Networked Infrastructures, Technological Mobilities and the Urban Condition*. London: Routledge, 2001.

Greenwood, Justin. "Organized Civil Society and Democratic Legitimacy in the European Union." *British Journal of Political Science* 37 (2007): 333–57.

Guttman, Amy, and Dennis Thompson. *Why Deliberative Democracy?* Princeton, NJ: Princeton University Press, 2009.

Habermas, Jürgen. *The Legitimation Crisis*. Boston: Beacon Press, 1975.

–. *The Structural Transformation of the Public Sphere*. Cambridge, MA: MIT Press, 1989.

Haddock, Mark. "Current Issues in Environmental Assessment in British Columbia." *Journal of Environmental Law and Practice* 21 (2010): 221–45.

–. *Environmental Assessment in British Columbia*. Victoria: Environmental Law Centre, 2010.

Hall, Matthew E.K. *The Nature of Supreme Court Power*. New York: Cambridge University Press, 2011.

Hamilton, Robert, and Joshua Nichols. "The Tin Ear of the Court: Ktunaxa Nation and the Foundations of the Duty to Consult." *Alberta Law Review* 56, 3 (2019): 729–60.

Harrison, Rowland. "The Elusive Goal of Regulatory Independence and the National Energy Board: Is Regulatory Independence Achievable? What Does Regulatory 'Independence' Mean? Should We Pursue It?" *Alberta Law Review* 50, 4 (2013): 757–82.

Hartley, Jean, Eva Sørenson, and Jacob Torfing. "Collaborative Innovation: A Viable Alternative to Market Competition and Organizational Entrepreneurship." *Public Administration Review* 73, 6 (2013): 821–30.

Henderson, James [Sa'ke'j] Youngblood. "Dialogical Governance: A Mechanism of Constitutional Governance." *Saskatchewan Law Review* 72 (2009): 29–73.

–. "Empowering Treaty Federalism." *Saskatchewan Law Review* 58, 2 (1994): 241–330.

Hennigar, Matthew. "Players and the Process: Charter Litigation and the Federal Government." *Windsor Yearbook of Access to Justice* 21 (2002): 91–110.

–. "Why Does the Federal Government Appeal to the Supreme Court of Canada in Charter of Rights Cases?: A Strategic Explanation." *Law and Society Review* 41, 1 (2007): 225–50.

Héritier, Adrienne, and Dirk Lehmkuhl. "The Shadow of Hierarchy and New Modes of Governance." *Journal of Public Policy* 28, 1 (2008): 1–17.

Hiebert, Janet. *Charter Conflicts: What Is Parliament's Role?* Montreal and Kingston: McGill-Queen's University Press, 2002.

–. "The Charter's Influence on Legislation: Political Strategizing about Risk" (Presidential Address to the Canadian Political Science Association, Regina). *Canadian Journal of Political Science* 51, 4 (2018): 727–47.

–. "The Notwithstanding Clause and Charter Compliance: Why Infrequent Use Should Not Be Equated with Charter Compliance." In *Oxford Handbook of the Canadian Constitution*, ed. Nathalie Des Rosiers, Patrick Macklem, and Peter Oliver, 695–714. Oxford: Oxford University Press, 2017.

Holliday, Ian. "Is the British State Hollowing Out?" *Political Quarterly* 71 (2000): 167–76.

Howlett, Michael. "Managing the 'Hollow State': Procedural Policy Instruments and Modern Governance." *Canadian Public Administration* 43, 4 (2000): 412–31.

Hulbert, Margot. "Evaluating Public Consultation in Nuclear Energy: The Importance of Problem Structuring and Scale." *International Journal of Energy Sector Management* 8, 1 (2014): 56–75.

Isaac, Thomas, and Anthony Knox. "The Crown's Duty to Consult Aboriginal People." *Alberta Law Review* 41, 1 (2003): 49–77.

Iusmen, Ingi, and John Boswell. "The Dilemmas of Pursuing 'Throughput Legitimacy' through Participatory Mechanisms." *West European Politics* 40, 2 (2017): 459–78.

Jackson, Laurie Skuba. "Contemporary Public Involvement: Toward a Strategic Approach." *Local Environment* 6, 2 (2001): 135–47.

Jacobs, Laverne. "Caught between Judicial Paradigms and the Administrative Stat's Pastiche: 'Tribunal' Independence, Impartiality, and Bias." In *Administrative Law in Context*, ed. Colleen Flood and Lorne Sossin, 233–78. Toronto: Emond Montgomery, 2013.

Kay, Adrian. "Tense Layering and Synthetic Policy Paradigms: The Politics of Health Insurance in Australia." *Australian Journal of Political Science* 42, 4 (2007): 579–91.

Kelly, James. *Governing with the Charter: Legislative and Judicial Activism and Framers' Intent*. Vancouver: UBC Press, 2005.

Kelly, James, and Matthew Hennigar. "The Canadian Charter of Rights and the Minister of Justice: Weak-form Review within a Constitutional Charter of Rights." *International Journal of Constitutional Law* 10, 1 (2012): 35–68.

Kirchoff, Denis, Holly Gardner, and Leonard Tsuji. "The Canadian Environmental Assessment Act 2012 and Associated Policy: Implications for Aboriginal Peoples." *International Indigenous Policy Journal* 4, 3 (2013): 1–16.

Klijn, Erik-Hans. "Analyzing and Managing Policy Processes in Complex Networks: A Theoretical Examination of the Concept Policy Network and Its Problems." *Administration and Society* 28, 1 (1996): 90–119.

Kohler-Koch, Beate. "How to Put Matters Right? Assessing the Role of Civil Society in EU Accountability." *West European Politics* 33, 5 (2010): 1117–41.

Krupta, Joel, Lindsay Galbraith, and Sarah Burch. "Participatory and Multi-Level Governance: Applications to Aboriginal Renewable Energy Projects." *Local Environment* 20, 1 (2015): 81–101.

Ladner, Kiera. "Colonialism Isn't the Only Obstacle: Indigenous Peoples and Multilevel Government in Canada." In *Federalism, Feminism and Multilevel Governance*, ed. Marian Sawer, Melissa Haussman and Jill Vickers, 83–96. London: Ashgate, 2010.

–. "Treaty Federalism: An Indigenous Vision of Canadian Federalisms." In *New Trends in Canadian Federalism*, 2nd ed., ed. Francois Rocher and Miriam Smith, 167–96. Peterborough, ON: Broadview Press, 2003.

–. "Up the Creek: Fishing for a New Constitutional Order." *Canadian Journal of Political Science* 38, 4 (2005): 923–53.

Laforest, Rachel. "Shifting Scales of Governance and Civil Society Participation in Canada and the European Union." *Canadian Public Administration* 56, 2 (2013): 235–51.

Lambrech, Kirk. *Aboriginal Consultation, Environmental Assessment and Regulatory Review in Canada*. Regina: University of Regina Press, 2013.

Larsen, Karin. "'We Are Moving Forward Together': Premier Urges Feds to Follow BC's Lead in Enshrining UNDRIP." *CBC News*, December 3, 2019. https://www.cbc.ca/news/canada/british-columbia/assembly-of-first-nations-recognizes-b-c-s-historic-undrip-legislation-1.5382649.

Latta, Alex. "Indigenous Rights and Multilevel Governance: Learning from the Northwest Territories Water Stewardship Strategy." *International Indigenous Policy Journal* 9, 2 (2018): 1–22.

Lavoie, Malcolm. *Assessing the Duty to Consult*. Vancouver: Fraser Institute, 2019.

Lawrence, Sonia, and Patrick Macklem. "From Consultation to Reconciliation: Aboriginal Rights and the Crown's Duty to Consult." *Canadian Bar Review* 79, 1 (2000): 252–79.

Leik, Robert K. "New Directions for Network Exchange Theory: Strategic Manipulation of Network Linkages." *Social Networks* 14, 3 (1992): 309–23.

Levesque, Mario. "Mapping a Way Forward: Interest Group Selection and Roles Performed in Engagement Processes." *Canadian Public Administration* 55, 4 (2012): 531–52.

Lightfoot, Sheryl. "Adopting and Implementing the United Nations Declaration on the Rights of Indigenous Peoples: Canada's Existential Crisis." In *Surviving Canada: Indigenous Peoples Celebrate 150 Years of Betrayal*, ed. Kiera Ladner and Myra J. Tait, 440–59. Winnipeg, ARP Books, 2017.

–. *Global Indigenous Politics: A Subtle Revolution*. London: Routledge, 2016.

–. "Indigenous-Crown Relations at the Sesquicentennial: An Opportunity for Real and Lasting Transformation." In *Policy Transformation in Canada: Is the Past Prologue?* ed. Carolyn Tuohy, Sophie Borwein, Peter Loewen, and Andrew Potter, 124–31. Toronto: University of Toronto Press, 2019.

Macfarlane, Emmett, ed. *Courts, Policy Change and the Canadian Constitution*. Toronto: University of Toronto Press, 2018.

Macklem, Patrick, and Douglas Sanderson. "Introduction: Recognition and Reconciliation in Indigenous-Settler Societies." In *From Recognition to Reconciliation: Essays on the Constitutional Entrenchment of Aboriginal and Treaty Rights*, ed. Patrick Macklem and Douglas Sanderson, 1–16. Toronto: University of Toronto Press, 2016.

Mahoney, James, and Kathleen Thelen. "Introduction: A Theory of Gradual Institutional Change." In *Explaining Institutional Change: Ambiguity, Agency, and Power*, ed. James Mahoney and Kathleen Thelen, 1–37. Cambridge, UK: Cambridge University Press, 2009.

Mayntz, Renate. "Legitimacy and the Directive Capacity of the Political System." In *Stress and Contradiction in Modern Capitalism*, ed. Leon N. Lindberg, Robert Alford, Colin Crouch, and Claus Offe, 261–27. Lexington, KY: Lexington Books, 1975.

McCrossan, Michael, and Kiera Ladner. "Eliminating Indigenous Jurisdictions: Federalism, The Supreme Court of Canada, and Territorial Rationalities of Power." *Canadian Journal of Political Science* 49, 3 (2016): 411–31.

Millar, Heather. "Comparing Accountability Relationships between Governments and Non-state Actors in Canadian and European International Development Policy." *Canadian Public Administration* 56, 2 (2013): 252–69.

Milward, H. Brinton, and Keith G. Provan. "Governing the Hallow State." *Journal of Public Administration Research and Practice* 10 (2000): 359–80.

Milward, H. Brinton, Keith G. Provan, and Barbara A. Else. "What Does the 'Hollow State' Look Like?" In *Public Management: The State of the Art*, ed. Barry Bozeman, 309–23. San Francisco: Jossey-Bass, 1993.

Monpetit, Eric. "Policy Design for Legitimacy: Expert Knowledge, Citizens, Time and Inclusion in the United Kingdom's Biotechnology Sector." *Public Administration* 86, 1 (2008): 259–77.

Moore, Mark, and Jean Hartley. "Innovations in Governance." *Public Management Review* 10, 1 (2008): 3–20.

Morgan, Douglas F., and Craig W. Shinn. "The Foundations of New Public Governance." In *New Public Governance: A Regime-Centred Perspective*, ed. Douglas F. Morgan and Brian J. Cook, 1–10. London: M.E. Sharpe, 2014.

Mullan, David. "The Supreme Court and the Duty to Consult Aboriginal Peoples: A Lifting of the Fog?" *Canadian Journal of Administrative Law and Practice* 24, 3 (2011): 233–60.

Murphy, Michael. "Culture and the Courts: A New Direction in Canadian Jurisprudence on Aboriginal Rights?" *Canadian Journal of Political Science* 34, no. 1 (2001): 109–29.

Murray, Cathryn, Janson Wong, Gerald Singh, Megan Mach, Jackie Lerner, Bernardo Ranieri, Guillaume Peterson St-Laurent, Alice Guimaraes, and Kai Chan. "The Insignificance of Thresholds in Environmental Impact Assessment: An Illustrative Case Study in Canada." *Environmental Management* 61, 6 (2018): 1062–71.

Newman, Dwight. "Consultation and Economic Reconciliation." In *From Recognition to Reconciliation: Essays on the Constitutional Entrenchment of Aboriginal and*

Treaty Rights, ed. Patrick Macklem and Douglas Sanderson, 207–22. Toronto: University of Toronto Press, 2016.

–. "Reconciliation: Legal Conception(s) and Faces of Justice." In *Moving toward Justice: Legal Traditions and Aboriginal Justice*, ed. John Whyte, 80–87. Saskatoon: Purich Publishing, 2008.

–. *Revisiting the Duty to Consult Aboriginal Peoples*. Saskatoon: Purich Publishing, 2014.

–. "The Section 35 Duty to Consult." In *The Oxford Handbook of the Canadian Constitution*, ed. Peter Oliver, Patrick Macklem, and Nathalie Des Rosiers, 349–65. New York: Oxford University Press, 2017.

Noble, Bram. *Introduction to Environmental Impact Assessment: A Guide to Principles and Practice*. 4th ed. Don Mills, ON: Oxford University Press, 2020.

Noble, Bram, and Courtney Fidler. "Advancing Indigenous-Community Corporate Agreements: Lessons from Practice in the Canadian Mining Sector." *Oil Gas and Energy Law* 9, 4 (2011): 1–30.

Noble, Bram, and Kevin Hanna. "Environmental Assessment in the Arctic: A Gap Analysis and Research Agenda." *Arctic* 68, 3 (2015): 341–55.

Noble, Bram, Skye Ketilson, Alec Aitken, and Greg Poelzer. "Strategic Environmental Assessment Opportunities and Risks for Arctic Offshore Energy Planning and Development." *Marine Policy* 39 (2013): 296–302.

Noble, Bram, and Aniekan Udofia. *Protectors of the Land: Toward an EA Process That Works for Aboriginal Communities and Developers*. Ottawa: MacDonald-Laurier Institute, 2015.

O'Faircheallaigh, Ciarian. "Environmental Agreements, EIA Followup and Aboriginal Participation in Environmental Management: The Canadian Experience." *Environmental Impact Assessment Review* 27, 4 (2007): 319–42.

–. "Extractive Industries and Indigenous Peoples: A Changing Dynamic?" *Journal of Rural Studies* 30 (2013): 20–30.

O'Faircheallaigh, Cirian, and Tony Corbett. "Indigenous Participation in Environmental Management of Mining Projects: The Role of Negotiated Agreements." *Environmental Politics* 14, 5 (2005): 629–47.

O'Rielly, Kevin. "Diamond Mining and the Demise of Environmental Assessment in the North." *Northern Perspectives* 24 (1996): 1–4.

Osborne, Stephen P., ed. *The New Public Governance? Emerging Perspectives on the Theory and Practice of Public Governance*. London: Routledge, 2010.

Paci, Chris, Ann Tobin, and Peter Robb. "Reconsidering the Canadian Environmental Impact Assessment Act: A Place for Traditional Environmental Knowledge." *Environmental Impact Assessment Review* 22, 2 (2002): 111–27.

Pape, Arthur. "The Duty to Consult and Accommodation: A Judicial Innovation Intended to Promote Reconciliation." In *Aboriginal Law since Delgamuukw*, ed. Maria Morellato, 313–31. Aurora, ON: Canada Law Book, 2009.

Papillon, Martin. "Adapting Federalism: Indigenous Multilevel Governance in Canada and the United States." *Publius: The Journal of Federalism* 42, 2 (2012): 289–312.

–. "Canadian Federalism and the Emerging Mosaic of Aboriginal Multilevel Governance." In *Canadian Federalism: Performance, Effectiveness and Legitimacy*, ed. Herman Bakvis and Grace Skogstad, 291–313. Toronto: Oxford University Press, 2008.

Papillon, Martin, and André Juneau. *Canada: The State of the Federation, 2013: Aboriginal Multilevel Governance*. Montreal and Kingston: McGill-Queen's University Press, 2015.

Papillon, Martin and Thierry Rodon. "Indigenous Consent and Natural Resource Extraction: Foundations for a Made-in-Canada Approach." *Institute for Research on Public Policy Insight* 16 (2017): 1–25.

–. "Proponent-Indigenous Agreements and the Implementation of the Right to Free, Prior and Informed Consent in Canada." *Environmental Impact Assessment Review* 62, 1 (2017): 216–24.

Patten, Steve. "Democratizing the Institutions of Policy-Making: Democratic Consultation and Participatory Administration." *Journal of Canadian Studies* 35, 4 (2001): 221–39.

Peach, Ian. "Who Speaks for Whom? Implementing the Crown's Duty to Consult in the Case of Divided Aboriginal Political Structures." *Canadian Public Administration* 59, 1 (2016): 95–112.

Peters, B. Guy, and Jon Pierre. *Comparative Governance: Rediscovering the Functional Dimension of Governing*. Cambridge, UK: Cambridge University Press, 2016.

Pierre, Jon. *Debating Governance: Authority, Steering, and Democracy*. Oxford: Oxford University Press, 2000.

–. "Public Consultation and Citizen Participation: Dilemmas of Policy Advice." In *Taking Stock: Assessing Public Sector Reforms*, ed. Guy Peters and Donald Savoie, 137–63. Montreal and Kingston: McGill-Queen's University Press and Canadian Centre for Management Development, 1998.

Pierre, Jon, and B. Guy Peters. *Governance, Politics and the State*. London: Macmillan Press, 2000.

Plate, Elmar, Malcolm Foy, and Rick Krehbiel. *Best Practices for First Nation Involvement in Environmental Assessment Reviews of Development Projects in British Columbia*. West Vancouver, BC: New Relationship Trust, 2009.

Potes, Veronica. "The Duty to Accommodate Aboriginal Peoples Rights: Substantive Consultation?" *Journal of Environmental Law and Practice* 17, 1 (2006): 27–45.

Pratchett, Lawrence. "New Fashions in Public Participation: Towards Greater Democracy?" *Parliamentary Affairs* 52, 4 (1999): 616–33.

Promislow, Janna. "Irreconcilable? The Duty to Consult and Administrative Decision Makers." *Constitutional Forum* 22, 1 (2013): 63–78.

Ratner, Robert. "Communicative Rationality in the Citizens' Assembly and Referendum Processes." In *Designing Deliberative Democracy: The British Columbia Citizens' Assembly,* ed. Mark Warren and Hilary Pearse, 145–65. Cambridge, UK: Cambridge University Press, 2008.

Rhodes, Roderick Arthur William. "The Hollowing Out of the State: The Changing Nature of the Public Service in Britain." *Political Quarterly* 65 (1994): 138–51.

Ritchie, Kaitlin. "Issues Associated with the Implementation of the Duty to Consult and Accommodate Aboriginal Peoples: Threatening the Goals of Reconciliation and Meaningful Consultation." *UBC Law Review* 46, 2 (2013): 397–438.

Rosenberg, Gerald. *The Hallow Hope: Can Courts Bring About Social Change?* Chicago: University of Chicago Press, 1991.

Rowe, Gene, and Lyn Frewer. "Public Participation Methods: A Framework for Evaluation." *Science, Technology and Human Values* 25, 1 (2000): 3–29.

Rudin, Jonathan. "One Step Forward, Two Steps Back: The Political and Institutional Dynamics behind the Supreme Court of Canada's Decisions in *R. v. Sparrow, R. v. Van der Peet* and *Delgamuukw v. British Columbia.*" *Journal of Law and Social Policy* 13 (1998): 67–94.

Russell, Peter. *Canada's Constitutional Odyssey: Can Canadians Become a Sovereign People?* Toronto: University of Toronto Press, 2004.

–. *Recognizing Aboriginal Title: The Mabo Case and Indigenous Resistance to English-Settler Colonialism*. Toronto: University of Toronto Press, 2006.

–. *Sovereignty: The Biography of a Claim*. Toronto: University of Toronto Press, 2021.

Salamon, Lester M., ed. *The Tools of Government: A Guide to the New Governance.* Oxford: Oxford University Press, 2002.

Scharpf, Fritz. *Governing in Europe: Effective and Democratic?* Oxford: Oxford University Press, 1999.

Scheingold, Stuart. *The Politics of Rights: Lawyers, Public Policy, and Political Change.* Ann Arbor: University of Michigan Press, 1974.

Schmidt, Vivien. "Democracy and Legitimacy in the European Union Revisited: Input, Output *and* 'Throughput.'" *Political Studies* 61, 1 (2013): 2–22.

Schmidt, Vivien, and Matthew Wood. "Conceptualizing Throughput Legitimacy: Procedural Mechanisms of Accountability, Transparency, Inclusiveness and Openness in EU Governance." *Public Administration* 97, 4 (2019): 727–40.

Scholtz, Christa. *Negotiating Claims: The Emergence of Indigenous Land Claim Negotiation Policies in Australia, Canada, New Zealand, and the United States.* Oxford: Routledge, 2006.

Simpson, Audra. *Mohawk Interruptus: Political Life across the Borders of Settler States.* Durham, NC: Duke University Press, 2014.

Skogstad, Grace. "Who Governs? Who Should Govern?: Political Authority and Legitimacy in Canada in the Twenty-First Century." *Canadian Journal of Political Science* 36, 5 (2003): 955–73.

Slattery, Brian. "Aboriginal Rights and the Honour of the Crown." *Supreme Court Law Review* 29, 3 (2005): 433–45.

–. "The Generative Structure of Aboriginal Rights." In *Moving toward Justice: Legal Traditions and Aboriginal Justice,* ed. John Whyte, 20–48. Saskatoon: Purich Publishing, 2008.

Slowey, Gabrielle. *Navigating Neoliberalism: Self-Determination in an Era of Globalization.* Vancouver: UBC Press, 2007.

Smith, Gavin. "BC's Proposed New Environmental Assessment Act: Some Things Have Really Changed ... Others, Not So Much." *West Coast Environmental Law Blog*, November 21, 2018. https://www.wcel.org/blog/bcs-proposed-new-environmental-assessment-act-some-things-have-really-changedothers-not-so-much.

Smith, Jackson, and Terry Mitchell. "Development of an UNDRIP Compliance Assessment Tool: How a Performance Framework Could Improve State Compliance." *International Indigenous Policy Journal* 11, 2 (2020): 1–23.

Snelgrove, Corey, and Matthew Wildcat. "Political Action in the Time of Reconciliation." In *Indigenous Resurgence in an Age of Reconciliation,* ed. Heidi Kiiwetinepinesiik Stark, Aimée Craft, and Hōkūlani K. Aikau, 3–20. Toronto: University of Toronto Press, 2023.

Somani, Nazneen. "Crown Policies on the Duty to Consult and Accommodate: Towards Reconciliation?" *McGill Journal of Sustainable Development Law* 13, 1 (2017): 1–54.

Song, Andrew, Owen Temby, Dongkyu Kim, Angel Saavedra Cisneros, and Gordon Hickey. "Measuring, Mapping and Quantifying the Effects of Trust and Informal Communication on Transboundary Collaboration in the Great Lakes Fisheries Policy Network." *Global Environmental Change* 54 (2019): 6–18.

Sossin, Lorne. "The Duty to Consult and Accommodate: Procedural Justice as Aboriginal Rights." *Canadian Journal of Administrative Law and Practice* 23, 1 (2010): 93–113.

–. "Public Fiduciary Obligations, Political Trusts, and the Equitable Duty of Reasonableness in Administrative Law." *Saskatchewan Law Review* 66, 1 (2003): 129–82.

Starblanket, Gina. "The Numbered Treaties and the Politics of Incoherency." *Canadian Journal of Political Science* 52, 3 (2019): 443–59.

Stark, Heidi Kiiwetinepinesiik. "Generating a Critical Resurgence Together." In *Indigenous Resurgence in an Age of Reconciliation,* ed. Heidi Kiiwetinepinesiik Stark, Aimée Craft, and Hōkūlani K. Aikau, 3–20. Toronto: University of Toronto Press, 2023.

Steffek, Jens. "The Limits of Proceduralism: Critical Remarks on the Rise of Throughput Legitimacy." *Public Administration* 97, 4 (2019): 784–96.

Stillman, Peter G. "The Concept of Legitimacy." *Polity* 7, 1 (1974): 32–56.

Streeck, Wolfgang, and Kathleen Thelen. "Introduction: Institutional Change in Advanced Political Economies." In *Beyond Continuity: Institutional Change in Advanced Political Economies,* ed. Wolfgang Streeck and K. Thelen, 1–39. Oxford: Oxford University Press, 2005.

Suchman, Mark C. "Managing Legitimacy: Strategic and Institutional Approaches." *Academy of Management Review* 20, 3 (1995): 571–610.

Susskind, Lawrence, Alejandro E. Camacho, and Todd Schenk. "A Critical Assessment of Collaborative Adaptive Management in Practice." *Journal of Applied Ecology* 49, 1 (2012): 47–51.

Thelen, Kathleen. "Institutional Change in Advanced Political Economies." *British Journal of Industrial Relations* 47, 3 (2009): 471–98.

Tollefson, Chris, and Karen Wipond. "Cumulative Environmental Impacts and Aboriginal Rights." *Environmental Impact Assessment Review* 18, 4 (1998): 371–90.

Truth and Reconciliation Commission of Canada. *Calls to Action.* Ottawa: Truth and Reconciliation Commission of Canada, 2015.

Tully, James. *Strange Multiplicity: Constitutionalism in an Age of Diversity.* Cambridge, UK: Cambridge University Press, 2010.

Tzimas, E. Ria. "To What End the Dialogue?" *The Supreme Court Law Review: Osgoode's Annual Constitutional Cases Conference* 54 (2011): 493–527.

Usher, Peter. "Traditional Knowledge in Environmental Assessment and Management." *Arctic* 53, 2 (2000): 183–93.

van Buuren, Arwin, Ingmar van Meerkerk, and Cecilia Tortajada. "Understanding Emergent Participation Practices in Water Governance." *International Journal of Water Resources Development* 35, 3 (2019): 367–82.

van der Heijden, Jeroen. "Institutional Layering: A Review of the Use of the Concept." *Politics* 31, 1 (2011): 9–18.

van Meerkerk, Ingmar, Jurien Edelenbos, and Erik-Hans Klijn. "Connective Management and Governance Network Performance: The Mediating Role of Throughput Legitimacy. Findings from Survey Research on Complex Water Projects in the Netherlands." *Environment and Planning C: Government and Policy* 33, 4 (2017): 746–64.

Veracini, Lorenzo. "Introducing Settler Colonial Studies." *Settler Colonial Studies* 1, 1 (2011): 1–12.

Verdun, Amy, and Donna Wood. "Governing the Social Dimension in Canadian Federalism and European Integration." *Canadian Public Administration* 56, 2 (2013): 173–84.

Vermette, D'Arcy. "Dizzying Dialogue: Canadian Courts and the Continuing Justification of the Dispossession of Aboriginal Peoples." *Windsor Yearbook of Access to Justice* 29, 1 (2011): 55–72.

Walters, Mark. "The Jurisprudence of Reconciliation." In *The Politics of Reconciliation in Multinational Societies,* ed. Will Kymlicka and Bashir Bashir, 165–91. Oxford: Oxford University Press, 2008.

Wellstead, Adam, Jeremy Rayner, and Michael Howlett. "Alberta's Oil Sands Reclamation Policy Trajectory: The Role of Tense Layering, Policy Stretching, and Policy Patching in Long-Term Policy Dynamics." *Journal of Environmental Planning and Management* 59, 10 (2016): 1873–90.

Wicks, Anthony. "Beyond Audi Alterum Partem: The Duty to Consult Aboriginal Peoples in Canada and New Zealand." *Journal of South Pacific Law* 13, 1 (2009): 40–46.

Wiebe, Sarah Marie, and Leah Levac, eds. *Creating Spaces of Engagement: Policy Justice and the Practical Craft of Deliberative Democracy.* Toronto: University of Toronto Press, 2020.

Williams, Meaghan, and Robert Scherzter. "Is Indigeneity Like Ethnicity? Theorizing and Assessing Models of Indigenous Political Representation." *Canadian Journal of Political Science* 52, 4 (2019): 677–96.

Legislation and Jurisprudence

Beckman v Little Samon/Carmacks First Nation, 2010 SCC 53.

Behn v Moulton Contracting Ltd., 2013 SCC 26.

Calder et al v British Columbia (Attorney General), [1973] SCR 313.

Canada (Minister of Citizenship and Immigration) v Vavilov, 2019 SCC 65.

Canadian Charter of Rights and Freedoms, Part 1 of the *Constitution Act, 1982,* being Schedule B to the *Canada Act 1982* (UK), 1982, c. 11.

Chartrand v British Columbia (Forests, Lands and Natural Resources Operations), 2015 BCCA 345.

Chippewas of the Thames First Nation v Enbridge Pipelines Inc., 2017 SCC 41.

Clyde River (Hamlet) v Petroleum Geo-Services Inc., 2017 SCC 40.

Constitution Act, 1982, being Schedule B to the *Canada Act 1982* (UK), 1982, c. 11.

Declaration on the Rights of Indigenous Peoples Act, SBC 2019, c. 44.

Delgamuukw v British Columbia, [1997] 3 SCR 1010.

Environmental Assessment Act, SBC 2002, c. 43.

Environmental Assessment Act, SBC 2018, c. 51.

Fort Nelson First Nation v British Columbia (Environmental Assessment Office), 2016 BCCA 500.

Haida Nation v British Columbia (Ministry of Forests), 2004 SCC 73.

Halalt First Nation v British Columbia, 2012 BCCA 472.

Kebaowek First Nation v Canadian Nuclear Laboratories, 2025 FC 319.

Ktunaxa Nation v British Columbia (Forests, Lands and Natural Resource Operations), 2017 SCC 54.

Lax Kw'Alaams Indian Band v British Columbia (Minister of Forests), 2002 BCCA 403.

Louis v British Columbia (Minister of Energy, Mines, and Petroleum Resources), 2013 BCCA 412.

Mikisew Cree v Canada (Minister of Canadian Heritage), 2005 SCC 69.

Mikisew Cree First Nation v Canada (Governor General in Council), 2018 SCC 40.

Musqueam Indian Band v British Columbia (Minister of Sustainable Resource Management), 2005 BCCA 128.

Neskonlith Indian Band v Salmon Arm (City), 2012 BCCA 379.

Nisga'a Final Agreement Act, RSBC 1999, c. 2, s. 3.

Nlaka'pamux Nation Tribal Council v British Columbia (Environmental Assessment Office), 2011 BCCA 78.

Paul v British Columbia (Forest Appeals Commission), 2001 BCCA 411.

Prophet River First Nation v British Columbia (Environment), 2017 BCCA 58.

R v Douglas et al., 2007 BCCA 265.

R v Sparrow, [1990] 1 SCR 1075.

R v Van der Peet, [1996] 2 SCR 507.

Reference re An Act Respecting First Nations, Inuit, and Métis Children, Youth and Families, 2024 SCC 5.

Rio Tinto Alcan Inc. v Carrier Sekani, 2010 SCC 43.

Royal Proclamation (UK), October 7, 1763.

Spookw v Gitxsan Treaty Society, 2017 BCCA 16.

Taku River Tlingit First Nation v British Columbia (Project Assessment Director), 2004 SCC 74.

Tsilhqot'in Nation v British Columbia, 2014 SCC 44.

Tsleil-Waututh v Canada (Attorney General), 2018 FCA 153.

United Nations Declaration on the Rights of Indigenous Peoples, GA Resolution 61/295, UNGAOR, 61st Sess., Supp. no. 49, UN Doc. A/61/49, September 13, 2007.

United Nations Declaration on the Rights of Indigenous Peoples Act, SC 2021, c. 14.
West Moberly First Nations v British Columbia (Chief Inspector of Mines), 2011 BCCA 247.
William v British Columbia (Attorney General), 2019 BCCA 74.
Yahey v British Columbia, 2021 BCSC 1287.

Index

Note: "(f)" after a page number indicates a figure; "(t)" after a page number indicates a table; BCCA stands for British Columbia Court of Appeal; EA stands for environmental assessment; UNDRIP stands for United Nations Declaration on the Rights of Indigenous Peoples.

Printed and bound in Canada
Set in Minion and Univers by Apex CoVantage, LLC
Copyeditor: Stacy Belden
Proofreader: Carmen Tiampo
Indexer: Patti Phillips
Cover designer: Will Brown
Cover image: Melody Charlie First Nation Photographer
Authorized Representative: Easy Access System Europe – Mustamäe tee 50, 10621
Tallinn, Estonia, gpsr.requests@easproject.com

FSC
www.fsc.org
MIX
Papier | Fördert gute Waldnutzung
FSC® C083411

Kolibri 360 GmbH
Ferdinand-Jühlke-Straße 7
99095 Erfurt, Deutschland
produktsicherheit@kolibri360.de